The Chronicles of Spirit Wrestlers' Immigration to Canada

Grigoriĭ Vasil'evich Verigin

The Chronicles of Spirit Wrestlers' Immigration to Canada

God is not in Might, but in Truth

Edited by Veronika Makarova and Larry A. Ewashen

Translated by Veronika Makarova

Grigoriĭ Vasil'evich Verigin (Deceased)

Editors
Veronika Makarova
Department of Linguistics
University of Saskatchewan
Saskatoon, SK, Canada

Larry A. Ewashen
Creston, BC, Canada

Translated by Veronika Makarova

ISBN 978-3-030-18524-4   ISBN 978-3-030-18525-1   (eBook)
https://doi.org/10.1007/978-3-030-18525-1

© The Editor(s) (if applicable) and The Author(s), under exclusive licence to Springer Nature Switzerland AG 2019
This work is subject to copyright. All rights are solely and exclusively licensed by the Publisher, whether the whole or part of the material is concerned, specifically the rights of translation, reprinting, reuse of illustrations, recitation, broadcasting, reproduction on microfilms or in any other physical way, and transmission or information storage and retrieval, electronic adaptation, computer software, or by similar or dissimilar methodology now known or hereafter developed.
The use of general descriptive names, registered names, trademarks, service marks, etc. in this publication does not imply, even in the absence of a specific statement, that such names are exempt from the relevant protective laws and regulations and therefore free for general use.
The publisher, the authors and the editors are safe to assume that the advice and information in this book are believed to be true and accurate at the date of publication. Neither the publisher nor the authors or the editors give a warranty, express or implied, with respect to the material contained herein or for any errors or omissions that may have been made. The publisher remains neutral with regard to jurisdictional claims in published maps and institutional affiliations.

This Palgrave Macmillan imprint is published by the registered company Springer Nature Switzerland AG.
The registered company address is: Gewerbestrasse 11, 6330 Cham, Switzerland

This book is dedicated to Pëtr Vasil'evich Verigin, a visionary of his time. The book is dedicated to his life, 16 years of his suffering in exile and his tragic still unresolved death in British Columbia. It is also dedicated to all the Doukhobors who underwent the burden of suffering for the Truth in Russia, and attempted to conquer evil with good. Many of them were sacrificed in their truly heroic and excruciating battle.

Preface by the Translator and the Editors

This book is a translation into English of the Russian original that describes the history of an ethnic and religious group known as Doukhobors (Doukhobortsy) or Spirit Wrestlers. The author portrays their life in the late nineteenth-century Russia and their immigration to Canada.

Doukhobortsy originated in Russia as a distinct Christian group in the seventeenth to eighteenth centuries. In Russian, "Doukhoborets" (Doukhobortsy in plural) means a Spirit Wrestler; subsequently the word got simplified to "Doukhobor." Their dissent with the Orthodox Church as well as their refusal to be conscripted into the army as this would violate the "thou shalt not kill" commandment led to their persecution in Russia that intensified at the end of the nineteenth century, the time when the narration of the book begins. In 1899, close to 8000 Doukhobors immigrated to Canada in search of a place where they could enjoy freedom of religion, exercise exemption from military conscription and work the land together in a commune. Today Doukhobors are still part of the multicultural pattern of Canada, and by the editors' estimate (other scholars' estimates may differ), about 3000 of them (in narrow terms of some affiliation with Doukhobor beliefs or activities) and up to about 30,000–40,000 (in terms of descent or heritage) currently reside mostly in British Columbia (BC) and Saskatchewan, as well as in other locations in Canada.

The book begins with the important years in reformation and consolidation of Doukhobor beliefs in the late nineteenth century initiated by Pëtr Verigin, the most famous Doukhobor leader, and the author's brother. It continues with the arrival of Doukhobors in Canada and closes in 1924 with Pëtr Verigin's tragic death in a still unsolved train bombing and his subsequent funeral.

This book was the first ever written by a Doukhobor, and one of the first immigrant narratives in Canada. It describes the survival of Doukhobor pioneers in the harsh climate of the prairies. It also reports a series of initial culture clashes and misunderstandings between Doukhobors and the Canadian government. This book is, therefore, of great interest to a wide range of scholars, including historians of Canada and Russia, political scientists, social scientists, ethnographers, anthropologists, specialists in Canadian and Russian studies, religious studies, social justice, as well as in communication and critical discourse. It is also of significance to the general public as it highlights the need for tolerance and diversity in Canadian society. The book is also an indispensable source of information for anyone interested in the history of early Western Canada's settlement during the crucial period of 1900–1920s on the Canadian prairies and in BC. The last, but not the least, for Canadian Doukhobors with no command of Russian, this book describes the lives and beliefs of their ancestors.

The author, Grigoriĭ Vasil'evich Verigin, was not only writing his personal recollections but he also interviewed many older generation Doukhobors and recorded their life experiences and stories. His brother Pëtr (Peter) Vasil'evich Verigin (Lordly)[1]—the Doukhobor leader—assisted him with information about his own life and events surrounding it and also with the descriptions of experiences during his 16-year exile in the remote regions of northern Russia and Siberia. He also approved his younger brother's literary work and encouraged him to share his historical information at community meetings.

Many pages in his writings contained details of events before and after Doukhobors burned their weapons in 1895, an event that changed their lives forever and led to the sufferings that they endured at the hands of the Russian tsar's military authorities. All these writings later became the major part of his book. The book also protocols the injustices and financial losses that Doukhobors were subjected to in Canada as they struggled for their religious rights against the assimilation policies of the Canadian government.

Very importantly for our day and age, the book time and again restates the most essential part of Doukhobor beliefs, their pacifism. In the author's own voice, in the testimonies of other Doukhobors and in their documents cited in the book, the senseless, brutal and barbaric nature of warfare is revealed; and people of the earth, no matter which religion, race, nation or creed, are called upon to lower their weapons and live together in peace, sharing resources that are otherwise wasted in bloodshed. The book highlights other aspects of Doukhobor beliefs such as their dream of a global community, brotherhood and equality of all the people on earth. The volume also describes their kind treatment of animals, vegetarianism, as well as abstinence from alcohol and tobacco. The narrative also calls for social justice, tolerance and diversity.

Grigoriĭ Vasil'evich completed his manuscript in 1929–1930 and asked a friend to type it. It was subsequently sent for publication to Pavel Ivanovich Biriukov in Switzerland who arranged publication in France. The original story was significantly abridged, as the author's niece, Fedos'ia Luk'ianovna Verigin(a) shared with Larry Ewashen in 1974. The original title of the book is "God is not in might but in truth," an old Russian saying.[2] In order to explain to an English speaking reader what the narrative is about, we decided to provide a new title for the book and keep the original one as a subtitle.

The translator and the editors attempted to make the text as comprehensible to a modern reader as possible, while at the same time preserving the authentic voice of the author.

The translation has been carried out by Dr. Veronika Makarova, a Professor of Linguistics, at the University of Saskatchewan. Her areas of expertise are linguistics, applied linguistics, Russian linguistics, as well as Doukhobor Studies. She directed and produced four documentary films about the National Doukhobor Heritage Village in Saskatchewan.

This book project was inspired by its literary editor, Larry A. Ewashen, Doukhobor historian, filmmaker and writer [http://www.larrysdesk.com/larry-a-ewashen%2D%2D-curriculum-vitae.html].

The American Library of Congress transliteration system is followed in the book (except for diacritic marks over "ia, iu and ts").[3]

Notes

1. "Lordly" is a somewhat controversial translation of his Russian nickname "Gospodniĭ" (God's) which indicates that his life was dedicated to God.
2. This proverb is attributed to the thirteenth-century Russian Prince and warrior Saint Alexander Nevskiĭ (Nevsky), who is famous for his multiple victories in battles, his wisdom, as well as for the strength of his Christian faith. It is possible that the author did not know the origins of this proverb.

3. American Library of Congress transliteration system for Russian is found at https://www.loc.gov/catdir/cpso/roman.html. For consistency, all the Russian personal names and place names were transliterated directly from Russian following the American Library of Congress transliteration system (with the exception of a few diacritic symbols). The traditional anglicized versions of the place names or personal were provided in Translator' chapter notes where important or relevant (e.g., Iakutsk (Yakutsk) for Якутск; Aleksandra Fëdorovna (Alexandra Feodorovna) for Александра Фёдоровна).

Preface by Pavel Biriukov,[1] the Editor of the Original Publication in Russian

Pavel Biriukov (Fourth person from the left, standing) with a group of Doukhobors

The author of this book, Grigoriĭ Vasil'evich Verigin, the youngest brother of Pëtr Vasil'evich,[2] asked me to write a preface.

I agreed because the subject of this book is dear to me, and the main character, Pëtr Vasil'evich, is undoubtedly an outstanding man.

The subject of this book is faith in the victory of kindness over evil and total renunciation of violence. It is beautifully elaborated in this simple presentation, sometimes moving you to tears, sometimes invoking touching stories about the people who boldly proclaimed their faith through deeds, and were not frightened of losing their property, of departing from their beloved and loving relatives, of being thrown into prisons, and into disciplinary battalions where they were humiliated and tortured with beastly cruelty. They were ready to die for this faith in the belief of the triumph of kindness, truth and love, and for its practice in life.

In this short essay we would like to pay attention to the unprecedented mass manifestations of those convictions which on the one side, evoked the beastly cruelty of people who strived to preserve the old dying foundations of violence and slavery as well as to intimidate and to force people into forgetting forever the law of kindness and love. On the other side, we see resolute faithfulness, faith in the triumph of these same ideas and a determined passionate desire to implement them in life.

On one side are the rulers of the states along with their servants executing their every will; on the other are illiterate peasants and farmers who face suffering and death with peace in their souls and joy in their hearts. And along with them, Tolstoy, the world's genius, worships the same idea of non-violent resistance.[3]

Neither the Doukhobors, who accomplished what nobody had dared before, nor Tolstoy who appealed to the whole world with the powerful gift of his word to follow this truth, did say anything new. More than 2000 years ago, this teaching was announced from the hills of the Himalayan mountains in Asia, and 500 years later, in Palestine, there appeared some carpenter's son who began to live in close communion with people, healing their spiritual and physical illnesses by the miraculous gift of love, and proclaiming by word and deed the new law of life. He touched the hearts of those who accepted his teaching by His profound truth. And the authorities captured him and crucified him alongside the robbers. The doctrine preached by that crucified carpenter was very simple: a person should not do violence to another.

The Doukhobors understood and remembered this teaching. For that teaching, they were deprived of their motherland and experienced much suffering. Perhaps more suffering awaits them. The essence of this teaching, from time to time, ignites humanity and it is impossible to extinguish it, it must triumph. "Everything passes, only the truth remains."[4] But in this case, something wondrous happened.

Almost at the same time as this movement, a great prophet who disrupted the human anthill, raised his voice. He discovered in the Gospel, that Jesus, that carpenter who many scholars had already put into the archives, was not as simple-minded as the scholarly people thought. Tolstoy said that the teaching of Christ, recognized as Divine, had been deliberately perverted and given a false interpretation. He articulated what had been long known by the ancestors of the Doukhobors, and for what they had suffered; that you do not need to create cathedrals and icons, burn incense, you do not need the complicated organization of priests, but the only thing each person needs is to understand and accept his teaching the way that he proclaimed it to the people: "A new commandment I give to you, that you love one another: just as I have loved you, you also are to love one another."[5] "You have heard that it hath been said, an eye for an eye, and a tooth for a tooth: but I say unto you, that you resist not evil: but whosoever shall smite thee on thy right cheek, turn to him the other also."[6]

This teaching, which Tolstoy reminded many people of, became a revelation and for many became a new faith which must renew the world. This truth was pronounced also by ancient wise men from the east. The proclaimers of this truth, Buddha, Krishna and others, were recognized for their divinity similarly to Christ. Temples were built in the name of Buddha and Krishna, as they were built in Christ's name. But in the lives of people who practised Buddhism and other religions as well as in the lives of those who called themselves Christians, violence of person over person continued to prevail.

The preaching of Tolstoy broke all exterior borders and enveloped the world. Over a distance, it reached Gandhi,[7] an Indian, who at the time lived in South Africa. For a long time he had the same thought ripening and the same passionate desire burning—to give to people the sacred ancient truth which they could implement in life. Tolstoy's words impressed him with their truth and strengthened his spirit. And now, in the east, in India, we see the glowing flames of this truth. The great spirit of Gandhi inspired the hearts of millions who struggle with their oppressors not with their weapons but with a firm and steadfast position for truth. And they are also not afraid of any suffering.

There were and there are many people practising this teaching. However, it should be noted that it was practised by the mass of several thousand people for the first time among the Doukhobors, a peasant mass who were born and died at their plough. They lived in this way and they live like this now. There are some exceptions, but there is no change.

This book is about a hero who gave himself to serve the people and inspired them to great feats for the truth—Pëtr Vasil'evich Verigin. Spiritual leader of the Doukhobors, Luker'ia Vasil'evna (Kalmykova),[8] who cherished in her soul the legacy of her ancestors, wanted the Doukhobors to continue in the same path, so that the fire that burned in the hearts of their ancestors would keep living in them. When Pëtr Vasil'evich Verigin was still a child, she noticed in him great mental and spiritual gifts. She envisaged that he could further inflame the holy fire within them, and she saw in him a fighter for virtue. It's a pity that we do not know more about this time of his life at Luker'ia Vasil'evna's. But we have the evidence that his spiritual growth was especially strong at the time. We can at least mention his talk with his brothers when after a long separation they showed him their wealth. The compiler of this book brings us his conversation with Luker'ia Vasil'evna. We can almost hear her voice and how movingly she instructed him on his difficult way to victory. Her premonitions and visions were fulfilled. Separated from the Doukhobors by force, Pëtr Vasil'evich fulfils his promise given to her—to call the Doukhobors to liberate themselves from militarism. "She, with tears in her eyes, was so glad to bless me to sacrifice my life if needed," Pëtr Verigin said in Shenkursk[9] to Ivan Evseevich Konkin, passing on to him an important message. And Konkin drove around all of the Doukhobor villages, disseminating the news about Pëtr Verigin's instructions everywhere. Without any fear of the presence of the authorities, he passed on all of the words of Pëtr Vasil'evich exactly and clearly about not becoming soldiers, giving up eating meat, drinking wine and smoking tobacco, and many other instructions.

And there was such a force of conviction as he passed the message that everyone who listened to him decided to fulfil all instructions, filled with happy, tender emotion, and many cried.

Ivan Konkin was arrested and exiled to Mezen'[10] and was liberated from exile after Pëtr Vasil'evich. In Canada, he became Pëtr Verigin's faithful friend and assistant. Ivan Konkin wrote many notes and expressions of general opinion. He was a man of pure and firm convictions. Long live his memory throughout the future generations.

I cannot help but mention two other associates of Pëtr Vasil'evich, his elder brother Vasiliĭ Vasil'evich Verigin and Vasiliĭ Gavrilovich Vereshchagin. They brought the most important instructions about the burning of the weapons and the rejection of military service from Peter Vasil'evich in exile.

Vasiliĭ Vasil'evich Verigin compiled the famous psalm with which many brothers entered their Way of the Cross. They both experienced prison and exile. Vasiliĭ Gavrilovich Konkin died on the way to Iakutsk[11] in the small town of Kerensk in prison. And Vasiliĭ Vasil'evich Verigin came to Canada from exile after Pëtr Vasil'evich had arrived there. He died in 1929 paralysed.

In this book, Grigoriĭ Vasil'evich Verigin compiled the description of those parts of his brother's life in which he directly took part; that is, the description of the last days of life in Shenkursk, his transport as a prisoner to Moscow, meeting with Leo Tolstoy and accompanying Pëtr Vasil'evich to Riazhsk where they parted company with Pëtr Vasil'evich and boldly went to the Caucasus to fulfil his instruction.

Worthy and loving brothers! Your life gave people lots of kindness, you have sewn good seeds, and they are already growing here and there in the field of life.

The ideal of Pëtr Vasil'evich is the same as that of Tolstoy. Both of them recognized that Christ's teaching must save the world.

At the meeting with Evgeniĭ Ivanovich Popov, Tolstoy's friend, at the Moscow Butyrskaia Transfer Prison, Pëtr Vasil'evich learned that he had a powerful companion in God's work, Lev Nikolaevich Tolstoy. He read *"The Kingdom of God is Within You"* passed on to him by Lev Nikolaevich, and since that time, they corresponded.

Tolstoy was struck with joy by the news of the burning of the weapons and the entire movement of the Doukhobors in the Caucasus and asked me to research these events. I went there and collected all of the evidence about what had happened. The material that I had gathered there was first published in the British newspaper, *Times*, with an afterword by Tolstoy. The Quakers joined Tolstoy and the resettlement was organized.

This book is about the life of the Doukhobors in Canada, which became especially exciting with the arrival of Pëtr Verigin from far away Siberian exile after 16 years of separation. I must also mention that the report of Tiflis[12] Governor Shervashidze says that, according to the replies of the Doukhobors he interrogated, among the books in circulation in their midst were the works of Socrates, Diogenes and Epictetus. Verigin and his comrades were exiled to Arkhangel'sk Region and then, even farther, but those stories about Socrates, Diogenes and Epictetus and many editions of *"Posrednik"*[13] founded by Tolstoy, were left in the Caucasus, and to say it more precisely, in the heads of those clever muzhiks whose brains were not twisted by the stories about Bogoroditsa Troeruchitsa (Three-handed Holy Virgin)[14] and so on. Those books did their task, preparing beneficial soil for the reception of those wholesome seeds of truth and kindness.

Thus by many different and invisible ways, the truth was disseminated. Not a single effort of people directed for good will be in vain. All of these aspirations for truth were united and reached more and more people just as the springs from different sites unite to form one powerful river.

In Siberia there is a communal settlement named after Tolstoy; there are already about 1000 people there. With the best aspirations of their souls they belong to the world brotherhood of people. Overcoming great difficulties, they are building a new free life without violence. Their sacrifices and labours for the benefit of future generations will not be in vain.

In the whole world, in all countries, among different people, we see the aspirations of people to free themselves from the old world of violence. The number of those rejecting military service is growing, young people go to prisons and subject themselves to deprivations happily, without hesitation. The time of mass refusals here and there in ways similar to that of the Doukhobors is not far away.

From this book we learn of many fearless fighters who sacrificed their lives for God's cause, who died in prison and on prison transports in wild cold uninhabited places of Siberia. They were the first to pioneer and point the way to the truth for future generations, for whom it will be easier to follow, because they will be more numerous and they will not be so unknown...

Eternal memory and eternal gratitude to those valiant fighters!

Switzerland   Pavel Biriukov
October 8, 1931

When the news about the burning of weapons by the Doukhobors and the cruelties perpetuated upon them by the government reached L. N. Tolstoy, he asked P. I. Biriukov to go to the Caucasus and find out exactly what happened. P. I. found the Doukhobors, visited them and learned all the details.

When Biriukov returned, he wrote a proclamation "*Help*" which was approved by Tolstoy. This appeal was signed by Chertkov, Tregubov and Biriukov. The appeal was sent to the tsar and other people close to the government. For that, Chertkov was exiled abroad, and Tregubov and Biriukov were exiled for five years to a small town in the Baltic region, but a year later Biriukov was also exiled abroad.

He passionately sympathized with the Doukhobors and their convictions against all violence and war, and he passionately desired to serve them as much as he was able to. He took an active part in their resettlement in Canada, lived with the Doukhobors in Cyprus, helping them as much as he was able to. He wrote many articles about the Doukhobors in Russian and other languages and organized conferences about them. In the last years of his life he, on the invitation of P. P. Verigin, came to Canada in order to help arrange the task of education and to serve the Doukhobors as much as he could, but in Brilliant, he suffered a stroke from which, after three years, he died in Switzerland. The preface to this book was written two days before his death.

Notes

1. Pavel Ivanovich Biriukov was a prominent Russian publicist, a follower of Tolstoy, as well as his friend and biographer. He was very interested in the Doukhobors and helped them to move to Canada.
2. Verigin, Pëtr Vasil'evich (1859–1924), the most famous Doukhobor leader.
3. Leo Tolstoy (Lev Nikolaevich Tolstoĭ) (1828–1910) was a famous Russian writer, the author of "War and Peace," "Anna Karenina" and multiple other novels. He also was a philosopher and thinker who developed the concept of not resisting evil with violence (non-violent resistance). He was a great sympathizer and supporter of the Doukhobors and assisted them in resettlement to Canada.
4. A quote from Dostoevsky's *The Karamazov Brothers*, taken from the famous *The Legend of the Grand Inquisitor* (cited by Dostoevsky, Fyodor. 2007. The Karamazov Brothers. Ware: Wordsworth Edition Limited, p. 340).
5. John 13:34.
6. Matthew 5:38.
7. Mohandas Karamchand (Mahatma) Gandhi (1869–1948), a famous Indian thinker and activist, who developed the idea of non-violent resistance and was in correspondence with Leo Tolstoy.
8. Lukeria Vasil'evna Kalmykova (Gubanova), 1841–1886, was the leader of the Doukhobors during their second exile to the Caucasus. She trained her nephew, Pëtr Vasil'evich Verigin, to be her successor.
9. Shenkursk is a town in Northern Russia; it was one of the places of exile of Pëtr Verigin.
10. Mezen' (Mezen) is a town in the Arkhangel'sk (Arkhangelsk) area in the north of the European part of Russia, close to the Arctic Polar Circle.

11. Iakutsk (Yakutsk) is a sub-Arctic city in Siberia with a harsh continental climate. During winters, it is one of the coldest cities in the world. It is the homeland of the Yakut (Sakha) people, the indigenous population of the area. It was used by the Russian government as a place of exile. Today it is the capital of Sakha republic.
12. Tiflis is the old name of modern Tbilisi, the capital of the country of Georgia. In the nineteenth century, it was the capital of Tiflis guberniia, which was a part of the Russian Empire.
13. "Posrednik" was a publishing firm founded in 1884 by Leo Tolstoy and a group of his friends and followers including P. Biriukov, the author of the preface to this volume. The publishing firm aimed at printing educational literature affordable for the common people.
14. The author of the preface refers to the allegedly wonder-working icon of Bogoroditsa Troeruchitsa (Three-handed Theotokos or the Three-handed Virgin Mary).

Introduction by the Author
Grigoriĭ Verigin

Grigoriĭ Vasil'evich Verigin, the author of the original volume

Doukhobortsy (Doukhobors) take their origins from Jesus Christ. The oral tradition passed by the Doukhobors through generations maintains that we, the Doukhobors, belong to a tribe of Israeli travellers, and descend from the three youths Ananiĭ, Azariĭ and Misail.[1] As their history recorded in the Bible shows, they did not consent to King Nebuchadnezzar's demands of worshipping an idol made by human hands and refused to partake of his table filled with animal meat. For this, Nebuchadnezzar's faithful servants threw them into a blazing furnace. According to the Biblical story, which may be a parable, they remained unharmed in it. Anything is possible for God. However, one can also presume that they died there in flesh, as all those who were burned in fire. But their spirit and state of mind passed over to the people and reached Jesus Christ, who described the spiritual and moral life of human beings in a more profound, clear and simple way than anyone else. Through this life, through the utmost perfection of human beings, the Kingdom of God on earth will be established, where boundless truth and love will reign supreme. This is what he expressed in his Sermon on the Mount and in two commandments, of which the first one is "Thou shalt love the Lord thy God with all thy heart, and with all thy soul, and with all thy mind." The second one is "Thou shalt love thy neighbour as thyself." This is the fulfillment of the Law and the Prophets.[2] Also "Do not do to others what you do not wish for thyself," as well as we are all "children of one God" and should live together as brothers[3] etc. These holy teachings passed from generation to generation until they reached our time. I will point out here the outstanding Doukhobor ancestors whose names I take from the oral tradition which is still maintained among the Doukhobors: Siluan Kolesnikov, Larion Pobirokhin and Saveliĭ Kapustin. They lived before the resettlement to the Taurida Guberniia[4] and suffered for Doukhoborism. Vasiliĭ Kalmykov (Kapustin) lived during the settlement in the Taurida Guberniia and died there. Larion Vasil'evich Kalmykov took over. He died in Transcaucasia[5] soon after the resettlement there. He was buried in the village of Goreloe. He was succeeded by his son Pëtr Larionovich. The latter also died in Goreloe. His wife Luker'ia Vasil'evna Kalmykova took over the leadership after his death, and after she passed away, it was the turn of Pëtr Vasil'evich Verigin.[6] These chronicles are recorded from his time.

As far as I know, Doukhobor history has been recorded, even if not in full detail, for 300 years. I have no evidence of records preceding this time.

Those earlier accounts were made not by the Doukhobors themselves, but by other people, and depended on the character of the writer. Those records can be found in extracts in journals and books, and they were mainly fair in their descriptions of how Doukhobors were tortured for refusing to revere and worship icons and to perform other church rites. Doukhobors themselves were not writing about their sufferings because those were cruel times. They already suffered because of not worshipping icons and they could suffer even more for making records of this. So they knew God's cause that had been entrusted to them through Jesus Christ and they believed that God knew about their sufferings. Moreover, these were olden days, when not only among the Doukhobors, but among other people as well, there were very few literate individuals.

Similar to the sufferings of our ancestors in the old times, in our time, Doukhobors have also been subjected to great sufferings for carrying out the cause of truth that was proclaimed by Jesus Christ: "you will know the truth and the truth will free you."[7] Doukhobors interpret this freedom in the spiritual sense, as liberation of oneself from an incorrect understanding of the true God, and for this, Doukhobors have to accept sufferings from the powerful of this age. The powerful of this age in their false teachings portray to people a directly opposite God and through this they enslave people into their power. The olden days are gone now.

This book is written by a Doukhobor, who was not only a witness but also a recipient of these sufferings. These chronicles are dedicated to the posterity of the whole humanity who will live afar in the future. These descendants will read my records with interest and horror. In their time humanity will have advanced considerably on the way to perfection, and they most likely will not experience any of those things that are recorded in this book.

The divine world swirls in its orbit and changes so fast, similar to the endless new views that a traveller sees from the window of a rapidly moving railway carriage.

I am talking about the divine realm for which there is neither limit nor measure. In our own lives we almost do not notice this, as we do not notice the movement of a clock's hand or the movement of the earth that revolves around its axis over one day and one night.

I hesitated to start these chronicles, as one needs a special talent for it in my understanding. One also needs free time to concentrate all the thoughts and reasoning on this writing, and honestly speaking, I do not have either prerequisite. However, things took their own course, and I felt obliged to write. Therefore, I request the readers of this book not to blame me for lack of rhetorical power that individuals with more talent and skills in writing would exhibit.

I come from a family of simple peasants and agrarians, and if my wordings are not in perfect style, please forgive me for this. I am not trying to be eloquent, but strive to be truthful, and truth is more precious than eloquence.

These notes were read and approved by Pëtr Vasil'evich in Columbia. Following his advice, it was read in four districts at meetings attended by many people in Uteshenie, Brilliant, Plodorodnoe and Lugovaia.[8] The purpose of the reading was to gather additional information from other people about the sufferings and death of their relatives that I did not know about and therefore could not include in the book. I also wrote to all the Doukhobors requesting them to send me the records of sufferings and death, if they know any more cases. If there are any gaps in my notes, please do not hold it against me.

Younger brother of Pëtr Vasil'evich[9] Verigin
Grigoriĭ Verigin

Notes

1. Ananiĭ, Azariĭ and Misail are legendary ancestors of the Doukhobors. The names are Russian versions of the names of the three Biblical youths, Hanania, Mishael and Azaria, also known under their Babylonian names of Shadrach, Meshach and Abednego. They were thrown into a blazing furnace for their refusal to worship the golden statue of king Nebuchadnezzar. The youths came out of the furnace unharmed as they were protected by God. This narrative is based on Daniel 3:23.
2. The Law and the Prophets refer to the two parts of the Old Testament: the Torah (Pentateuch) and the books of Prophets.

    Matthew 7:12.
3. Matthew 22:37; Matthew 22:36–40; Matthew 7:12.
4. Taurida guberniia (governorate) was one of the administrative units of the Russian Empire that comprised the Crimean peninsula, the basin of the lower Dnieper river and the coasts of the Black Sea and Azov Sea.
5. Transcaucasia is an area in and around the Caucasus mountains (located between the Caspian and the Black Sea). It is comprised mostly of the territories of the modern states of Russia, Georgia, Armenia and Azerbaijan. At the time of the narrative, it was the territory of the Russian Empire.

6. The author lists the names of some Doukhobor leaders. We provide here the dates of their births and deaths:

   Siluan Kolesnikov (17??–1775);
   Ilarion (Larion) Pobirokhin (17??–1791);
   Saveliĭ Kapustin (1743–1820);
   Vasiliĭ Kalmykov (Kapustin) (around 1790–1832);
   Ilarion (Larion) Vasil'evich Kalmykov (early 1800–1841);
   Pëtr Ilarionovich Kalmykov (around 1836–1864);
   Luker'ia Vasil'evna Kalmykova (1841–1886);
   Pëtr Vasil'evich Verigin (1859–1924).

7. John 8:32.
8. The names of Doukhobor villages in British Columbia in the early twentieth century. Some of them still exist (e.g., Uteshenie, Brilliant are a part of modern Castlegar), but some of these toponyms (place names) are spelled differently from Russian transliteration system followed in this volume (e.g., Uteshenie is spelled in Castlegar as Ootischenia).
9. A respectful and formal way to address adults in Russia is by their first name and patronymic (a derivative from the name of the father). Patronymic is also included in all official records, for example, Vasil'evich (for men) and Vasil'evna (for women) indicate that the name of the person's father is Vasiliĭ.

Contents

1   Resettlement from Taurida Guberniia to the Caucasus   1

2   Pëtr Vasil'evich Verigin   5

3   Life and Death of Luker'ia Vasil'evna Kalmykova   9

4   The Arrest of Pëtr Vasil'evich and His Exile from the Orphans' Home   19

5   His Exile According to the Administrative Order to Arkhangel'sk Guberniia for Five Years   23

6   The Transfer of Pëtr Vasil'evich from Shenkursk to the Island of Kola. The Extension of His Exile for Five More Years. The Return to Shenkursk   27

7   What Happened to the Orphans' Home. Division of the Doukhobors   31

8   My Trip to Shenkursk and My Communal Life There   35

9   Pëtr Vasil'evich's Message to the Doukhobors Through Ivan Evseevich Konkin   43

10	The Relaying of the Message and Its Fulfilment by the Doukhobors. The Exile of Ivan Evseevich Konkin	51
11	The New Exile of Pëtr Vasil'evich to Obdorsk of the Tobol'sk Guberniia for Five Years. The Trip by Vasiliĭ Gavrilovich Vereshchagin and Brother Vasiliĭ Vasil'evich to Shenkursk to Visit Pëtr Vasil'evich and Their Receipt of a Message for the Doukhobors	55
12	Prisoner Transport of Pëtr Vasil'evich to Obdorsk, Tobol'sk Guberniia	61
13	Accomplishment of the Mission. Letter of Pëtr Vasil'evich to the Doukhobors. Doukhobors' Refusal of Military Service. Imprisonment of Vasiliĭ Verigin and Vereshchagin	67
14	The Burning of Weapons in Three Guberniias and the Return of the Reserve Conscription Cards	75
15	The Burning of Weapons in the Akhalkalak Area and the Brutal Massacre by the Government	81
16	The Destruction of Livelihood and Possessions; Resettlement Among the Indigenous Peoples	85
17	My Arrest and Life in Prisons	89
18	Torments in the Ekaterinograd Disciplinary Battalion	105
19	Exile to Iakutsk Area. The Description of the Prisoner Transport to Nizhneudinsk	119
20	The Continuation of Prisoner Transport. The Last Words and Death of Vasiliĭ G. Vereshchagin	129
21	Life in Nel'kan	139

22	Life in Notor, Iakutsk and Other Areas	143
23	A Trip to Russia	153
24	A Trip Abroad	159
25	Arrival in England. Meeting the Chertkovs	165
26	A Request for Relocation. A Letter by Pëtr Vasil'evich to the Empress Aleksandra Fëdorovna Romanova	171
27	The Relocation	175
28	A Letter of Anastasiia Vasil'evna Verigina to Empress Aleksandra Fëdorovna Romanova	181
29	The March of Brothers and Sisters for God's Cause	183
30	The Release of Pëtr Vasil'evich Verigin by the Russian Government and His Journey to Canada to the Doukhobors	187
31	Pëtr Vasil'evich Travels Around All the Villages. His Speeches and His Advice to the People	191
32	The Congress for the Discussion of the Land Issue. Acceptance of Land	197
33	Starting the Communal Household. The Life of Pëtr Vasil'evich in Otradnoe	203
34	Cancellation of Land Entries by the Government for Non-acceptance of Allegiance to the British King Edward	207
35	A Letter to the Government and the People of Canada Regarding Cancellation of Land Entries	211

36	A Move to British Columbia. An Explanation to the Government	219
37	Detailed Inquiry and Investigation by Royal Commissioner William Blakemore	225
38	The Explanatory Letters of Doukhobors to Blakemore	231
39	The Inquiry Report and the Recommendation of the Royal Commissioner William Blakemore	239
40	A Conversation Between Military Minister Bowser and the Doukhobors About Registries and Schools	245
41	The Resolution by Soldiers Who Returned from the War Reached at a Big Meeting in Nelson on February 13, 1919	259
42	Canada and Doukhobors	265
43	Death and Funeral of Pëtr the Lordly	271

Addendum 1: A Visit of Molokan Brothers and Sisters by Pëtr Vasil'evich	279
Addendum 2: The Last Poem by Pëtr Verigin, "Oh, Lord, you are the light of my life"	285
Appendix 1: The Author's Appendix Information	287
Appendix 2: Oath of Allegiance (the Early Twentieth Century)	289
Appendix 3: The English Original of a Letter by James Mavor	291
Name Index	297
Subject Index	301

CHAPTER 1

Resettlement from Taurida Guberniia to the Caucasus

A group of Doukhobors in the Caucasus

Taurida guberniia (governorate) was one of the administrative units of the Russian Empire that comprised the Crimean peninsula, the basin of the lower Dnieper river and the coasts of the Black Sea and Azov Sea.

When the Doukhobors were expelled from the Taurida guberniia by the government in 1840, they were resettled to the Tiflis guberniia, Akhalkalak District[1] to the so-called Wet Mountains, 10 miles[2] from the Turkish border. The government expelled them from the Taurida guberniia because of their religious convictions. They were settled on the Turkish border with the aim of weakening their religious spirit. The climate there was very severe, winters were long and cold. Because of the spring and autumn frost, wheat did not ripen at all, but barley did. For the most part, people ate barley. After two or three years, a small part of the Doukhobors resettled to the Elizavetpol'[3] guberniia, three hundred miles to the east. Our parents were among those who resettled there; they lived in the village of Slavianka. The climate here was tolerable: winters were not as severe and grains would ripen in a satisfactory way.

Most of the Doukhobors stayed in the Wet Mountains. They formed up to ten villages there, and in spite of the severe climate, began to make themselves at home and to cultivate the land in earnest. The land was free and virgin. They began to breed cattle and horses, and soon life improved.

In the village of Goreloe, a so-called public Orphans' Home was built. Orphans' Homes had existed from ancestral times, and the Doukhobors considered this a necessity. An Orphans' Home had been built through communal effort, the material wealth was donated. The Doukhobor leader lived in this house; besides him the old people and orphans who had no other housing lived there as well. That is why the house was called the Orphans' Home. As I recall, in my lifetime, Luker'ia Vasil'evna Kalmykova, the ruler and leader of the Doukhobors, lived there. The house was co-owned with the resettled Doukhobors of Elizavetpol' guberniia where there were four Doukhobor villages. Donations were given by them as well. Donations consisted mostly of money, but wheat was also brought in moderate amounts, because in the Wet Mountains it was not available.

After 40 years of living there the Doukhobors completely felt at home and became well-to-do people. The Orphans' Home was also increasing its resources, and during this time, a capital of 100,000 roubles had accumulated there. There were 150 head of cattle, about 100 horses and about 2000 select sheep. Such an enterprise must be ruled by a reliable person who was elected from the society and was like an *ataman*,[4] one who kept all in order. He made all the decisions he was able to, but whenever he could not cope, he asked for advice from Luker'ia Vasil'evna and she advised him. For the most part, the Doukhobors who lived there looked after the household, but other Doukhobors often worked there as volunteers. They were paid 25 roubles a year. In addition to this, all of their regular needs including clothing were taken care of. At that time, the government did not bother the Doukhobors very much. Not only the Doukhobors but all of the population of the Caucasus were not required to perform military service because, aside from the Doukhobors and Molokans,[5] all of the population was Asian. Since the population consisted of Moslems, Armenians and Georgians, they were granted the privilege of not performing military service until a specific time. Now I will stop and begin writing about Pëtr Vasil'evich Verigin.

Notes

1. Akhalkalak (modern Akhalkalaki) is an administrative district in the country of Georgia. Now an independent state, in Imperial Russia, Georgia constituted Tiflis guberniia.
2. Here and elsewhere, the Russian word "versta" is translated as a "mile." Verst (versta) is an old Russian measure of distance, one verst equals 1066.8 m.
3. Elizavetpol' (later Kirovabad, since 1989, Ganja) was the capital of Elizavetpol' guberniia in the Russian Empire. Since the separation of Azerbaijan from the Soviet Union, it is one of the largest cities in Azerbaijan.
4. Ataman (particularly among the Cossacks) is a leader of a closely connected group of people such as a village or a family clan.
5. Molokans are a sectarian religious group that split off from the Russian Orthodox Church. At present, Doukhobors of Canada and Molokans of the United States retain amicable relationships and send representatives to each other's major events.

CHAPTER 2

Pëtr Vasil'evich Verigin

Pëtr Vasil'evich Verigin

Pëtr Vasil'evich was born in the Caucasus, in the Elizavetpol' guberniia,[1] in the village of Slavianka in 1858 on the 29th of June, on the saints' day of Peter and Paul, into the peaceful and devout family of Verigins.

© The Author(s) 2019
G. V. Verigin, *The Chronicles of Spirit Wrestlers' Immigration to Canada*, https://doi.org/10.1007/978-3-030-18525-1_2

This name originates from the word *verigi* [chains]. Our ancestor, Fëdorushka, from the Old Believers, was the *bearer of chains*. As far as we remember, our heritage begins with him. Upon accepting Christ, he had his second birth in the Holy Spirit baptized in the name of the Father, the Son, and the Holy Spirit. Fëdorushka's son was Prokof'iushka. Prokof'iushka's son was Luk'ianushka. Luk'ianushka's son—Vasil'iushka—this is our immediate parent.

Our mother, Anastasiia Vasil'evna, originated from the family of Kapustin. Father Verigin was of stern and just character, neither coveting nor envious of other people's possessions. He always used to tell us: "Look children, if you desire wealth, then attain it through a just way through your own labour. Don't covet others' possessions. And especially, do not steal. If a lost object lies on the road, drive around it at a distance of a few feet in order not to be tempted. If that object was discarded by someone as unnecessary, you do not need it either. But if however, someone has dropped it by mistake, he will look for it and find it." He always used to say: "Look children, the man may be naked but righteous. Avoid drunkenness as you would avoid hell."

In the religious sense he was a true Doukhobor. The resettlement of the Doukhobors from Taurida guberniia[2] to the Caucasus was done by the government with the purpose of weakening the Doukhobor spirit in the realization of their true path. The government announced: if someone does not want to resettle, they may stay, but they must become Orthodox. Such an offer was more for the rich people; and this related to Vasiliĭ Luk'ianovich as well. His father, Luk'ian Prokof'evich, was still alive. They had their own land, several tens of thousands of high bred sheep named *shlyonka*. It would be a great carnal temptation for a secular person, but Vasiliĭ Luk'ianovich did not waiver in spirit, he neither held onto anything nor regretted anything, he was only concerned with the preservation of Doukhoborism.

Our mother had a meek and peaceful character and she approached every being with love. In her family, she maintained Christian order, always mentioned God and His power. She hardly ever scolded us and never beat us. If we didn't listen to her at times, and she was trying to influence us, it was with her meek request and prayer. Sometimes we didn't listen to that either. In that case, she would tell us: "Or else I will tell your father of your disobedience." The word "father" influenced us more strongly and we would always settle down. It happened like that only when we were small and didn't know what it meant not to listen to your own mother. However, when we began to understand these things, then we always tried to fulfil her personal request, without waiting for the word "father" from her. But to tell the truth, our father never beat us either, although he was stern. Both of them, mother and father, were solidly built; there was no lack in physical beauty, they were, as they say, blood with milk.[3] Pëtr Vasil'evich originated from those parents.

Our parents had seven sons and two daughters. The eldest was Ivan, the second one was Fëdor, the third was daughter Anna, the fourth was Lukeian, the fifth was Prokofiĭ, the sixth was Varvara, the seventh was Vasiliĭ, the eighth was Pëtr and the ninth was Grigoriĭ. All of them were built well, but Pëtr Vasil'evich stood out with the slenderness of his body, the beauty of his face and his moral and spiritual being. From childhood, he had an inclination towards the holy church, which means a disposition towards the prayers and spiritual sobraniia[4] meetings of the brothers and sisters, he studied all the significant Doukhobor psalms. The three of us, Vasiliĭ, Pëtr and Grigoriĭ, studied in school; Ivan Evseevich Konkin and others studied with us. In all, there were about ten students. The school was a simple village school and was located in our house. In studies, Pëtr Vasil'evich was also ahead of others; in oral lessons, he was better than we were; his drawing turned out more properly than ours. Our teacher always reprimanded us pointing at him: "Look how studious Petrusha[5] is, how everything turns out neat and well in his work." And he told me, "You, Grisha, you are only concerned with filling your tummy." For my inept studiousness, our teacher often put me on my knees and so on. We learned mathematics well, and also learned to read and write, but as soon as we completed our grammar, our school was over, which meant we stopped studying and entered into household duties.

Our parents did not live in a very wealthy fashion, but not poorly; they were engaged in growing grain, had 3000 sheep, 100 cattle, about 70 horses, a water mill with two grinders and a general store. According to his age, Pëtr Vasil'evich participated in all of these affairs: he pastured the calves, the cows, the sheep, he ploughed the land, managed the mill, and for some time, worked in the general store. Without exaggeration, I would say all turned out better with him than with the other brothers. This happened because, besides his abilities to tend to each affair, he had a great love and willingness for each job. He always did his best to have everything in good order so that neither his father nor his elder brothers who visited him could find any fault with his work.

During this period of his youth, one event threatened him with death. This was during the Russo-Turkish war near Kars.[6] Soldiers wounded in the war were stationed in our village of Slavianka as well and were ill with typhus. He also contracted this disease. He had a strong fever, and for two weeks he suffered from a frightening severe delirium. He could not be left without care; he could wander off anywhere. In order to reduce this strong fever at least a little, we collected snow in small sacks and took turns putting them on his head. He was in such a state for two weeks. Then he became very weak and it seemed that his life was over. They were already reading funeral psalms and preparing the burial clothes; they expected his death any moment. All were impossibly sorry for him and with sincere tears, we appealed to God in prayer. Whether it was because God heard our prayers or because Pëtr Vasil'evich was destined not to die but to perform great deeds in his life, he conquered death. His condition slowly improved and he began to recover, and after some time, he recovered completely. He was 16 years old then.

Time passed and he turned 21. It was necessary to marry. He married Avdot'ia Grigor'evna Kotel'nikova.

Notes

1. Elizavetpol' (later Kirovabad, since 1989, Ganja) was the capital of Elizavetpol' guberniia in the Russian Empire. Since the separation of Azerbaijan from the Soviet Union, it is one of the largest cities in Azerbaijan.
2. Taurida guberniia (governorate) was one of the administrative units of the Russian Empire that comprised the Crimean peninsula, the basin of the lower Dnieper river and the coasts of the Black Sea and Azov Sea.
3. "krov's molokom" ("blood and milk," in reference to white complexion and rosy colour of cheeks) is a Russian expression indicating both beauty and health.
4. Sobranie (sobran'e, sobraniia in plural) is a Doukhobor Assembly that typically started with "molenie" (molen'e) (including prayers, psalms and hymns) and continued with the resolution of pertinent matters by the assembly.
5. Petrusha is one of diminutives of endearment that can be formed from the Russian given name Pëtr.
6. Kars is a town in Turkey. With its surrounding area, at the time of the narrative, it belonged to the Russian Empire. It was one of the areas of the Transcaucasian exile of the Doukhobors. Since 1921, it has been a part of Turkey.

CHAPTER 3

Life and Death of Luker'ia Vasil'evna Kalmykova

Luker'ia Vasil'evna Kalmykova, Doukhobor leader

Now I will begin to describe Luker'ia Vasil'evna Kalmykova's visits to the Doukhobors who lived in Elizavetpol'[1] guberniia. I remember three visits. Luker'ia Vasil'evna always stayed with the Verigins. Our mother was Pëtr Larionovich Kalmykov's[2] aunt. Thus Luker'ia Vasil'evna visited her as the aunt of her late husband. Her first visit was when Pëtr Vasil'evich and I were children. I remember how every morning she invited us to her room and asked us to stand beside her, with arms folded on our chests. This was in preparation to read the children's psalms. And we began to recite them. When we finished she thanked us and said, "These are clever boys." And she gave us candies and nuts. We bowed in thanks and left in triumph.

Her second visit was when we had already finished school. She again invited both of us to her room and asked us to read a book, to write, to make arithmetical calculations, to draw and so on. To tell the truth, Pëtr Vasil'evich's work turned out better than mine and received more approval, but she didn't want to offend me because I was the youngest and she told us, "How well you read, write, calculate and draw, all is very good!" When she was leaving for her home in Goreloe all the Doukhobors were supposed to see her off to a certain place. She had her own covered buggy with four good horses. When the buggy was sent to the house, she said good-bye to the Verigin family, got into the buggy, and asked my mother and us to get into the buggy as well. I was placed beside the coachman and Pëtr Vasil'evich was seated beside her. Overall, she liked him more than me. I was a great fan of the horses and looked at them for the most part, but I also occasionally looked at Luker'ia Vasil'evna and my mother and brother. They spoke about something in a low voice but I was able to overhear and understand the conversation. Luker'ia Vasil'evna said, "Nastiusha," this is how she addressed our mother, "Cherish Petrusha,[3] love him, bring him up in the Christian spirit, know that he belongs to me. The time will come and I will call for him. I will need him for God's work, but you should keep it a secret." I heard that but I was not as interested in that as much as in the horses. From those two visits, there is little else left in my memory. When she arrived the third time, Pëtr Vasil'evich was already married and I was 18 years old.

All the Doukhobors loved, respected, and to some degree, adored Luker'ia Vasil'evna. She was their leader. She was a tall and slender woman. Her face was indescribably beautiful. She was of a tender character and never resorted to any severe measures. If the Doukhobors wavered from justice and virtue sometimes, she pleaded with them, provided explanations and guidance, and always succeeded. And I would again repeat that the Doukhobors loved her so much, not only the elders and adults but all the children loved her.

During her visits, no one stayed at home to look after the household. The news about her arrival spread quickly throughout all of the villages and everyone who possibly could went in a hurry to Slavianka to meet her. The first meeting took place 30 miles ahead. In front, there were about 20 people on horseback, and then everyone who could be there from Slavianka and other villages went to meet her about eight miles ahead of their land boundaries. They always met her with bread and salt and the singing of spiritual psalms. When her buggy appeared about one mile ahead, people would start to move. On the one side there was joy, on the other there was concern that everything must be in order. I was a coachman for my parents. A light buggy was led by dark stallions and I stayed in the buggy steering the horses. When Luker'ia Vasil'evna's buggy was approaching, people stood on both sides singing. Then the singing ended. Luker'ia Vasil'evna, not leaving the buggy, greeted everyone: "How are you? Are all in good health? Is everyone well?" All replied in a loud chorus "Slava Bogu [Glory be to God]! Happy arrival, you are welcome!"

She spoke a little, invited my mother to her buggy and drove on. My father came, got into the buggy as well, and I took my place behind the buggy. At our place, Luker'ia Vasil'evna touched upon the subject of Pëtr Vasil'evich's marriage. She spoke to our parents thus, "I warned you of this earlier, that I will take him for my own. For what task you do not need to know, but I wished that he were not tied to any worldly attachments. Nothing should hinder him in the task that I am taking him for. He should even consider his father and mother as a secondary matter. In a word, he must sacrifice himself for God, that is for serving God. As for the divorce of his marriage, this is your personal matter: if there is agreement from both sides they may divorce." Thus, having visited for some time, she said good-bye to everyone and left. And she never returned to Slavianka.

The divorce began. It lasted for a long time. The parents of Avdot'ia Grigor'evna Kotel'nikova didn't give their permission, but finally she realized the impossibility of their life together, she collected all her belongings, her clothes, and other things and left forever for her parent's home. This matter did not end there. Pëtr Vasil'evich kept offering her the divorce. At Kotel'nikov's house she gave birth to a boy, they called him Pëtr.

Finally the day came, a day when her parents, along with her, agreed to the divorce, with the payment of 500 roubles to her. Then Pëtr Vasil'evich announced that matter in the regional village court, and in the presence of the village starosta,[4] starshina[5] and other elected members, he received the legal divorce certificate with the official seals of the starosta and starshina, and thus the marriage became void.

On February 29, 1882, Pëtr Vasil'evich set out for Luker'ia Vasil'evna Kalmykova's Orphans' Home in Goreloe. His departure was reported to the local society. Vasia Kabatov let his eldest son Fadeĭ accompany him and also provided a horse for the trip. My parents also let me go with them. We took a wagon with three horses and on the fourth day arrived in Goreloe. We went directly to Luker'ia Vasil'evna's home. She was very happy to see Pëtr Vasil'evich. We visited for two weeks and returned to Slavianka.

During his stay there she respected him and loved him. She advised him not to interfere with household affairs and he was to work only with her. Often she sent him to other villages on some errands, often he wrote letters she dictated to the government and to the Doukhobors. If she left somewhere on business or visits, he was always with her.

Seeing such a good relationship of Luker'ia Vasil'evna with Pëtr Vasil'evich, most Doukhobors also respected him. The more she loved him, the more he was hated by her relatives and those close to her. They kept this to themselves and did not discuss this openly because Luker'ia Vasil'evna scolded them for every offensive word directed at him and said, "He has a father, mother, brothers and sisters whom he has forsaken for the call of God, for our mutual well-being. And you look at him in this way, and you are even ready to offend him—this should not be done." With such approval from Luker'ia Vasil'evna, he stayed with her until her death.

For five years of his stay there he only came to Slavianka once. This was at the beginning of September in 1886. Luker'ia Vasil'evna went to Tiflis[6] because of her illness and from there she sent him to visit his parents and relatives. A telegram arrived, "Send horses to the station Dzegam.[7] Pëtr Verigin." Our oldest brother Ivan went there and took me with him. We came to Dzegam. Pëtr Vasil'evich met us and kissed us and soon by nightfall we were at home. The meeting with parents and relatives was not without tears of joy. On the second day, he wanted to observe all of the household, whether it had grown or decreased since his departure. All the seven brothers rode on horseback along with the brother-in-law Ivan Konkin and the closest childhood friend of Pëtr Vasil'evich, Fëdor V. Konkin.

All nine people went to the farm. They had to cover six miles to the rented land where we had farms for sheep, horses and cattle and there was also a house. They had sent a man there to prepare for our arrival. When we arrived there, Pëtr Vasil'evich observed everything and said, "It is good that you have such wealth but it is not good that you did not earn this through your own labour. You are here as overseers, of course, you observe all of this, and maintain order, but the labour comes more from your workers." He pointed at them. They were Tatars, of a poor class, some had families, some were seasonal workers and there were others. There were about 12 people. Among them were also women. Many of them remembered him and were curious to see him. He pointed at them, saying that to keep them as labourers was bad, wrong, and not the Christian way. "The word Christians derives from the word Christ. You believe in Him, but that is not enough, you must practise what you preach. Christ said, "All are children of God and should live like brothers." Christ said, "Feed the hungry, and help the poor. If you have two shirts, give one to those who have none." Christ called all people to be equal so there would be no poor and no rich. Although you pay them a legal salary, your position is quite different from their position. My brotherly, most sincere desire is that you will understand this. Let your property be half of what it is now, as long as you would become Christians in deed and not only in words. This will bring you greater benefits, the spiritual side is more important than the material. The material side is temporary, the spiritual is eternal, what profit is there to have the whole world and to harm your soul." And he spoke of many other things.

All the brothers listened attentively and did not say anything other than words of gratitude. We understood immediately that he was calling us to fulfil the teaching of Christ. From his youth, Pëtr Vasil'evich had led the same life as we had and even approved of it, but now he had adopted a spiritual life and he invited us to do the same. And for all of us, the question was answered as to why Luker'ia had invited him to her home. He was born in the flesh as Verigin, but his spiritual rebirth in the Holy Spirit came from Luker'ia Vasil'evna Kalmykova. He spent three days with us, and then as he was ordered, said good-bye to all of us and left for Tiflis.

For 23 years in her office, Luker'ia Vasil'evna did not have any conflicts or disagreements with the government. She was well known to Aleksandr Nikolaevich and acquainted with Mikhail Nikolaevich,[8] who was the chief commander in the Caucasus and lived in Tiflis. He and his wife visited Luker'ia Vasil'evna several times. When Luker'ia Vasil'evna sent the deputies personally to the emperor in St. Petersburg for community reasons, Mikhail Nikolaevich made a report to the emperor about this, and the deputies had a personal audience with the emperor and explained why they were sent, and always returned with a satisfactory answer.

When the Russo-Turkish war began near Kars in which Mikhail participated, and there was some assistance needed to transport weapons and other war materials, Mikhail came to Luker'ia Vasil'evna personally. He explained his difficult situation and asked for assistance. Luker'ia Vasil'evna reminded him that the Doukhobors, according to Christ's teaching, considered it a great sin to take part in military action. Mikhail was personally acquainted with her and sincerely respected her and agreed with that. But at the same time he asked Luker'ia to understand his and her positions: "You should understand, Luker'ia Vasil'evna, that with all your Doukhobors you will become the first target for Turkey. If only the Turkish regiments advance ten miles you will be the first to suffer. I do not ask you to take up arms and to enter the ranks of the army, I only ask you to give us the wagons to transport the military munitions. The battles and the front will be in the distance. Your wagons will be far away and it is likely that no one from the Doukhobors will be injured. And the most important aspect in your understanding of Christ's teaching is that the Doukhobors must not kill a person—so this cannot ever happen."

Because of this necessity, Luker'ia had to give in to his entreaties. Immediately, she called a convention and offered this matter for discussion by all the Doukhobors.

Up to 400 wagons went to Aleksandropol',[9] and from there, on demand, they carried out what they were called for.

As they were leaving, they first had to drive to the village of Goreloe to see Luker'ia Vasil'evna. She gave them necessary advice about the trip. She said, "You go to help the military action, even if indirectly. Your ancestors avoided this, and in our time we also have to resist. But because of the known reasons, as a woman, I neither insist on it, nor oppose it. But I warn you this may be the last illegal deed in the history of the Doukhobors, this is service to Baal.[10] I ask you not to forget about it and always remember God. To remember God means not to do bad things, which may bring harm to yourself. First, don't drink wine. Second, be careful. Care is your best and true friend, which will save you from unfortunate events. If you are called to help collect casualties, whether Russian or Turkish, if someone is alive, help them as much as possible. God forbid that you will search the pockets of the dead. Do not do this under any circumstances: people have sacrificed their lives, and without thinking about that, you will search their pockets tempted by a rouble or two. Besides that, during that awful action, there could be a stray bullet that will hit you. What then will be more precious to you, your life or those two roubles? I ask and warn you, all that I have said fulfill in detail and you will be fortunate. According to Christ, one hair from your head will not be harmed."

Thanking their spiritual leader for such advice, they bid her a tearful farewell.

Living among the Doukhobors, Luker'ia Vasil'evna, from time to time, reminded them about all of their failings such as drunkenness and other matters. She also raised the issue of military matters because the time of recruiting young people for such awful and wrong deeds was approaching. She spoke seriously about this with Pëtr Vasil'evich and, in particular, she wanted to know his opinion about this.

Pëtr Vasil'evich studied the history of the Doukhobors from his childhood, read all of the psalms in which all this [military action] is denied and he also read the Gospel about the life and teaching of Jesus Christ. In the refusal of military action, Pëtr Vasil'evich saw the service of God. Christ said, "who loves their father and mother more than me is not worthy of me," and so on. Pëtr Vasil'evich faced the alternative: obedience to the government or service to God. As usual he chose the second, service to God. Luker'ia Vasil'evna was happy for his choice and at the same time she cried a lot.

Sometimes she called him Zhurushka.[11] The word "Zhurushka" meant that occasionally he was in a sad mood. It happened probably when he had a conflict between flesh and spirit. She cried saying, "What is ahead of you only God knows. They may put you in prison, you will be separated from your relatives and all the Doukhobors, you will be deprived of freedom. I will not be here anymore to comfort you, as I am doing now. But know and remember for sure, Zhurushka, that if you fulfil God's will, He will comfort you and help you more than any one of us could. He will visit you in prison, He will preserve your well-being, He will help you everywhere and with everything. Only do not forsake Him and listen to His voice which will originate from your own soul and reason. Let our heavenly Father help you first to have victory over your body, to subdue body to spirit. Then it will be easier for you to conquer the Prince of Darkness of this world. When the victory is complete and you are free, how pleasant it will be then to remember me and all your difficult path to victory. We will meet in the future. There Christ awaits you and will congratulate you on the great victory of the glorious fighter for truth."

On December 15, 1886, Luker'ia Vasil'evna died. From the day of her passing, the Doukhobors had a big change in their lives. I will now tell you about that.

Most of the Doukhobors wanted Pëtr Vasil'evich to remain in the Orphans' Home and to govern there as Luker'ia, who died at the age of 46, had done for 23 years. But about one-sixth or one-seventh part of Doukhobors, including her relatives, did not agree to this. Luker'ia Vasil'evna had a brother, Mikhail Gubanov, two sisters, Praskov'ia and Tat'iana, and an uncle Ignat Gubanov. At that time, the elder was Alekseĭ Zubkov who occupied this position for 25 years and knew all of the government officials. Ivan Vasil'evich Baturin was *ataman* and they were all against Pëtr Vasil'evich. A small group joined them.

Two parties appeared among the Doukhobors. The majority of the Doukhobors belonged to a party legally insisting that Pëtr Vasil'evich should govern the Doukhobors and demanding that all matters should be delegated to him. They were trying to prove that he was invited by Luker'ia Vasil'evna for that very purpose, and after he had spent five years there honourably, he became aware of all of the rules and customs of the Orphan's Home, and from the moral character perspective, he also definitely deserved that position.

The other party included a minority of the Doukhobors. None of them distinguished themselves in any way in the community and they were driven by mercenary motives. They captured the financial assets. They appealed to the government for help, and they began to tell lies saying that all the inheritance belonged to the relatives of Luker'ia Vasil'evna. The government didn't interfere in that matter as they knew very well that the house and all the property belonged to all the Doukhobors, and that those informers were after other people's belongings. Then the minority party attempted to bribe the government officials on the condition that the officials would accept lies and slander by the minority party as true statements, and that these officials would always take the side of the minority party whenever necessary before the higher authorities.

Prince Sumbatov, Akhalkalak Region authority, received 10,000 roubles. When Prince Sumbatov left his position, his successor was D'iachkov-Tarasov who received 5000 roubles. Tiflis Governor Zissermann received a gift of a pair of Voronezh stallions priced at 2000 roubles. After that, the authorities began to side in their reports with the lies and slander.

Notes

1. Elizavetpol' (later Kirovabad, since 1989 – Ganja) was the capital of Elizavetpol' guberniia in the Russian empire. Since the separation of Azerbaijan from the Soviet Union, it is one of the largest cities in Azerbaijan.
2. Pëtr Ilarionovich (Larionovich) Kalmykov (around 1836–1864) was a leader of the Doukhobors and the husband of Lukeria Kalmykova, who took the role of a Doukhobor leader after his death.
3. Petrusha is one of the diminutives of endearment that can be formed from the Russian given name Pëtr.

4. "Starosta" in Imperial Russia was the head of self-governance of a Russian village endowed with the power of registering marriages and divorces.
5. "Starshina" in Imperial Russia was a head of the Cossack unit. The word also means a person in charge. It can also relate to a low military rank.
6. Tiflis is the old name of modern Tbilisi, the capital of the country of Georgia. In the nineteenth century, it was the capital of Tiflis guberniia, which was a part of the Russian Empire.
7. Dzegam most likely refers to modern Dzagam (Dzegam), a town in Azerbaijan. At the time of the narrative, Azerbaijan was a part of the Russian Empire.
8. Aleksandr Nikolaevich Romanov and Mikhail Nikolaevich Romanov were Grand Dukes of Russia. The author omits their last name and their titles in the narrative. The omission of the titles may be due to the Doukhobor belief in the equality of all people. The omission of the last names could be due to the author's understanding that this was common knowledge in the days the narrative took place.
9. Aleksandropol' at the time of the narrative was a town in Imperial Russia. After the collapse of the Soviet Union and the independence of Armenia, it was renamed Giymri. Giymri is the second largest city of Armenia.
10. Baal is an ancient god of storm and fertility worshipped by the Canaanites (Ancient Phoenicians). Baal is mentioned in the Bible; and in the Christian tradition, he became an allegory of a false God, a blood-thirsty demon and one of the Princes of Hell.
11. Pëtr Verigin's nickname "Zhurushka" given to him by Luker'ia Kalmykova is a diminutive form from the word "zhuravl'," a crane. Cranes are often associated with sadness and grief in Russian culture probably due to the perceived sadness of their calls.

CHAPTER 4

The Arrest of Pëtr Vasil'evich and His Exile from the Orphans' Home

January 26, 1887, according to the Doukhobor custom, was a memorial day for Luker'ia Vasil'evna Kalmykova. On this day, all the Doukhobors gathered at her graveside. After the liturgy was over, they arrived at the Orphans' Home where she had lived. There was a dinner prepared for everyone, and at the conclusion, Ivan Fadeevich Makhortov called upon all of the brothers and sisters to give thanks to God according to Doukhobor beliefs, and then depart for their homes.

First, they bowed to the Lord in thanks for their present life. The second bow was for the soul of Luker'ia Vasil'evna to rest in peace and enter the Kingdom of Heaven. With the third bow, they wished Pëtr Vasil'evich to take over the position of Luker'ia Vasil'evna in this house. The police chief Prince Sumbatov was also present. He had been purposely invited by the opposite side in order to support their lies. Sumbatov saw that from Pëtr Vasil'evich's side nothing illegal had been done. If Pëtr Vasil'evich was delegated with anything, it was done by the majority of the people. But because Sumbatov had been bribed and had decided to make an arrest, he demanded that Pëtr Vasil'evich should show his passport that he had while living there. But his passport had already been stolen by Mar'ia Tikhonovna, a housemaid of Luker'ia Vasil'evna. When the passport did not appear, Sumbatov required Pëtr Vasil'evich to go with him to Akhalkalak[1] regional office for further investigation of this case. That very evening they left the Orphans' Home, to which he never returned. He had spent five years in this house without offending or harming anyone. Luker'ia Vasil'evna was no longer there to defend him. The dissenters treated him so heartlessly and unfairly.

Thus began the troubles of a young 28-year-old man who was innocent before God and man. People began to persecute him because of their jealousy and with the purpose of gaining control of all of the community property obtained via the sacrifices of all the Doukhobors. And in order to gain it, they were prepared to put an innocent person to death.

Through such devious means, the story of Jesus Christ was repeated. Those nearest to Him, His own kin, came to betray Him to Pilate and demanded to have Christ crucified. They understood that the leadership, that is, Luker'ia Vasil'evna's place, was now his, and this did not agree with their taste. So they were preparing even more evil plots as if the leadership depended upon people or that man who was destined to inherit it.[2]

It is impossible for man to reach that which is unattainable for him. This is what happened in this case. It looked as though, albeit illegally, they had attained their desired purpose to gain in material wealth. But the real spiritual leadership remained with the one who was visited by the Heavenly Father. And the one visited by such a heavenly spirit will overcome all the troubles and survive all the perils on his way, and in the end, he will nevertheless reveal in himself the power of God not available to everyone.

When they arrived at the Akhalkalak Regional office, the local police chief Sumbatov held Pëtr Vasil'evich there for three days, then required him to resettle to Slavianka and passed him and his packaged case file to a policeman who accompanied him as far as Elizavetpol'.[3] There he introduced him to the Governor Nakashidze, who after looking into the case, sent him to Slavianka. Pëtr Vasil'evich arrived at his parent's house and lived there for some time. The majority of the Doukhobors did not find anything bad about him and wished he were in charge of the Orphans' Home. Sometimes sobraniia (Doukhobor assemblies) were held. The opposite side was concerned that he would create some unrest among the people. At the head of this small party were Andreĭ Markov, who was starshina[4] at that time, Evseĭ Konkin, Grigoriĭ Kotel'nikov, Vasiliĭ Streliaev, Vasiliĭ Agafonov and others. They began to report that Verigin was a great threat. The money pursued its own ends again. The money was transferred from the Orphans' Home in Goreloe.

On March 5, the Elizavetpol' Governor Nakashidze ordered the district police officer Asak-bek to deliver Pëtr Vasil'evich and his father Vasiliĭ Lukianovich to Elizavetpol' and announced that they must stay in town under police surveillance. An Armenian, Efrem Nanasov, a good acquaintance of Verigin's, bailed them out into his care and took them to his house. They spent four months at his place. The Elizavetpol' guberniia is a very hot area, so Pëtr Vasil'evich appealed to the assistant of the chief commander, General Peshcherov, pointing out that the climate was unsuitable for them and asked for permission to return to Slavianka. General Peshcherov considered this request and ordered Governor Nakashidze to release them from surveillance and allow them to go to Slavianka.

When they came back to Slavianka, the opposite side became agitated and started to report various perjuries to the government (via a court official).

Notes

1. Akhalkalak (modern Akhalkalaki) is an administrative district in the country of Georgia. Now an independent state, in Imperial Russia, Georgia constituted Tiflis guberniia.
2. The author means that spiritual leadership is in God's and not in human hands.
3. Elizavetpol' (later Kirovabad, since 1989, Ganja) was the capital of Elizavetpol' guberniia in the Russian Empire. Since the separation of Azerbaijan from the Soviet Union, it is one of the largest cities in Azerbaijan.
4. "Starshina" in Imperial Russia was a head of the Cossack unit. The word also means a person in charge. It can also relate to a low military rank.

CHAPTER 5

His Exile According to the Administrative Order to Arkhangel'sk Guberniia for Five Years

On August 1, the Governor once again ordered the delivery of Pëtr Vasil'evich to Elizavetpol'[1] under convoy. Upon his arrival, the Governor, without interrogation, put him into prison. On August 15, Pëtr Vasil'evich was transferred to Tiflis[2] and was imprisoned in Metekh[3] Castle in solitary confinement. No one was allowed to see him. His parents arrived, but all their efforts to meet with him were to no avail. On September 10, Pëtr Vasil'evich was secretly taken from Metekh Castle. At midnight, a covered wagon arrived at the castle accompanied by two gendarmes.[4] The prison guard ordered Pëtr Vasil'evich to get dressed explaining that by a special order an official required to see him at the regional municipal office for interrogation. Not suspecting anything, Pëtr Vasil'evich got in the wagon and it drove on. As they were passing the regional municipal office, Pëtr Vasil'evich became frightened and he asked the gendarmes: "Where are you taking me? The office is behind us and it is midnight." Realizing their behaviour was inhuman, the gendarmes tried to calm him down, saying: "Calm down, Pëtr Vasil'evich, nothing of harm will come to you, we are only transferring you to Dushet[5] Prison three stations from Tiflis, on government order." Pëtr Vasil'evich, believing them, calmed down. They arrived at the first station, changed horses, and drove on, then Pëtr Vasil'evich relaxed completely. They brought him to Dushet Prison. The gendarmes apologized, justifying their actions by higher government orders.

This secretive undertaking disturbed all his relatives and the Doukhobors. But soon they discovered his location and visited him. In this prison, it was even easier because the guard was a good-hearted person and didn't have anything against him. He was there until October 10, 1887, when on an administrative order, he was exiled via Vladikavkaz[6] to the town of Shenkursk,[7] Arkhangel'sk[8] Region. A close relative, Ivan Stepanovich Verigin, expressed a wish to accompany him on such a distant journey. Pëtr Vasil'evich agreed. The second man who expressed his eager desire to accompany Pëtr Vasil'evich on his way to the place of his exile was Emel'ian Dmitrievich Dmitriev of the Orthodox persuasion, resident of Tiflis and a close acquaintance of Luker'ia Vasil'evna. Both of them, with the agreement of the Doukhobors, set off on the long journey with him. These two men followed him of their own will. Where it was possible to visit him in prisons, or way stations, they visited him. On the way, Pëtr Vasil'evich had to stay in many prisons and to experience hardships, not only from the prisoners but also from the convoy soldiers, who, following their violent and illegal orders, behaved in the most inhumane fashion with the people. He lived through all of the unsanitary conditions of the stage stops. After six months of such a trip, he arrived in Arkhangel'sk.

The governor of Arkhangel'sk decided upon Shenkursk as his place of exile. In order to get there, they had to retrace the same route for 400 miles. Pëtr Vasil'evich decided to travel there by post horses. The governor was not against this and gave his permission. A gendarme officer was appointed as his convoy, and upon arrival, he passed over Pëtr Vasil'evich to the surveillance of the Shenkursk municipal policeman.

Those two men accompanying him on behalf of the Doukhobors arrived at Shenkursk as well, but they only spent a short time there. The government did not allow them to remain. They parted with Pëtr Vasil'evich and returned to the Caucasus where they reported on his journey in complete detail, and his settlement in Shenkursk, and how they left him there alone.

His relatives, especially his parents, and all the Doukhobors who knew only too well that he suffered innocently, and was separated from them by such a long distance, were sad and disheartened. There was nothing to be done, and they had to accept such an unjust fate and hope that in the future the government would understand that they were wrong and would return him to his homeland.

At the same time, with Pëtr Vasil'evich, five elders from Kholodnoe were exiled for defending the community property and capital. The first one was Ivan F. Makhortov, 70 years old, the second was Fëdor Rybin of the same age, the third one was Ignatiĭ Argatov of 65 years, the fourth was Nikolaĭ Tsybul'kin at 67 and the fifth was Alekseĭ Zubkov. They were all sent by administrative order to Olonets Region,[9] the town of Pudozh, for a term of five years.

Living in Shenkursk, Pëtr Vasil'evich wrote letters to his relatives and all the Doukhobors about his health and well-being and asked them not to worry and grieve about him too much because "All is well so far, Thank God, as to the future, leave it to God's will." All his letters and letters to him were carefully censored by the government, and he was under strict surveillance. His relatives and all the Doukhobors wrote letters to him as well. They even sent people to see him as well as the elders in person, and they also sent money. The Doukhobors thought it was necessary because Pëtr Vasil'evich and the elders were exiled because of matters relating to the entire community.

At first, the Caucasian government officials didn't allow trips and refused to give passports. The Doukhobors understood their greed for money very well, and gave them, instead of one rouble, 45 kopecks—legal price for the annual passport—25 roubles and got the passport; they gave 50 roubles, 100 roubles, and when Ivan Konkin needed a passport to submit a petition in St. Petersburg and to visit Pëtr Vasil'evich, he gave 200 roubles. The Shenkursk and Olonetsk governments did not oppress the visitors any more.

Pëtr Vasil'evich, in his youth, was a passionate horse rider. That is why his parents and relatives sent him a bay trotter stallion at a cost of 500 roubles from the Caucasus. It was delivered by his older brother Ivan Vasil'evich. The government did not like this.

Sometime later his sister, Varvara Vasil'evna, married name Konkina, and his cousin and childhood friend, Fëdor Vasil'ievich Konkin, acquired passports in order to spend some time there.

There were some political exiles in Shenkursk: Nikolaĭ Ivanovich Voronin and others. Pëtr Vasil'evich became acquainted with them. Though in the area of spiritual understanding he didn't have much in common with the political exiles, they all had the same outlook at the injustice of the government.

All these actions did not suit the Shenkursk government and the officials began to report more lies to the higher government in order to exile Verigin to a more distant, remote place. The higher government fulfilled this sly intent. The Minister of Interior ordered Verigin to be exiled to Kola.[10]

Notes

1. Elizavetpol' (later Kirovabad, since 1989, Ganja) was the capital of Elizavetpol' guberniia in the Russian Empire. Since the separation of Azerbaijan from the Soviet Union, it is one of the largest cities in Azerbaijan.
2. Tiflis is the old name of modern Tbilisi, the capital of the country of Georgia. In the nineteenth century, it was the capital of Tiflis guberniia, which was a part of the Russian Empire.
3. Metekh (Metekhi) castle was a strongly fortified nineteenth-century prison in the Metekhi area of Tiflis (modern Tbilisi), the capital of Georgia (in the nineteenth century it was a part of the Russian Empire).
4. Gendarmes were a Special Corps of military police in Imperial Russia.
5. Dushet (Dusheti) is a town in Georgia. At the time of the narrative, it was a part of the Russian Empire.
6. Vladikavkaz (the name means in Russian "owner of the Caucasus") is a town located north of Georgia in the north of the Caucasus Mountains. It is currently the capital of North Ossetia-Alania Republic, a subject of the Russian Federation.
7. Shenkursk is a town in Northern Russia; it was one of the places of exile of Pëtr Verigin.
8. Arkhangel'sk (Arkhangelsk) is a city in the north of the European part of Russia.
9. Olonets is a town in the Republic of Karelia, a subject of the Russian Federation. It is located in the Karelian peninsula.
10. Kola is a town in Kola peninsular, Murmansk area, a remote location in the north of the European part of Russia.

CHAPTER 6

The Transfer of Pëtr Vasil'evich from Shenkursk to the Island of Kola. The Extension of His Exile for Five More Years. The Return to Shenkursk

At the beginning of May 1890, Pëtr Vasil'evich was informed by the Shenkursk[1] Municipal Chief of Police that he had to leave for Kola.[2] At the time, his brother Vasiliĭ and Konkin were in St. Petersburg[3] on business regarding a petition. Pëtr Vasil'evich sent a telegram to his brother Vasiliĭ to come to Shenkursk immediately. As for Pëtr Vasil'evich himself, he left for Arkhangel'sk[4] by post horses[5] accompanied by a gendarme[6] who was appointed by the government. From Arkhangel'sk the governor sent him to Kola by ship. Pëtr Vasil'evich was not at all disturbed by this, and on parting with the Shenkursk authorities, he asked them a question, "What does it mean that they are now taking me off your hands?" They shrugged their shoulders and said, "We do not know anything." To which he said, "If you do not know then who does? But that is fine. I have lived here for three years and was looking forward to some changes as I am young and I want to see vast lands and experience as much as possible in my life." Brother Vasiliĭ, upon receiving the telegram, immediately left for Shenkursk where his sister Varvara and Vasiliĭ Ob"edkov were staying with horses and domestic necessities.

Fëdor Vasil'ievich Konkin had already returned home to the Caucasus. Upon leaving Shenkursk Pëtr Vasil'evich asked them to wait for his brother Vasiliĭ and to proceed to Kola after taking the horse and necessary items. This was done. When they arrived in Kola, Pëtr Vasil'evich met them at the dock and they all left for the accommodations together. Everyone was overjoyed with this meeting.

In the Kola police department, the senior policeman in charge was Aleksandr Vertsynskiĭ, an elderly person of about 60 years of age. As it turned out in the conversation with Pëtr Vasil'evich, Vertsynskiĭ was from the Caucasus and a very close acquaintance of our father, Vasiliĭ Luk'ianovich. Vertsynskiĭ treated Pëtr Vasil'evich not as an official but as a very close friend and a good man. Even among the police, there are good people, but they must carry out bad laws. When possible, they leave the law aside and then a good, hearty and kind man appears with whom one can talk about God and about the good qualities of mankind. He was very kind to the visitors and allowed them to stay as long as they wished. After having spent some time there, brother Vasiliĭ and sister Varvara returned home, while Ob"edkov remained with Pëtr Vasil'evich. Even if Vertsynskiĭ did report anything to the higher government about the life and behaviour of Pëtr Vasil'evich, he only reported the best and the fairest. Pëtr Vasil'evich, after having lived there for two years, completed his term in Kola. The order followed to proceed to Arkhangel'sk in order to return home.

Upon Pëtr Vasil'evich's arrival in Arkhangel'sk, the Governor detained him for two weeks, explaining that "the official papers about your release have not arrived from the ministry." These two weeks Pëtr Vasil'evich lived as a free man at the Fedoseev hotel. When the papers arrived, instead of being allowed to go home, he received instructions to continue his exile for a further five years in the Arkhangel'sk region.

Such a brutal and illegal statement was not explained in any way. Maybe it was caused by the government's will or by another request of the illegal claimants of the communal property. There was nothing to be done. A person had to submit to fate. The governor granted the right to Pëtr Vasil'evich to choose where he would prefer to spend his new term. He chose his former place of living in Shenkursk. The governor allowed him to go there on his own. In Shenkursk, though there were problems with the government, he had friends among the exiles who were still there. As for the government, you could mostly ignore it there.

The elders, Makhortov, Rybin, Tsybul'kin and Lezhebokov, were still in Olonetsk guberniia. They also received an additional five-year sentence. Only Argatov, with the permission of the government, had left earlier for Astrakhan'[7] guberniia because he was ill and the government respected his request and allowed him to go to a warmer climate. There, in accordance with God's will, he ended his days.

Upon his arrival in Shenkursk, Pëtr Vasil'evich wrote a letter to the elders. He wrote that if they wished they could apply to the government to resettle to Shenkursk. They did, and the government soon sent them to Shenkursk.

Now a whole family of Doukhobors was settled there. The elders were quite advanced in years, they needed care, food and clothes. The elders were settled in a neighbouring separate accommodation which was used as their dormitory. However, they all dined together at the accommodation of Pëtr Vasil'evich. A female cook was hired. Then they took in two young girls, both orphan beggars. One was 13 and the other was 11, they were sisters. The Doukhobors bought them clothes, footwear and all they needed and paid them a modest salary. For the most part, the girls looked after the bedding and the linen, and helped the cook. The family was enlarging. They found it suitable to buy three Kholmogory milk cows[8] and a horse which was used for their transportation and work in the household. They built greenhouses in which they planted melons, watermelons and cucumbers. Everything grew very well. For the most part, Pëtr Vasil'evich worked on the greenhouses himself. For the Shenkursk inhabitants, such plants were a great curiosity and surprise.

Notes

1. Shenkursk is a town in Northern Russia; it was one of the places of exile of Pëtr Verigin.
2. Kola is a town in Kola peninsular, Murmansk area, a remote location in the north of the European part of Russia.
3. St. Petersburg was the capital of Imperial Russia in 1713–1728 and 1732–1918. It was also called Petrograd and Leningrad during some periods in the twentieth century. Now, it is the second largest city in Russia with a population of over 5 million people. It is known for its museums, architecture, music, theatre and other cultural attractions. Its historic centre is a UNESCO World Heritage Site.
4. Arkhangel'sk (Arkhangelsk) is a city in the north of the European part of Russia.
5. Post horses were a form of public transportation in Imperial Russia. Carriages delivering mail between postal stations were also used as a way of transporting people.
6. Gendarmes were a Special Corps of military police in Imperial Russia.
7. Astrakhan' (or Astrakhan) is a town in southern Russia located in the delta of the Volga river where it flows into the Caspian Sea.
8. Kholmogory milk cows are known as one of the best breeds in Russia. They originated in the town of Kholmogory in Northern Russia.

CHAPTER 7

What Happened to the Orphans' Home. Division of the Doukhobors

All the capital and the community property of the Orphans' Home fell into the hands of the Gubanovs and their followers. Most Doukhobors had made contributions to this home and they earnestly asked the Gubanovs not to pursue such a course because it was not good or moral for several people to take over the belongings of the entire community. All these entreaties did not have any effect, and in spite of everything, the Gubanovs took over all of the community property which had belonged to all the Doukhobors.

The Doukhobors were left unsatisfied and decided to apply for court action. Pëtr Vasil'evich on his behalf advised them not to continue with this action. This could be seen from his first letter to all the Doukhobors from his exile. I present this letter here word by word.

The first letter to the Doukhobors of the large party, of March 6, 1888.

"To beloved brothers and sisters in spirit, all those residing by the city of Jerusalem, those who remember our Lord Jesus Christ, and are awaiting His return with His saints on this earth. In the first lines of this letter, my dear brothers and sisters, I bow to the ground before you, and wish you the best in the world from our Lord in both this life and in the future one. Oh Lord, take care of us and pardon us, with thy mercy, bestow upon us the ray of thy true light and envelop us with it. And let our God, the merciful Father, send you the thoughts and the desire to walk without discontent the path that has its gates covered with thorns of wild roses. And if you feel the strength and fortitude, and if hope accompanies you, then let the Lord send you more and more love and patience. Oh, Lord, close those charming but deceitful gates that lead to a wide and soft way and protect us from it. Because, my friends, this way ends with the void of Tartarus, where the pain is endless and eternal. Oh Lord, save and protect us from this awful and terrifying afterlife. The other path is very hard and narrow, but once you pass through the gate covered with thorns, you walk into clear even fields, where those who have walked through these narrow gates along the true earthly path of sorrows and grief and suffered in the name of our Lord and his glory, enjoy the eternal blissful life. There they live and enjoy the eternal peace, the vision of God the Lord and the pleasant singing of light bearing angels.

My beloved friends, many of you may be frightened of that tempting and treacherous way that ends in misfortune, and you would rather walk through your earthly lives on the needles of steel[1] and bear everything, as our forefathers did before us. But you may have lost the understanding that our ancestors had, and you may say, 'Lord, how can we differentiate between these two ways, how can we walk through the gate that leads to the field of eternal peace and the luminous kingdom of God?' I can tell you, my beloved brothers and sisters, that every person can easily and freely identify and know the path. One only needs to have a passionate and strong faith and love our God the Lord, who for our salvation did not abhor appearing through a maiden's womb and suffered for us. Why won't we love God our Lord with our whole hearts and souls? Our love of Him will be even stronger, if peace, unity and love of one another will abide among us.

I wish it for you, dear brothers and sisters, and bequeath you to carry it out, and if you do so, my heart will rejoice for you with all its might and my soul will glorify my heavenly Father from the edge of the earth to the edge of heaven. I also request you, my dear ones, not to argue among you and not to trespass against those who hurt you, but pray to God for them, for they do not know what they are doing. And Oh Lord, it must have been predestined that the Doukhobors should split, and I fear, my friends, and I am horrified by what has transpired, but let there be the will of our Heavenly Father in everything. But I fear for many of you, dear brothers and sisters, I am afraid that your will may be weak and indecisive, and that many of you will do what Lot's wife[2] did. And here again I tell you, my friends, that if any one of you is truly troubled by doubts, then I wish you from all my heart to strengthen in your faith in the Unknowable Father. And I will say to you that in the flock of the Heavenly Father's sheep, there has never been and will never be anything forced. Each one of you can select one's path according to one's understanding, because now you can think in secret, because in your heart you may not believe that everything hidden will become revealed.

About the Orphans' Home possessions, my dear friends, even in those times I strongly wished against this matter being subjected to Caesar's trial.[3] Lord, this must have been destined, so now await till the end of it [trial], and do not start anything new. Let it be in possession of those who dared to commit such a blasphemy. Perhaps, this is not the first case of this nature among the Doukhobors, but I fully believe, my friends, that the assembled silver and gold will lead them to peril.

Finally, my dear brother and sisters, I received in full amount all your charity assembled in the name of our saints. God save and bless you for your great and much appreciated gifts, and I request you not to send me anything else here, since I have everything in abundance, and every minute I thank the Lord and all the kind people, God save you all. Farewell. I remain alive and healthy, thank God.

Willing you all the best and loving you forever,

Pëtr Vasil'evich Verigin"

However, the Doukhobors still decided to apply in court in order to become better acquainted with the government laws. The Orphans' Home and all the property was given over to the regional Tiflis court. The court then decided in favour of the majority of the Doukhobors. The small party was not satisfied and appealed to the Chamber. There, they decided in favour of the Gubanovs. Then the Doukhobors, seeing this injustice of the government law, decided to give up this case. And they decided to have as little as possible to do with the government. When they were offended by the indigenous population, even then they did not report it to the local government, following the teachings of Christ: if someone takes your shirt, give him your coat also, and so on.

It meant that the Gubanovs and their followers took over the capital of 100,000 roubles, the Orphans' Home and the entire property. Due to their illegal and immoral takeover of the community property, it was decided to completely split up with them, not to deal with them and not to participate in prayer meetings with them. They [the two parties] stopped visiting each other, as they say, there was no reason and no purpose for it. In this division, there were many cases like these: parents were divided from their children, husbands from wives, brothers from sisters, and so on. They received different names: the majority of the Doukhobors who held to the truth were called the "large," "written" or "Verigin" party. The small party, who betrayed their brothers because of jealousy and greed for money, was called the "Zubkov" party.

Notes

1. This may be an allusion to the saying attributed to Jesus Christ, "It is easier for a camel to go through the eye of a needle than for a rich man to enter the kingdom of God." The eye of the needle stands for a narrow path to heaven described by Pëtr Verigin.
2. An episode from the Bible (Genesis) where Lot was told by angels to flee the corrupt city of Sodom which was about to be destructed and not to look back. However, his wife looked back and was turned into a pillar of salt.
3. "Caesar's trial" refers to the government court trial since the Russian word "tsar'" originates from Latin "Caesar."

CHAPTER 8

My Trip to Shenkursk and My Communal Life There

The elders living in Shenkursk,[1] along with Pëtr Vasil'evich, advised him to invite a lady from the Caucasus, who would look after the elders and housekeeping. The lot fell to the wife of Dmitriĭ Vasil'evich Lezhebokov. His wife was Arina Vasil'evna, middle-aged, energetic, wise and industrious, and well versed in housekeeping and related duties. She was exactly the kind of person needed there. However, such a long journey was not suitable for a lady travelling alone. Pëtr Vasil'evich wrote to our parents and asked them, if possible, to allow me to travel with her, as a guide, so that Pëtr Vasil'evich and I could meet in person, as true brothers should.

Our parents gladly agreed to let me go, and on September 12, we said our good-byes and began our journey. We travelled by railroad to Tiflis[2] and from Tiflis to Vladikavkaz[3] by baggage van. From Vladikavkaz, we purchased railway tickets to Moscow. In Moscow, there was a transfer and new tickets to Vologda.[4] At Vologda, the railroad ended and we travelled by the postal system on horses for 300 miles. We travelled by carriage and found the trip extremely arduous, especially Arina Vasil'evna, as a lady would. We were surrounded by swamps, nearly the entire road was bogged down, covered with logs and the travel was shaky and difficult in the autumn. When we were 100 miles from our destination, snow fell on the ground, and we continued by sleigh. Near Shenkursk there was a large river, the Vaga, which we crossed by ferry. A severe squall with sludge ice began which made it dangerous to proceed. This was on September 29.

We had our belongings with us, and we crossed safely and were left on the shore, awaiting further transport. Others crossing with us lived in Shenkursk, and when they learned from our conversation that we were travelling to see Pëtr Vasil'evich, they assured us that as soon as we disembarked, they would let him know.

After some time, a conveyance arrived, and in it was Dmitriĭ Vasil'evich, someone I did not know in person as he was from the Akhalkalak area. His wife also did not recognize him. He did not tell her immediately, and it was only after some talk that his wife recognized her own husband! After that, we kissed him, loaded our luggage unto the sleigh and left for our quarters. There, Pëtr Vasil'evich and the elders greeted us with heart-felt enthusiasm and were extremely gratified to see us. First they enquired about our route, whether we made it safely and comfortably, then about the life of our parents and relatives, and all of our brothers and sisters in spirit. We gave a full account. Pëtr Vasil'evich, along with the elders, was very pleased to hear that all were healthy and well and had begun living as Christians. And this is how we started living there, spending the time happily.

They all seemed to live well. They lived in two accommodations about 70 feet apart, one from the other. The elders lived in one accommodation. Their household consisted of Makhortov, his elderly wife who had come from home, Rybin and Tsybul'kin. Also living with them was Nikolaĭ Ivanovich Voronin with his wife. His wife was a dear old lady, Katerina Vasil'evna, many years his senior. Voronin was of middle age, a full, handsome man of Russian background, kind and with good humour; he was not very well off, and the elders asked him to live in their quarters without payment; he ate separately buying his own food. He was banished administratively and belonged to the political exiles.

Pëtr Vasil'evich, along with Lezhebokov, lived in the other accommodation. There was a kitchen and a dining room, and they ate together with the elders. There was a hired cook and two orphan girls, of whom I have written earlier; there were two young lads about 16 years of age, one cared for the horses and the other for the cows, of which there were four of Kholmogor[5] breed. There were also about 20 geese which grandfather[6] Makhortov minded. He loved them a lot and they were his entertainment. He tended them with kindly care. He had a bell with which he called them for feeding. As soon as he rang, they would surround him. He gave them their feed, and if they began to nip at each other, he would reprimand them saying that such behaviour is not necessary; they seemed to listen to him, they would stop their strife and stretch their necks towards him as an indication that they would no longer fight. The geese were well bred, large and very gentle. I often watched and admired how he handled them. One time I said to him, "Grandfather, could we butcher that one that is lagging behind? What a tasty noodle soup that would be!" He replied, "Enough, enough! Let them live and rejoice under God's grace! We can do without that." By this time, grandfather Makhortov was a complete vegetarian.

In the winter time, the nights were long, and there was little to do. It was not good for the elders to stay indoors all the time, so every morning we went for a walk for an hour and a half, or even two. This was good for our health, especially for the elders. After such a walk we had a good breakfast and then retired to our quarters to rest.

In the evening, after dinner, when the cooks cleared the tables and all was in order, Pëtr Vasil'evich, and all of us, except for Lezhebokov, went to the elders, and there we read the New Testament. This was for everyone, and especially for the elders, as they had suffered for truth. It gave them some comfort in their difficult circumstances when they heard how Christ had said, "They persecuted me and they will persecute you, fear not them which kill the body, but are not able to kill the soul; My yoke is tolerable, I carry my cross with ease; Learn from me and you will no longer live in darkness," etc.

Voronin attended these meetings without fail and so did Ivan Semënovich Tikhomirov of the political exiles. He was a moral, goodhearted person and eventually left his former beliefs and joined the teachings of Christ. The reading was often followed by discussion. If some text of Christ's teachings was not understood, it was examined and dissected from different directions until we all agreed on one conclusion, and this went on until 11 pm. Then after goodnights were exchanged, we departed to our respective quarters.

There was also Vasiliĭ Ob"edkov. He was always near Pëtr Vasil'evich like a brother and a true and faithful servant.

On Sundays, not always but often, we would hitch up the horses for a sleigh ride. The horses were hitched singly. Such a trip included the entire family; the family consisted of all at home: the cook, the girls and the youngsters. We did not look at them as outsiders but as members of our own family. If anyone was ever left at home and did not go on the ride, it was Lezhebokov who looked after the homes. This was our entire assembly: the three sleighs, horses which were racers and pretty as a picture. Two horses were from the Caucasus: one was sent by our parents, the other was from Ivan Ivanovich Ponomarëv. He wished to give the stud racehorse as a gift to Pëtr Vasil'evich. The third horse was purchased there in Shenkursk. Such rides were looked upon with envy by the administrators, police, gendarmes and others; they had not even seen such horses before, let alone ride with them. Occasionally this disturbed them—how was it that the banished, inferior to them, enjoyed such rides?

I will give you another instance. People here live poorly; children from around Shenkursk often come to town to beg in the name of Christ. Upon a suggestion of the elders, Pëtr Vasil'evich decided that twice a week they would prepare a hot meal for the children. Some 40 or more began to show up. This developed into a completely new story. The priests stirred this up. They reported to the Chief of Police that "our Orthodox children are going to the sectarians for dinner, and that through this dinner they are being seduced into becoming sectarians." The Chief of Police summoned Pëtr Vasil'evich and warned him that he must not let the children gather around him and he must not prepare any more meals for them. Pëtr Vasil'evich replied, "How can I deny those children who ask in the name of Christ? You are warning me against it, but this is the command of Christ, in whom you probably believe yourself: 'ask and it shall be given you'. Such a request from you is unseemly—if you have the authority, you may place a policeman at my gates to prevent the children from entering. Once they are in my yard, and ask for food in the name of Christ, then please forgive me but in this matter I cannot obey you, and I must listen to Christ rather than to you." Hearing this, the commander raised his voice: "I will write about this to the minister." Pëtr Vasil'evich replied, "That is your business," and walked away.

Whether or not the Chief of Police did write to the minister, we do not know, but they could not forbid the cooking of dinners. However, as soon as the children's dinner started, a senior administrator would come to observe how children pray before and give thanks after the dinner. The children, though young, were accustomed to icon worship, and at first, did not want to pray and give thanks. Then the cook, who had been an Orthodox believer, but who already understood through Pëtr Vasil'evich that one could pray to God in spirit and truth without any icons, told them: "It is possible to pray without icons, let one of you look at salt and bread and say the prayer out loud, the others recite silently." This is exactly what they started doing. The observer could not object to the children praying, even if without icons; he came with nothing and left with nothing. This really was one stupid attempt on the part of the priests and the Chief of Police to find some fault with us.

Children that are begging in the name of Christ are hungry and are asking for their daily bread, and such children aren't interested in preaching, they only need bread. With grown-ups, however, Pëtr Vasil'evich often discussed the teachings of Christ whenever possible, and pointed out the errors of the priests who for the sake of their own earthly gains and an easy good life ruin the world and misrepresent the teachings of Christ. They fool the people, and the people for some reason are easily fooled. Some agreed with Pëtr Vasil'evich, and four families stopped going to church, and they were subjected to secret surveillance. Of course, the authorities suspected that Pëtr Vasil'evich was responsible. I will only name here one of these families: the Krasnikovs: a man, his wife, and their 18 year old daughter, whom I had seen as guests at Pëtr Vasil'evich's.

Many agreed with Pëtr Vasil'evich in words only, but they were afraid to take action because of the fear of exile and suffering. Until people hold onto worldly life and plans, they cannot decide to follow. But when people understand that man's major destination is the spiritual life that should merge with the timeless existence of our essence, they will not fear suffering for the truth. Our material life is secondary, it is confined by time. Today we're here, tomorrow we're gone—I am talking here of the flesh. Spirit is without beginning or end, it is timeless. And when people understand that, they will no longer be detained by fear or suffering. We see the example and proof of this in the life and death of Jesus Christ.

Life in Shenkursk in the home of Pëtr Vasil'evich and the elders continued joyfully. There was one thing that bothered me: Pëtr Vasil'evich and the elders were already fully vegetarian, and because of that, no meat was prepared, neither for themselves nor for the guests. Even if someone wanted meat, it was not allowed. For me this did not feel right and was unsettling as at home I ate meat. However, their food was very good and nutritious, there was enough butter and milk. Every morning coffee with cream and leavened bread was served. They often had pies with cheese and potatoes. There was also tasty borsch, good soup with various grains and they served noodles. You couldn't ask for better. But my heart was not at ease: I wanted to eat meat. Pëtr Vasil'evich saw this and noticed it. One day he asked me, "How do you like our food? Can one live without meat?" I answered, "The food is very good, but it's impossible to live without meat."

He laughed, I was a little embarrassed, and he, wanting to ease me out of my embarrassment, said, "I noticed that your body seems to be weakening." I answered, "Yes, I live here as a guest, and do almost no work, yet I noticed that I feel weaker." I did feel weaker, but it was not the result of the food but because I felt dissatisfied and my heart was not at ease, as I did not have the understanding of the proper attitude to living creatures. Pëtr Vasil'evich sympathized with me because I was feeling weaker. However, there was nothing to do but for me to get used to it [vegetarianism].

He said, "We got used to it. It occurs to me that at our table there is surplus food, enough to get fat on, not to get weak on. In my understanding, we could cut back a little at our table, but it would be difficult for the elders and they might start weakening. This depends on one's convictions. For example, I now hold this belief that all beings on earth including humans were created for life. A man can be considered a form of life with more reasoning power compared to other creatures only when he acts like a human being. For example, man is not a carnivore. This is illustrated in his body and his organism. Don't give him a knife or a weapon he invented and turn him out with a bull or a ram. What will he do with them? Nothing. But let the bull in with an enraged lion or tiger, or the ram with a wolf, and quicker than the eye can see, all will be over. Man has strayed from nature and natural legitimate food, and with such violent ways, is bringing himself down to the level of animals. Is this a good or reasonable direction for mankind, for a human who is made in the image of God? If one has anything of God within him, he must look at all creations with love, admiration, and compassion. And for all this world's bounty, he must glorify and thank God. In this way, he will stand out from the rest of the living creatures as an intelligent being. By contrast, in such bloodthirsty behaviour as the eating of meat, a human does not distinguish himself from the fierce animal, and to satisfy his Mammon-like craving, decides to destroy what God has created. I will repeat again; everything is created for life, not for death. If it were for death, then people should be fattened as a person fattens oxen, cows or rams, especially older ones that are no longer fit for physical labour. I don't know how true this is, but they say human flesh is the best and the tastiest of all meats, and we could use this for ourselves, and for sale. I suppose people would then cry out and protest in every which way that this is not good, and even sinful. How could we do this with people? This is how animals behave, this is frightening. They would be offering all sorts of arguments to save and protect their own lives.

And if through this reasoning, we would be saving our own lives, why shouldn't we think seriously about all other lives, the lives of all creatures? Perhaps they are also pleading and proving in various ways that it is not right and it is even sinful to end their lives, they want to live as much as people do, but we don't understand their language; we get strong ropes ready for them and continue to sharpen knives. In such circumstances where we do not understand each other's language, we must speak with the language of the heart and soul, especially because the heart of a human should understand and communicate with the swiftness of a telephone, which can transmit sounds over several dozens or hundreds of miles. This invention is made by a human being and yet has such a strong effect. However, in a person, who has the spark of God's love and compassion within him, this spark is definitely there, but he does not feel it. Sometimes when they fall such a huge animal as an ox for slaughter, tie down his feet tightly, and he feels he is going to die, the ox often cries with tears, but nothing helps, the man nevertheless continues with what he shouldn't. The man should understand this with his heart. But where to find such a heart, when all is lost, and the man only in shape is human, but that God's sparkle is lost? And this state of man is pitiful."

He said a lot more about this subject, which made me turn away from my desire for meat. And after that I began to develop a more reasonable attitude to vegetarian food. After some time even my weakness disappeared—Pëtr Vasil'evich really affected me in this matter. And this only makes sense: where there is a non-credible weakness, you need a serious strengthening.

Notes

1. Shenkursk is a town in Northern Russia; it was one of the places of exile of Pëtr Verigin.
2. Tiflis is the old name of modern Tbilisi, the capital of the country of Georgia. In the nineteenth century, it was the capital of Tiflis guberniia, which was a part of the Russian Empire.
3. Vladikavkaz (the name means in Russian "owner of the Caucasus") is a town located north of Georgia in the north of the Caucasus Mountains. It is currently the capital of North Ossetia-Alania Republic, a subject of the Russian Federation.
4. Vologda is a town in Central Russia on the Volga river.
5. Kholmogory milk cows are known as one of the best breeds in Russia. They originated in the town of Kholmogory in Northern Russia.
6. In Russian, any elderly man can be referred to as "grandfather," and any elderly woman as "grandmother."

CHAPTER 9

Pëtr Vasil'evich's Message to the Doukhobors Through Ivan Evseevich Konkin

Sometime later, Ivan Evseevich Konkin arrived in Shenkursk.[1] He arrived from the Far East and Siberia. He had been in the Akmalinsk Region,[2] Irkutsk,[3] Vladivostok,[4] on the Amur river, and on the Sakhalin Island. He met with the Governor-General. He was sent there by Pëtr Vasil'evich to look for free, suitable land. If such suitable lands were found, under favourable circumstances, the Doukhobors could have resettled there. He was accompanied by a comrade, a Polish man, Evgeniĭ Avsinskiĭ. Avsinskiĭ had completed his exile in Shenkursk and was free. He was a close acquaintance of Pëtr Vasil'evich and upon his request went with Konkin because he understood land matters and was a good agronomist. Pëtr Vasil'evich's plans were as follows: they were supposed to travel to the Eniseĭ Area, Krasnoiarsk[5] and other places. There was no railroad then, only a post track. From that track, they were supposed to go 500 miles to the south where it was possible to find out whether there were any "cabinet" lands[6] available, and if so, inspect them thoroughly. They were not able to go as far for several important reasons and they returned with no results. This is how their journey ended.

Ivan Evseevich spent two weeks here at Shenkursk. He enjoyed vegetarian food immediately and resolved to continue to eat the food that had not been killed. Pëtr Vasil'evich advised Konkin to go to the Caucasus to visit his parents as well as his wife and sick daughter. Pëtr Vasil'evich gave him an important message for all of the Doukhobors. These instructions were made in the presence of all of the elders:

Makhortov, Rybin, Tsybul'kin, Lezhebokov and Ob"edkov. I was also there.

Pëtr Vasil'evich began thus:

"You will go to the Doukhobors, Vaniusha. Visit all of them, as you are able. First of all, convey our brotherly kind greetings[7] and best wishes with everything in their lives to all of the spiritual brothers and sisters including my relatives and the relatives of the elders. Tell them that all of us, who live here, feel tired. Particularly, the elders miss all the relatives and spiritual brothers and sisters, and the elders would need to be freed from exile. Tell all the Doukhobors that I also miss everyone, but I remain cheerful. The spiritual communion with God supports me and gives me strength for the future. I sincerely ask all the elders not to weaken spiritually. Our struggle with militarism is still ahead of us, and for our suffering not to be in vain, we must persevere. Our ancestors suffered a lot in order to free themselves and their descendants from the false interpreters of the true path of God, from the priests and all church ceremonies. They were also exiled, as we are, but to even more distant and worse places, such as Kola and Kamchatka. They were imprisoned in stone towers where they survived for up to twelve years and died. They were beaten and tortured mercilessly, they had strips of skin cut off their backs, but they persevered through this without looking back and died in body only. Our ancestors could have been punished less severely, but at that time people were not enlightened by the spirit of virtue, their heart was cruel and their hands didn't tremble at such doings.

In our time, all the Doukhobors have a direct duty to free not only themselves but also their descendants from militarism, that is, not to join the soldiers. It is my duty to tell all the Doukhobors about this. I promised the late Luker'ia Vasil'evna to do this. I must fulfil this immediately. With tears in her eyes, she seemed content, and blessed me to sacrifice myself if need be. When I began my position I was to begin with this sacrifice, but the internal conflicts between the Doukhobors created delays. But it doesn't matter. Throughout this time, we learned many things, and sincerely understood the essence of a sinful undertaking of militarism. God will assist us. This I have only explained to you," said Petr Vasil'evich.

"But the time to address this is yet to come, and now we must prepare ourselves, and to prepare sincerely and conscientiously the mind of every single person to bring forth the love to God and aversion to anything that serves against love. This is clearly said in the commandments of Moses. Christ shortens them and gives us two commandments: first, you must love God with all your heart, soul, and reason. Second, you must love those near you as yourself, and not wish upon them what you do not wish upon yourself. This is the Law and the Prophets.[8] So, dear Vaniusha, one must not only understand this in words, but apply it in deeds. Love God, whom the Doukhobors from the beginning of time and till the present day recognize in spirit, whom one cannot see with physical eyes but has to comprehend with one's heart, soul, and reason. This is according to Christ's words, the second birth from above, from the Holy Spirit. Those who are not born from above, from the Holy Spirit, will not enter the Kingdom of Heavenly life. But they must aspire to attain the area of the eternal being, which could be reached through perfection, efforts, mercy, compassion, and boundless love, not only to human beings, but to all who inhabit the earth. All seen by us on earth could be compared to a splendid museum in which the amazed spectators glorify and thank the Creator of all this.

Tell all the Doukhobors from me that they should strive to reach the Kingdom of Heaven through perfection and love, and the rest will be provided. You must work and labour, for it was said, 'by the sweat of your brow you will procure your food from the earth'. But this labour must be honest and just. To use the labour of other people is reprehensible, for example, for a Christian to exploit the labour of his own brothers, or of a stranger, even though he is paid a salary. If a labourer works only enough to cover his own salary, it makes no sense for the employer. Correspondingly, the labourer must work not only to cover his own salary, but also to work twice or thrice more for his owner, and this is not compatible with Christianity. One may include Christ's words here that if you want to eat, work: a working man deserves to eat. This refers to each person, rich or beggar, it doesn't matter. If a person is poor and you are a Christian, give something from your wealth to the beggar. If you have two shirts, give one to the pauper. In this way, there would not be any rich or poor among the Christians. Pass this over from me to all the Doukhobors, and explain to them that this is my well-meaning advice, and that those who follow it, won't have any labourers. If you have extra property, you may share it with the poor. If the rich lent money to the poor, they should forgive the debt. The poor will then thank Christ who lived nineteen centuries ago and brought this holy sacred teaching through which the Kingdom of God could be created on earth and in heaven."

From a human being, the talk then passed on to all of God's creations on earth.

"All of creation received its life's beginning from the same power as man did. Consequently, each and every creature has the full and legal right to live, which is not dependent on anyone. To annihilate this creation for the sake of Mammon is reprehensible and contrary to the nature of a human being. Clarify this on my behalf for everyone. The same goes for the use of alcohol and tobacco. Not only is it uncharacteristic of Christians to use such harmful substances, but it does not befit even an unreasoning man who doesn't recognize moral law but who still must recognize and understand the harm to his body. However, an individual who is a Christian even to the smallest degree, and understands the law of nature, must not do this under any circumstances, because through this a person harms oneself. There is a saying: don't over indulge in wine because it results in lust, harm, vice and drunkenness. Avoid it as you would hell, the abstinent live well and in good health. From indulgence, illness is born, and from illness, death. Our ancestors did not use it, and we gradually made it a habit about which our ancestors said: 'Nothing is more dangerous than getting used to bad things'. We, their descendants, not only stopped being afraid of this bad habit, but made it a custom and elevated it to a high place when partaking food. We should begin with bread and salt but we begin with this poison, to drink a little glass to stimulate the appetite, and this leads to more and more. Dinner is not over and all the people are drunk, and they become fearless and can then do all types of wretched things.

As for smoking and the harm of tobacco, it goes without saying. It is mankind stooping to its lowest level. If someone does not understand this, then what kind of a person is he? I understand that these are not righteous habits. In no way should they be followed by a person. However, if a person allows such habits, in a period of time, they become embedded, and grow strong. That is why for overcoming this you need an effort to gain victory.

My sincere and well-meaning wish is for the Doukhobors to come to their senses and forsake such habits forever. Tell all this to the Doukhobors.

You must keep your household matters restrained. Every household should have what is needed, and what is essential for life. From my childhood, the country life is well known to me. For example, they have sheep and what profit do they receive? Absolutely nothing: suffices if the worker can survive and his work pays only for his salary. I know this very well, as when I lived with my parents and brothers, we had up to 3000 sheep, and when it was time for the annual budget, the profit hardly covered the expenses. How many efforts and troubles all wasted in vain!

While ploughing the land, you harness five or six pairs of oxen, and what an exhausting ploughing it is! Why not have three or four pairs of good horses? The work will be done three or four times quicker than with oxen. This is how our grandfathers worked, but we must improve ourselves spiritually and practically and choose the useful."

Then he spoke in relation to the life of husband and wife, and was expressing his opinion on this subject. "I understand," Pëtr Vasil'evich said, "if people come together for mutual life, then this is for upholding humankind on earth. This is the most important, otherwise mankind could come to an end, though nowadays there are so many people there is no fear for the end of mankind. In this matter also, humankind has gone too far and absolutely does not understand its own purpose and spends its lives worse than any other creature. Here I speak in relation to husband and wife as reasonable creatures. From such lack of understanding, humankind itself suffers and oppresses the rest of God's creation that was created by the same God and has its own rightful share of life on earth. From the unlawful propagation of people, the man lives where he should not, where his life is poorly suited and hard. He should live in moderate countries but not in the hot and severe ones. However, nowadays not only moderate countries are inhabited by people but already hot and severe ones are overpopulated. The man comes there without shame, pushes away every creature living in nature and settles there as if he were the rightful owner. Surprisingly, lions, tigers, and other strong animals avoid meeting with a man. It indicates that a man has little physical strength, but by his cruelty, surpasses all these animals. Mating is seen in the entire surrounding world, even if you are talking about cattle as if they are a lower creation in the eyes of a man.

When the time calls, a female finds a male in order to leave progeny. When a female understands that there is an embryo, then they discontinue their relations and live quietly till a female gives birth to the progeny. After a while, the same is repeated. A female finds a male. The female feeds the baby and looks after it. Sometimes she is prepared to die for it. When the time of upbringing is over, she leaves the offspring. Whether this is in the wild or among humans, we see that when the mother leaves its offspring and no longer gives it milk, it means that this time is up, and she has done all that was required, and now the offspring must look after themselves. If you want to eat, you must find food for yourself, and so on. As the mother frees herself from the offspring, so the offspring free themselves from the mothers, but in humankind, we see the opposite.

I repeat, husband and wife often do not understand the purpose for which they have come together. For the most part they say: from this the children appear. Before two years are over, there are more children, then more and more. The first child asks, 'Mom, give me some bread, it is high up a shelf' and the child can't reach it. The second says, 'Clean me, dress me'. The third asks to put him down on the floor pointing down with his finger—the child cannot speak yet. The fourth lays in the cradle not knowing anything and crying loudly. I ask you: what is the mother to do and where is she to go?

All the children know nothing and if their desires are not satisfied immediately, they will all burst into crying, the mother rushes here and there as she feels sorry for the children, but she does not improve anything. However, everyone knows that if the children are upset, it is difficult to please them.

The mother is beside herself and begins to hit them with whatever she lays her hand on. Is it reasonable? Through this fuss, the human life goes on. If the parents are not able to organize children even in a material way, and if they are, as it was said above, they do it with great difficulty, even with beating, can the parents think about spiritual and divine life? Can they teach the children and show them the first steps of the divine law? But this is the obligation of the parents. But after a beating, how will you teach the children this divine Law, the essence of which is love, meekness, humility and so on, when in practice, the mother herself does not follow such a law and behaves in the opposite way? I repeat this is not reasonable for a man. You may pass this on from me as brotherly and well-meaning advice.

I will tell you more. I advise you to stop physical relationships and child bearing for a while, since the time is near when Doukhobors must begin their struggle with the Prince of Darkness. There will be a fearsome battle, and at that time the children, who are supposed to be born for the Glory of God and for the joy of the parents, may be an obstacle for the divine cause. Because it would be very hard for the parents, and through this they may curtail the divine work which happened to be their lot from the Father of all centuries and which they must fulfil to the most for the glory of God and for future generations. Don't be shy to speak of this, explain reasonably and clearly that this is temporary and this will make it easier for all people. I repeat, those who understand will understand. Such people will be free and will go forward and not look back.

I also ask you, Konkin, to inform the higher authorities, beginning with junior policemen and up to the ministers, of all their illegal actions which they exercised over us. It is well known to you that I was exiled only because of the bribery, and the money. They did not convict me in a court of law because there was no case, and after me you suffered from the authorities as well. For example, let's consider the matter of passports. When you wanted to leave to submit a petition, you were not allowed to have a passport, but when you paid 50 or 100 instead of the legal cost of 1 rouble, 45 kopecks, you received the passports. You paid 200 roubles for your passport—is this legal? All this should be brought to the attention of the ministers. Listen, do not add anything, or you will spoil the case, tell the truth, do not be shy and do not be afraid of anything. Even if you have to suffer for this, this wouldn't matter, through this you will reveal their dishonesty. Many people will understand you and tell you that Konkin suffers for truth, and not everyone can suffer for truth but only the courageous individuals who love truth."

When Pëtr Vasil'evich delivered this message and expressed his testament, all the elders were sitting. Konkin was standing upright and was trying to perceive everything very attentively in order to memorize and pass every detail to the Doukhobor brothers and sisters. During his speech, Pëtr Vasil'evich did not sit either, and when the talk became serious, he walked about the room in spiritual ecstasy and spoke fervently. Occasionally, he asked Konkin if he understood everything in order to pass it on to the Doukhobors, not only the words but the clear sense of the matter, so that Konkin would not deviate from the true sense of his message. If Konkin did not understand something, Pëtr Vasil'evich repeated it.

After a week of rest after the long journey, Konkin bid farewell to everyone and set out for the Doukhobors. This was on December 10, 1893. Konkin was supposed to get to Slavianka by Christmas. Vasiliĭ Ob"edkov left with him as his travelling companion. Ob"edkov went to see his parents, and after some time, he was supposed to come back to Shenkursk.

Notes

1. Shenkursk is a town in Northern Russia; it was one of the places of exile of Pëtr Verigin.
2. Akmalinsk region possibly refers to Akmolinsk, an area and town of Russian Empire, now Astana, the capital of modern Kazakhstan. The city of Akmolinsk was renamed Tselinograd (Virgin lands city), then the name was changed to Akmola and finally, to Astana.
3. Irkutsk is one of the largest cities in Siberia, located in Southern Siberia close to Baĭkal Lake.
4. Vladivostok is a major city of the Russian Far East.
5. Krasnoiarsk (Krasnoyarsk) is one of the major cities in Siberia located on the Eniseĭ (Yenisei) river.
6. "Cabinet lands" are the lands in the private property of the emperor of Russia, along with other imperial properties they were managed by the Imperial Cabinet, hence the name. Since 1860s, they could be made available for rent or resettlement, and for this reason, the Doukhobors were interested in them.
7. The text says "pass over our brotherly heart-felt bow (poklon)." Passing a "bow" (poklon) to relatives and family is a typical form of Doukhobor greetings originating in old Russian tradition of bowing to each other in greetings.
8. The Law and the Prophets are two parts of the Bible (the Torah that describes the laws of Moses and the Prophets that relates to the other books of the Bible).

CHAPTER 10

The Relaying of the Message and Its Fulfilment by the Doukhobors. The Exile of Ivan Evseevich Konkin

Vasiliĭ Verigin and Ivan Konkin

Konkin and Ob"edkov both arrived in Slavianka, Elizavetpol'[1] guberniia. Everyone was pleased to see them, including relatives and spiritual brothers and sisters. The Doukhobors from other villages arrived in Slavianka to meet them. They were also invited to other places. They travelled and discussed everything. Konkin began each conversation with the message of Pëtr Vasil'evich. After reciting the message in detail, sometimes he also asked the Doukhobors if they understood what he had told them on behalf of Pëtr Vasil'evich. They asked for some elaboration and he explained precisely what Pëtr Vasil'evich had said. The Doukhobors thanked Pëtr Vasil'evich for sincerely wanting them to become good Christians and to fulfil the teachings of Jesus Christ for which He was crucified on Golgotha Mountain. Konkin was a wise man, he behaved with honesty and dignity. After passing over Pëtr Vasil'evich's message, he continued the conversation in a serious and solemn manner. His speech touched people's hearts so strongly that it brought forth tears. In conversation, Konkin was not intimidated by anyone, not even by the presence of government officials. Governments detest any divine sermons because they destroy their way of life. Of course, for the most part he spoke of Christ's teachings and exemplary life, and this did not make him uneasy, and he was not afraid of any suffering, relying upon God's will and providence.

Meantime, the government attended to its business through secret observation. When he and Ob"edkov decided to go to Kars[2] Region, the government did not allow him to go, warning him that if he went without government permission, he would be arrested and imprisoned. Ob"edkov started out by himself, while Konkin remained at home. He sent a message with Ob"edkov requesting three respected elders from Kars Region and from Akhalkalak Region to arrive at Slavianka to receive the message from Pëtr Vasil'evich. They all arrived and Konkin relayed all in detail.

In this way, after many discussions and interpretations, all the Doukhobors in all three guberniias began to embrace the life which Christ taught and which Pëtr Vasil'evich reminded them of. At first they paid all their debts. If some were in debt to their own brothers, it was decided not to demand payment. Those Doukhobors who were in debt to people of other ethnic groups, willingly collected sufficient money among themselves to pay off all the debts. Then the rich began to give horses, oxen, cows, wagons and all that was needed to the poor people. Observing such generous behaviour, other groups such as the Molokans,[3] Armenians and Moslems also decided to appeal for help; and they were provided with whatever was available. I know that Molokans who asked for help were given a pair of good oxen and a wagon full of wheat. With all this, the Molokans went home to their poor family glorifying and thanking Jesus Christ. This was in the Kars Region.

After this the Doukhobors decided to absolutely stop drinking vodka and smoking tobacco regarding them as two unnecessary items which are not only useless but also harmful. This habit was mostly ingrained in the elders and for them it was the most difficult to eradicate. Nevertheless, the Doukhobors heroically overcame these bad habits. It was well done.

Next, Konkin wrote an explanatory letter to the Minister of the Interior, in which he described in detail the bribes for the passports and other illegal acts and sent it off by mail. This took some time. And then, the Minister ordered the Governor of Elizavetpol' to arrest Konkin immediately and put him in prison. For this purpose the Governor sent a special courier, a kind of policeman who arrested Konkin at once and brought him to Elizavetpol'. There he was imprisoned awaiting special orders. Sometime later he was interrogated. The interrogation was carried out by the local administration by the district Chief of Police who was involved in this case himself. The district Chief of Police read Konkin's letter to the Minister and asked, "Did you write this?" Konkin answered, "Yes, I wrote it."—"Could you confirm what you wrote about?"—"With pleasure, I ascertain that all I have written here is the essential truth. Some received this amount, others that amount, and you—some amount. Do you remember it, or maybe you will investigate this as well?" The district Chief of Police had nothing more to say, and did not interrogate further, as it would be extremely shameless from his side. He began to give Konkin advice: "I advise you, Konkin, to disavow this letter, and things will go easier for you, you would be soon released from the prison and you would be free. But if you insist on this letter, you might be exiled farther than Pëtr Verigin." Konkin rejected this proposition and insisted on his statements. After this, he was detained in prison for two more months, and was transported by administrative order to Arkhangel'sk Region to the town of Mezen'[4] for five years. This was on September 20, 1894. Thus, Konkin who stood for justice had to undergo five years of punishment far from his home and relatives. This is what's happening on earth in God's world! Where is truth, where is justice? The truth suffers, justice bears heavy shackles and the lie triumphs! Then how can people live well?

The Doukhobors stopped eating meat on the day of great holiday of Michael the Archangel, November 8, 1894.

Notes

1. Elizavetpol' (later Kirovabad, since 1989, Ganja) was the capital of Elizavetpol' guberniia in the Russian Empire. Since the separation of Azerbaijan from the Soviet Union, it is one of the largest cities in Azerbaijan.
2. Kars is a town in Turkey. With its surrounding area, at the time of the narrative, it belonged to the Russian Empire. It was one of the areas of the Transcaucasian exile of the Doukhobors. Since 1921, it has been a part of Turkey.
3. Molokans are a sectarian religious group that split off from the Russian Orthodox Church. At present, Doukhobors of Canada and Molokans of the United States retain amicable relationships and send representatives to each other's major events.
4. Mezen' (Mezen) is a town in the Arkhangel'sk (Arkhangelsk) area in the north of the European part of Russia, close to the Arctic Polar Circle.

CHAPTER 11

The New Exile of Pëtr Vasil'evich to Obdorsk of the Tobol'sk Guberniia for Five Years. The Trip by Vasiliĭ Gavrilovich Vereshchagin and Brother Vasiliĭ Vasil'evich to Shenkursk to Visit Pëtr Vasil'evich and Their Receipt of a Message for the Doukhobors

As already mentioned, Pëtr Vasil'evich had already been suspected by the priests of converting four families from Orthodoxy. Apart from that, the government had another reason for persecuting Pëtr Vasil'evich. He wrote to his parents about this: "The reason for my transfer from Shenkursk[1] to Obdorsk[2] was that several times I received warnings not to feed the beggars and not to help the needy. Recently, I finally answered, 'I cannot listen to you more than to our Lord Jesus Christ. That is why I am doing this—because He calls us to behave in such a fashion'. Secondly, I had earlier sent a request to the minister, who was originally from the Caucasus, in which I indicated the unprincipled bribery by the Caucasian officials." Pëtr Vasil'evich informed his relatives and all the Doukhobors about his transfer and asked that two people would come to meet him in Vologda and Moscow and so on. He believed that it would be possible to meet in Vologda.

Upon receiving this news, the relatives and all the Doukhobors immediately selected two people to apply for passports. At that time, the Doukhobors were not permitted to receive passports. Vasiliĭ Gavrilovich Vereshchagin and my brother Vasiliĭ, both from Kars[3] region, were nominated for the trip.

Vereshchagin was a person known to the local government. Everyone knew him well, even the Governor Tomich was a close acquaintance of his and respected him very much. When Vereshchagin applied to the chancellery in Kars for passports, the district Chief of Police Shagubov refused him, explaining that chief official Sheremet'ev prohibited the granting of passports to Doukhobors. Vereshchagin appealed to the governor and asked him to telegraph the chief commander about this with the reply to be paid by Vereshchagin. In about three hours, the reply came: to grant the passports to the Doukhobors. They received their passports and in a short time they were off for Vologda, the specified place. They arrived in Vologda, and enquired in the transfer prison if Pëtr Vasil'evich was transported from Shenkursk. They were informed that Verigin was still in Shenkursk and that they could go there. They arrived in Shenkursk and found Pëtr Vasil'evich there.

I write from Vereshchagin's and brother Vasiliĭ's words, why he had remained there for so long. Pëtr Vasil'evich himself told them: "On being informed about my transfer, it was immediately suggested that I go at my own expense, to which I agreed. When Shenkursk gendarme Captain heard about it, he began to report that such a dangerous man as Verigin must not be allowed to transfer with only one guard but should travel with two and with gendarmes as well.

The correspondence about it continued the entire month, and suddenly they announced that I had to pay for two guards, there and back, and that the gendarmes will also come with us. Of course I was very much bewildered, could the minister have backed off on his promise? When I knew that he certainly had done this, I definitely refused to go at my own expense. Moreover, financially, it was a great difference. According to the first budget, I was supposed to pay 220 roubles for transportation to Tobol'sk with one guard, and we were still able to go partly by ship—as it was still the fall. According to the second budget, I had to pay 450 roubles. Fearing to be considered a miser in this particular case, I bought felted boots and clothes for 450 roubles and gave them to the poor of the Shenkursk district. As for myself, I had decided to be transported administratively on foot, and thank God, that is how it happened. I invited you to come here on important business which I will pass on to you to relay to all the Doukhobors." Vereshchagin and brother Vasiliĭ spent two weeks with Pëtr Verigin. The government did not bother them and they lived together with Pëtr Vasil'evich and discussed everything.

During their stay there, the people had to swear the oath of allegiance to Nikolaĭ Aleksandrovich Romanov.[4] This oath concerned Pëtr Vasil'evich and all of the elders. All of them, based on the teaching of Jesus Christ, refused to swear the oath. The first conversation of Pëtr Vasil'evich with the elders was about the oath. He began with the following words,

> It would not be good for us as Christians to swear the oath to a mortal man. Christ in His teaching does not permit the swearing of the oath, and we, if we believe in Him, we must uphold that, and if needed, we must sacrifice our lives. For example, during a transportation to exile as was given to me, I have to walk for several thousand miles of the prisoner transport in the winter season and I must stay in several prisons. You of course did not experience these prisons, transportation, and treatment there, but I am very familiar with this. Everywhere, the treatment is very harsh and for the most part, they treat the convicts not as people but as animals, and from such treatment you may become ill and die. I accept all of this and cannot do otherwise, as not to heed Christ's teachings is not at all good. He suffered and died on Mount Golgotha. He was crucified announcing the virtue and truth of God to the people through which the people would find salvation. The matter here is about the oath which Christ forbade in His teaching, saying: 'But I say to you, make no oath at all, either by heaven, or by the earth, or by Jerusalem, nor shall you make an oath by your head, for you cannot make one hair white or black. But let your statement be, 'Yes, yes' or 'No, no'. Anything beyond this is evil.' In order to ascertain or to agree to some dealing, you may finish it with only two words, 'yes' or 'no', as Christ teaches. In the oath we were supposed to sign, there are not two words but maybe one hundred and two or even more, and all of the words are against Christ's teachings. Then how could you agree to such a signature? This would mean that you listen more to other people like you rather than to Christ. I repeat, though earlier I was ordered to be transferred to the district town of Berëzov, for this action, they add on Obdorsk for me, but it only means that you should not pay any attention to either such transfers as I had been sentenced to or to the entire matter. Moreover, you must sacrifice yourself as Christ did.

After this, the discussion passed on to the question of military service. Pëtr Vasil'evich began to disapprove of the following delusion:

> People entering the military service usually say that they join the Christ loving ranks. This is the doctrine of priests and this is the biggest deceit on their part by which they live. Such a deceit, especially in our time, is out of place

in Christianity. Any person, who knows at least something about the teaching and life of Christ, must not agree to this deceit. But people even in our time so easily succumb to this and accept this as a correct teaching. In the meantime, Christ in His teaching criticized and destroyed militarism, which serves only violence, and for this, these same soldiers crucified and killed Him. In our time, if the same Christ came with His tidings to the same world, I am sure that now, they would treat Him in the same way as they did 1900 years ago. Could this be considered a Christ loving army? You would sooner consider it the army of Nikolaĭ and it looks like a big band of robbers, headed by Nikolaĭ. As I understand the life and teaching of Christ, we must free ourselves as much as possible of such a misconception and not participate in such matters. It would be appropriate for the Doukhobors, as Christians of our time, to reject the military service completely. I consider it my obligation to tell them this because I am in the first rank among the Doukhobors. And if I do not tell them this, I may answer for this before God. That is why my direct obligation before God and the Doukhobors is to tell them this in order that they, according to the teaching of Jesus Christ and my personal advice, would reject military action and would not become soldiers and would not participate in any military actions, even indirectly. All weapons belonging to the Doukhobors, for example, rifles, revolvers, sabres, swords, which they had acquired distancing themselves from the teachings of Christ, must be gathered in one place. As a symbol of the refusal to fight evil with evil and in fulfilment of the commandment not to kill, Doukhobors must set all these weapons on fire. They should burn these weapons, remembering the words of Christ that those who take up the sword will perish by the sword.

The day of the burning of weapons, simultaneously in all three areas, was decided upon as June 29, 1895, midnight. It was the day of the apostles, Saint Peter and Paul, and the birthday of Pëtr Vasil'evich.

I advise those who are now among the ranks of the army, Pëtr Vasil'evich said, to return their weapons including their uniforms and to announce that they are Christians and all this does not befit them, and that from this day onwards they can no longer serve in any violent actions of the army, since their own conscience and the teaching of Jesus Christ contradicts it.

Such a lawful and just refusal to follow the official power in the state with a population of 180 million people must be heroic. It may produce persecution, suffering, even death, as they did with Christ and all of His true followers. Therefore, all of this must be admitted for their consideration and they must discuss it within their hearts seriously and reasonably in order to come to the final conclusion. I repeat again that you must explain to them my extreme conviction and understanding about Christ. Now they are doing military service—it means they are serving Nikolaĭ and obeying him as a sinful and mortal man who does not have anything in common in his life with Christ. That is why if they understand this and want to come from serving Nikolaĭ to serving Christ, they must change their life. Maybe they have already become proud, as the discipline is based on that. If so, they must forsake their pride and become meek and humble, as Christ showed us. And most important, they must be satisfied with their position whatever might happen to them. They must look upon all this as temporary and this is the most important turn in their lives. This is my brotherly advice to them. Please tell them: if they accept this and will behave according to my brotherly advice which is centred on the teachings of Jesus, let them begin without any fear remembering the words of Christ that you may kill the body but not the soul. Let them rely upon God because this is God's cause and in our weakness, we must appeal to Him. He will help all of us to discover the path of truth and virtue, that is, it will relieve our hard situation and sooth our souls.

The day selected for this action was the first day of Easter of 1895; on this day at least one of them must do this, and the rest may do it gradually.

Such an unexpected request from Pëtr Vasil'evich to Vereshchagin and brother Vasiliĭ puzzled them because they were not prepared for this. They did not know what to do, whether to take up this task upon themselves or to refuse. That was a moment of struggle between the spirit and the flesh. The flesh was unsettled because no matter whatever happens or does not happen to those who receive this message, the messengers must be the first to face their fate. Flesh itself began to ask the question of what will befall them and to seek the answers. Thus, for some time they remained uncertain. Pëtr Vasil'evich immediately noticed their flagging spirits and said, "I see that you are doubtful." For the truth's sake, they had to reveal what went on in their hearts, and they told him, "Yes, it is true." Pëtr Vasil'evich then told them, "I cannot pass this message with you. While entrusting this message, first, I must be sure of the messengers, and secondly, I must have a hope that you will deliver everything to the Doukhobors in detail. Otherwise, I repeat, I cannot give you this message. I will give you one day to decide yes or no. In making this decision, do not forget what is most important. When you raise the question of flesh, give more room for the decision for Spirit, which lives in you, and then I am sure you will conquer the weakness of your flesh and you will receive my message with joy." Then he let them go, and they left.

Such a decision must not be postponed for a day. When the victory of spirit over flesh is revealed—this continues only for a moment—all is fulfilled in spiritual ecstasy. In two hours, they arrived energetic and joyful, and for this message, they were now prepared to look into the eyes of death without any fear and be triumphant in spirit. Pëtr Vasil'evich was very glad for this and again began to repeat his message, which they had already received and it was inscribed on the tablets of their hearts.

Notes

1. Shenkursk is a town in Northern Russia; it was one of the places of exile of Pëtr Verigin.
2. Obdorsk (now Salekhard) is a town in north-western Siberia on the Ob' river. It was often used as a place of exile in Imperial Russia.
3. Kars is a town in Turkey. With its surrounding area, at the time of the narrative, it belonged to the Russian Empire. It was one of the areas of the Transcaucasian exile of the Doukhobors. Since 1921, it has been a part of Turkey.
4. Nikolaĭ (Nicolas II) Romanov was the last Russian tsar who succeeded the throne in 1894 and was officially crowned in 1896.

CHAPTER 12

Prisoner Transport of Pëtr Vasil'evich to Obdorsk, Tobol'sk Guberniia

The day of scheduled prisoner transport had arrived, and Pëtr Vasil'evich bid his farewell to all his friends and the residents of Shenkursk.[1] There were also many brothers and sisters who came from the neighbouring villages in order to see him off and tell him for the last time: "Good luck [Dobryĭ chas] to you, Pëtr Vasil'evich, and may our Lord bless you and grant you well-being on every day of your life. You are leaving good memories behind you that we will never forget. You comforted us in our privations and poverty not only with your words, but with your deeds as well." While saying this, many people wept.

At last, the hour and the moment came; the guards gave out the command: "Prisoners, line up for the check-up and departure!" Pëtr Vasil'evich joined the rows of thieves and murderers, and the word of Christ came to pass that He would be treated the same as villains and lawbreakers. However, this did not humiliate Pëtr Vasil'evich at all, and he was like the Lamb of God before the people. All the kind-hearted individuals felt sorry for him as they felt for Christ when he was crucified. They could not assist him in any other way, as they were powerless, and only felt sorry for him and cried. Those who did not know him were often struck by the expression in his eyes and were confused. They spoke to each other, "Why is this man mixed up with this group? It seems by the looks in his eyes that he does not deserve it." Simple folk understood it in their hearts but hardened governmental officials did not feel it. If sometime in these officials' hearts the innocence of Pëtr Vasil'evich were proven, they always shrugged off accountability, explaining it in the following way, "There are higher authorities responsible for this, and we are only doing what they assign to us."

The prisoner transport group moved ahead, and from the crowd, Pëtr Vasil'evich said for the last time, "Farewell, brothers and sisters, remember me well." Everyone answered with tears in their eyes, "Good luck [Dobryĭ chas], may God bless you."

This was on November 5, 1895. The frost was extremely severe. The snow was quite deep, and it was very difficult and painful to walk. Prisoner transport quarters were always very cold. As soon as prisoners were brought there, they would start taking care of everything themselves: they started the stoves, cooked the food or boiled water for tea. The guards were appointed to go from Shenkursk to the first regional town Vel'sk.[2] The guards did not change along the way and were instructed in Shenkursk to keep an eye on Pëtr Vasil'evich and not to allow anyone to meet with him. The guards followed these orders as far as Vel'sk. Vereshchagin, brother Vasiliĭ and Ob"edkov rented a wagon and followed the prisoner transport.

When they approached Vel'sk, the guards were changed, and another group of guards took over. Then matters improved. Vereshchagin and brother Vasiliĭ could visit the prisoner transport and stay there for a long time in the soldiers' quarters. The guards did not constrain them in any way, and they could freely talk about anything. They would always bring him a bottle of milk or some bread to eat or some other things. In this way, they freely went as far as Vologda. Pëtr Vasil'evich never got on the wagon, not even once. Vereshchagin and brother Vasiliĭ offered him a ride on the wagon, and the guards permitted it. But Pëtr Vasil'evich declined this offer saying, "I promised to God that I would walk all the way." They did not bother him about it anymore. Because of the torturous walk he was not accustomed to, Pëtr Vasil'evich developed blisters on his feet that caused him much pain. The blisters were bleeding and nobody knew how to help him. They stayed for one day in a village. Vereshchagin and brother Vasiliĭ invited two Russian women who were knowledgeable in such matters to come to the prisoner transport.

The guards allowed the women to walk in, and one of them attended to this concern. She took a needle with a thread, rubbed the thread with coal and pierced the blister with the needle, dragging the thread all the way through. The blister stopped bleeding, the pain ceased, and since that time, until the end of the prisoner transport, the pain never came back. Pëtr Vasil'evich was very grateful to them and gave them whatever was due. They also thanked him and left. They arrived in Vologda safely. Pëtr Vasil'evich was not affected by walking all the way. He always remained cheerful and happy.

In Vologda, Pëtr Vasil'evich spent four days in prison, and the prisoner transport continued by railway as far as Iaroslavl'.[3] In Iaroslavl', they also stayed for four days.

They arrived in Moscow in the evening. There he was placed in the central transit Butyrskaia[4] prison. He stayed there for five days and brother Vasilii visited him there when it was allowed. During the first visit, while Vasilii Vasil'evich was talking with Pëtr Vasil'evich, right there next to them separated by a double common grid, a free Tolstoyan[5] conversed with someone, I think it was Iziumchenko. Pëtr Vasil'evich got to know Iziumchenko in prison and while saying his good-byes to his brother, Pëtr Vasil'evich said, "Get acquainted with that other Tolstoyan and talk with him in detail about everything without any inhibitions." That Tolstoyan was Evgenii Ivanovich Popov[6] with whom we walked together as far as my hotel. Then he went to Lev Nikolaevich[7] and told him, "I was visiting the prisoners and the brother of Pëtr Vasil'evich was next to me and we had a conversation. I personally saw Pëtr Vasil'evich, and he also saw me and he told his brother to make my acquaintance, and this is what we did. I invited Pëtr Vasil'evich's brother to visit you, but he refused saying that he was staying at the hotel 'Petersburg', close to the Red Gate."[8] Vasilii Vasil'evich said, "I have two comrades there: Vasilii Grigor'evich Vereshchagin and Vasilii Ivanovich Ob"edkov, who are waiting for me, so if you want to meet them, please come and visit us." Upon hearing these words, Lev Nikolaevich sent to us Pavel Ivanovich Biriukov and Evgenii Ivanovich to invite us to visit him. We should not have refused this invitation by Lev Nikolaevich, but we had already been entrusted with the message from Pëtr Vasil'evich to all the Doukhobors, and we were afraid that we could be arrested because of this visit, so we refused their invitation. Before leaving they asked us to make an appointment for another time they could visit us. We suggested the next day at four in the afternoon after dinner. It was on December 8.

By this time, a few people headed by Lev Nikolaevich came to see us. We received them very amiably, and Lev Nikolaevich started asking us about our lives. Most questions by Lev Nikolaevich about violence, property, church and vegetarianism received our complete agreement.

Lev Nikolaevich asked about Pëtr Vasil'evich and we briefly informed him that he had been in exile for seven years already: first, he was exiled to Shenkursk, stayed there for three years and was then transferred to Kola.[9] He stayed there for two years, and then left for Arkhangel'sk[10] with the understanding that he had finished his term and would be free to go back to his homeland. However, in Arkhangel'sk, the governor announced that the ministry detained him there for five more years. Pëtr Vasil'evich decided to settle again in Shenkursk and spend his sentence time there. However, now again, his staying in Shenkursk was considered dangerous and he was being transported for settlement in Siberia. We talked with them for about an hour and a half. They gave us a book "*The Kingdom of God is Within You*" written by Lev Nikolaevich, said their good-byes and left.

The prisoner transport to which Pëtr Vasil'evich was assigned was scheduled to leave for Tula the next day, December 9.[11] The transport was scheduled to leave at 9 pm, and by this time, Lev Nikolaevich went to the railway terminal in the hope of seeing Pëtr Vasil'evich personally, even if from a distance, and of saying at least a few words to him. At 9 in the evening we learned that the transport would leave at 11 pm. Therefore, Lev Nikolaevich decided to go home; he gave me the box that he brought for Pëtr Vasil'evich, we said our good-byes and he left.

The train with the prisoner convoy left Moscow at 11 at night. The three of us took the same train to Tula. Pëtr Vasil'evich stayed there in prison for four days and then left for Riazhsk,[12] Riazan' guberniia, where we finally bid our farewell to Pëtr Vasil'evich and Ob"edkov. Their train left for Siberia, and we took another one to Transcaucasia, our homeland. This was on December 15th.

As a free man, Ob"edkov followed the prisoner transport to Obdorsk. They arrived safely in Obdorsk. The journey lasted for six months. After living together in Obdorsk for six months, Pëtr Vasil'evich decided to return Ob"edkov to his family and home. Pëtr Vasil'evich stayed there alone. During his whole stay in Obdorsk he lived alone, had a small apartment and did some work depending on the time of the year. He had a carpenter's bench that he made himself and some necessary equipment. He made some house trimmings, made doors, window frames and such other things. He made brick stoves, and in summer, he got together with a group of three or four men, and they cut the grass and stacked it in haystacks, for which they were well paid. He had a boat and he often took a ride along the river with some company of close friends. The boat was called "The Free Yacht."

He wrote letters to his relatives and all brothers and sisters, although rather infrequently. All his letters as well as letters to him were checked by the government, so he always wrote very briefly referring only to his health and well-being. These notifications still helped to support his relatives, particularly his father and mother who missed him dearly. If while checking his letters the government found anything suspicious, the letters were forwarded to the ministry. Knowing this, Pëtr Vasil'evich sometimes wrote letters with deep content, blaming and reprimanding the government, as was appropriate, and sent them off with the understanding that they should reach the minister. He did not suffer any ramifications for this. The local administration treated him politely in consideration of the fact that he could write about them as well, as he was not intimidated by anyone. And this is where I pause my narrative for the time being with Pëtr Vasil'evich staying in Obdorsk until his term finishes.

The elders were also sent away from Shenkursk for not swearing the oath of allegiance. Makhortov and Lezhebokov were sent to the town of Mezen',[13] Rybin was transported to Olonets,[14] where he soon passed away. Tsybul'kin, who was sick, stayed in Shenkursk hospital, and when he became better, his son who arrived from Transcaucasia,[15] Akhalklakh[16] region, took Tsybul'kin back home to the village of Bogdanovka.

Notes

1. Shenkursk is a town in Northern Russia; it was one of the places of exile of Pëtr Verigin.
2. Vel'sk (Velsk) a town in the South of Arkhangel'sk region.
3. Iaroslavl' (Yaroslavl) is a city on the Volga river, about 250 km to the north-east of Moscow.
4. Butyrskaia (Butyrskaya) prison or Butyrka (for short) is a prison in Moscow that was the central transport prison in Imperial Russia.
5. "Tolstoyan" means a follower of Tolstoy's teachings.
6. Evgeniĭ Ivanovich Popov was a man of letters, a vegetarian and a friend and follower of Tolstoy.
7. Leo Tolstoy (Lev Nikolaevich Tolstoĭ) (1828–1910) is a famous Russian writer, the author of "War and Peace," "Anna Karenina" and multiple other novels. He also was a philosopher and thinker who developed the concept of not resisting evil with violence (non-violent resistance). He was a great sympathizer and supporter of the Doukhobors and assisted them in resettlement to Canada.

8. Red Gate was a triumphal arch celebrating a Russian victory in an early eighteenth-century battle with Sweden. It was pulled down in 1920s.
9. Kola is a town in Kola peninsular, Murmansk area, a remote location in the north of the European part of Russia.
10. Arkhangel'sk (Arkhangelsk) is a city in the north of the European part of Russia.
11. Tula is a town in Central Russia about 200 km to the south of Moscow.
12. Riazhsk is a town in Riazan' region, located to the south of Moscow.
13. Mezen' (Mezen) is a town in the Arkhangel'sk (Arkhangelsk) area in the north of the European part of Russia, close to the Arctic Polar Circle.
14. Olonets is a town in the Republic of Karelia, a subject of the Russian Federation. It is located in the Karelian peninsula.
15. Transcaucasia is an area in and around the Caucasus mountains (located between the Caspian and the Black sea). It is comprised mostly of the territories of the modern states of Russia, Georgia, Armenia and Azerbaijan. At the time of the narrative, it was the territory of the Russian Empire.
16. Akhalkalak (modern Akhalkalaki) is an administrative district in the country of Georgia. Now an independent state, in Imperial Russia, Georgia constituted Tiflis guberniia.

CHAPTER 13

Accomplishment of the Mission. Letter of Pëtr Vasil'evich to the Doukhobors. Doukhobors' Refusal of Military Service. Imprisonment of Vasiliĭ Verigin and Vereshchagin

Vasiliĭ Grigor'evich Vereshchagin and my brother Vasiliĭ Vasil'evich returned home from the trip safely, thank God.[1] All the Doukhobors waited for them impatiently. When they arrived, there were big conventions and sobraniia assemblies, where they spoke in detail about their trip, and about the health and well-being of Pëtr Vasil'evich. They also explained in detail why he was being transferred for such a long distance and to such a remote place as Obdorsk.[2]

Of course that transfer accompanied by much suffering made everyone sad, but life and the course of events soon took another turn. Vasiliĭ Grigor'evich Vereshchagin and Vasiliĭ Vasil'evich Verigin brought regards and best wishes from Pëtr Vasil'evich, and without any hesitation presented his advice for the life of the Doukhobors concerning the burning of weapons and rejection of military service and other related matters. Over the next while, they went to Elizavetpol'[3] Region, to Slavianka, and to the other villages. They saw everyone there and delivered all the necessary messages.

From there they went to Akhalkalak[4] district where the majority of the Doukhobors lived. They went through all the villages safely and discussed all pertinent matters. But the police followed them closely. If they were not as careful as they were, they could have been arrested and imprisoned. They avoided this successfully keeping in mind the words of Christ: "Be wise as the snakes, and you will be safe as the doves." They returned home to the village of Terpenie of Kars[5] Region safely. When the police learned about the delivery of Pëtr Vasil'evich's messages, they became concerned. Alekseĭ Vorob'ëv, who was considered to be the closest friend and even the brother of Pëtr Vasil'evich (the late Luker'ia Vasil'evna called them brothers), became intimidated along with the small party of the Doukhobors, because they feared punishment by the government. That segment of the Doukhobors, headed by Vorob'ëv, did not accept the message and advice of Pëtr Vasil'evich. They did not stop eating meat, did not participate in the burning of the weapons and did not reject military service. If they only had refused to participate, it would have been all right, but they went so far as to make reports to the government. In these reports they said that some people were going around the villages creating disturbances. Christ's words are true which take on a meaning today. He said, "Those who are not with me are against me." But let them do as they wish, and we will continue with God's work. Vereshchagin and brother Vasiliĭ asked their relatives to go to those who were in military service as soldiers and inform them of Pëtr Vasil'evich's advice. Brother Vasiliĭ passed on a letter to them personally where the message was explained. I quote this letter, word for word.

> Beloved brother in our Lord Jesus Christ, I would like to talk to you, dear brother, about what constitutes my faith. I believe in the law of our Lord Jesus Christ and comprehend it not superficially but at its core. When we live according to the will of our Father, our Lord, then our Lord lives in us reviving us and enlightening our reason with a radiant light. Those who wish to fulfil the will of our heavenly Father must bend their hearts to God's will. Our Lord speaks to us: you were bought at an expensive price, do not be slaves of human beings. Learn the truth and the truth shall make you free.
>
> Undertaking such a great course we must totally realize that our sincerity may be subjected to cruel tests. Our task may bring upon us insults, offences, suffering and even death. Misunderstanding, false interpretations and lies will await us. A storm will arise against us: pride, pharisaism, ambition, cruel rulers, authorities; all of these may unite to eradicate us. In the same way did they treat our Lord, Jesus Christ, whom we try to emulate as much as possible, according to our abilities. We should not be frightened by these horrors. Our hope is not for the people but for the almighty God. If we reject human protection, what would support us, save the singular faith, which

conquers the entire world? We will not be surprised by those trials to which we are exposed. We will be glad to have the honour to share the sufferings of our Lord Jesus Christ. Because of all this, we give our souls to God and believe what was said: 'The one who leaves one's home, brothers, sisters, mother, father, or children or possessions for the sake of God will get one hundred times more, and will inherit eternal life in the Kingdom of Heaven.' So firmly believing in the certain triumph of truth, in spite all that could stand against us, we trust reason and the consciousness of humanity, but most of all, God's power to which we must subject ourselves. For a Christian to promise to obey people or human laws is the same as for a hired worker to promise to follow not only his employer's orders, but also orders given by other people. You cannot serve two masters. A Christian liberates himself from human power when he recognizes only the power of God over himself and the law which was revealed by the Lord Jesus Christ. He realizes it within himself and abides by it. Human life consists of following not your own will but the will of God. A Christian may be subjected to exterior violence and may be deprived of physical freedom, and at the same time could be freed of his passions. The one who sins is the slave of sin. A Christian is meek and humble, does not argue with anyone, does not attack anyone, does not use violence against anyone, and on the contrary, without resentment he endures violence and through this overcomes evil.

Vasiliĭ Vasil'evich Verigin

They travelled, met with everyone and did their task so well that those who chose to reject military service selected a specific day, as I explained above. If they consider this seriously and come to an understanding, then they must take action on the first day of Easter. Perhaps not everyone at once, but the beginning must take place on that day, when the commander of the squad comes and congratulates his soldiers on this great holiday in the world, saying, "Christ has arisen." The soldiers must answer, "In the righteous, Christ has arisen." Then the ones with the hearts filled with the spirit of God must prove this by telling the commander, "I believe in Christ in deed and will serve Him, and reject your whole violent regime. Therefore I ask you to accept this rifle from me along with your other things that are useless for me, since they contradict my consciousness and the spiritual feeling of my soul."

Matveĭ Vasil'evich Lebedev[6] was the first to commit this action. His brave endeavour became known to the whole regiment and everyone questioned, "What happened to him?" Some people said he went insane, while others said, cautiously, that he was correct in his actions. He was tortured, beaten and put into the punishment cell, where he was not given any food other than bread and water. Others followed his example, and soon in all of the three guberniias, all the Doukhobor soldiers returned their weapons and equipment. They were all arrested, beaten, tortured and put into isolation away from the other soldiers. But nothing worked. Finally, they were all sent to the disciplinary battalion to Ekaterinograd[7] Fortress for more cruel punishment. In all, there were 33 of them.

When the above-mentioned brothers returned their weapons and ammunition to the government, the government did not let it go and began to investigate and search for reasons and sources for this behaviour. Although they were not certain, they suspected Vasiliĭ Vereshchagin, my brother Vasilii Verigin, and I do not know why, myself.

On July 10, 1895, all three of us were summoned by gendarme[8] officer Astaf'ev and Assistant Procurator Stepanov to the Argeno station. The above-mentioned persons took another road to come to our village with horsemen and began to search our houses. They did not find anything suspicious, came back and began to interrogate us. Because there was no direct evidence against us to enable them to arrest and imprison us, they began to question us about our convictions and whether we recognize our sovereign and all existing authorities. Without any hesitation, we informed them of our convictions, "We recognize the sovereign as sovereign, authorities for authorities, but in no way will we abide by their demand if it were against the law of God. We deeply believe in our Lord Jesus Christ, who came to the world to redeem the sin of the forefathers. He gave the entire human race the commandment and presented the testament, not to sin and not to perform unlawful actions. The foundation of his teaching consists firstly, to love God with all your heart, with all your soul and with all your reason. Secondly, love your neighbour as you love yourself. This is the foundation of the Law and the Prophets. Also in the Gospel of Matthew, Chapter Five, verse 38, Christ says to the people, 'You have heard the law as it was pronounced: an eye for an eye, and a tooth for a tooth. But I say unto you, that ye resist not evil, but whosoever shall smite thee on thy right cheek, turn to him the other also. And if any man will sue thee at the law, and take away thy coat, let him have thy cloak also'. The sixth commandment of the law of Moses says, 'Do not kill'. And based on this, we should not kill people, moreover, according to Christ, we should love our enemies. Those were the words of our Lord Jesus Christ, that He carried out in life being the son of God, but He was banished and put on trial, endured all sorts of persecutions and sufferings, and died on the cross. With His example, He inspired His followers, who were tortured before and now. So those who believe in Him, must accept His teaching, that is to implement His teaching in their life's actions, since without deeds, a faith is dead. The deeds that are required from us are: be meek, humble and love not only humans, but all the living things on earth, be compassionate, do not avenge evil with evil, but conquer evil with goodness."

From what we said, the Gendarme Officer and Assistant Procurator sensed that somehow we didn't belong to them anymore, and they said, "It means that you won't abide by the laws of the sovereign?"—"Yes, if the laws of the sovereign are connected with murder and violence, we cannot participate in them." After that, they compiled our case files and announced that, "now you are arrested and tomorrow you will be sent to Kars to the Karadakh prison." My brother Vasiliĭ addressed them with the following words: "Because our parents are old, our wives are unable to take care of the household, and the children are very small, would it not be possible to liberate our youngest brother till the special order, to let him look after the old parents and small children?" They agreed to do this on payment of 500 roubles bail. Ivan Ivanovich Usachëv agreed to bail me immediately, and in the morning they freed me. I went home, and the same day my brother Vasilii and Vereshchagin were sent to Kars under strict convoy and put into the Karadakh[9] prison in solitary confinement. Chief Commander Sheremet'ev was informed about them and he resolved to put both of them under military tribunal in order to frighten all the rest; and to prove that, I quote excerpts from Tregubov's and brother Vasilii's letters: "Once there was a rumour that they wanted to sentence some Doukhobors to death by hanging or shooting. Their friends informed the Doukhobors about this. They replied with a dignified letter that we quote here."

> Today we received a letter from Ivan Mikhaĭlovich Tregubov in which he greets us with brotherly wishes and regards, may God save him. He writes that allegedly me and Vereshchagin were sentenced to hanging; he also says that he and Vladimir Grigor'evich Chertkov wrote to the Chief Commander in the Caucasus, Sheremet'ev, with a request to pardon us. I do not know from whence this rumour reached them, we have not heard this yet, but it may as well be that there is such an evil plot against us. It is up to them. Our task is to fulfil the work of the Lord, who gave us life and light. Of course, we are thankful to our brothers who care about us with hearts overflowing with love.

Save them Oh, Lord. But according to our understanding, it is not appropriate for a Christian to bend one's will in front of a human and ask for pardon.
(From the letter of Vasiliĭ Verigin to Dmitriĭ Aleksandrovich Khilkov)

Besides Treguboff and Chertkov, Georgiĭ Aleksandrovich Dadiani also wrote to Sheremet'ev. Dadiani was adjutant to Sheremet'ev but later on he gave up all his ranks and rewards and became a Christian. Georgiĭ Aleksandrovich, a Georgian prince by inheritance, only a year ago was an adjutant to Sheremet'ev; and brother Vasiliĭ Vasil'evich knew him personally. Georgiĭ Aleksandrovich was a Tolstoyan.[10] When he received that resolution, he immediately wrote a letter to Sheremet'ev in which he said, "I received awful news that you have resolved to put Vereshchagin and Verigin before a military tribunal and it all depends on your signature. This is awful. How immoral this is. How low this is. Haven't those times come to an end? We are living in the twentieth century after the birth and the horrible death of our great teacher of truth Jesus Christ who desired brotherhood and peaceful life for all humanity, and thanks to that the Kingdom of God will come to earth as it is in heaven. And for this sacred teaching you dare to publicly shoot these innocent people. Moreover, you believe in this doctrine yourself, as you are considered a Christian. You think that by such a cruel action as to spill the blood of the innocent you will intimidate people who are fulfilling the will of God expressed by Jesus Christ, for which He laid down His life and bequeathed His followers to do the same. Perhaps you think that in such a way you will intimidate these two fighters for truth. I am telling you as my former friend (now I stand in the ranks of Christ)—by this action, you will stain not only yourself but the entire country of Russian people with innocent blood. The greater part of these people, in one way or another, believe in Christ, and you will bury these individuals for Christ. As for Vereshchagin and Verigin, I know Vasiliĭ Vasil'evich personally. They will not give in and will abide by your resolution with joy. The rest of the Doukhobors who have already accepted the spirit of Christ, will not be intimidated. Quite the opposite, they will be even more inspired. Because these individuals whom you wish to execute will be revered as holy. And in fact these people deserve this name because they are dying for the teachings of Christ and for the common brotherly unified course. They themselves will abide by your resolution."

This is exactly what Georgiĭ Alksandrovich Dadiani wrote. Of course such people have a great force in God's work, maybe this helped the salvation of the accused and they were not executed.

Notes

1. Sobranie (or sobran'e, sobraniia for plural) is a Doukhobor Assembly that typically started with "molenie" (molen'e) (including prayers, psalms and hymns) and continued with the resolution of pertinent matters by the assembly.
2. Obdorsk (now Salekhard) is a town in north-western Siberia on the Ob' river. It was often used as a place of exile in Imperial Russia.
3. Elizavetpol' (later Kirovabad, since 1989, Ganja) was the capital of Elizavetpol' guberniia in the Russian Empire. Since the separation of Azerbaijan from the Soviet Union, it is one of the largest cities in Azerbaijan.
4. Akhalkalak (modern Akhalkalaki) is an administrative district in the country of Georgia. Now an independent state, in Imperial Russia, Georgia constituted Tiflis guberniia.
5. Kars is a town in Turkey, With its surrounding area, at the time of the narrative, it belonged to the Russian Empire. It was one of the areas of the Transcaucasian exile of the Doukhobors. Since 1921, it has been a part of Turkey.
6. Matveĭ Levedev (we are not sure why he is referred to as Timofeĭ in the text) was one of the first Doukhobor soldiers to lay down his weapons. He survived the brutal punishment and exile and immigrated to Canada with other Doukhobors. He is buried in Nadezhda cemetery in Saskatchewan (close to the National Doukhobor Heritage Village site in Veregin).
7. Ekaterinograd is modern Ekterinogradskaia or Yekaterinogradskaya village in Kabardino-Balkaria, a republic of the Russian Federation; it is located to the north of Georgia.
8. Gendarmes were a Special Corps of military police in Imperial Russia.
9. Karadakh is a town in the modern Republic of Dagestan, a subject of Russian Federation. It is located in the north Caucasus region.
10. "Tolstoyan" means a follower of Tolstoy's teachings.

CHAPTER 14

The Burning of Weapons in Three Guberniias and the Return of the Reserve Conscription Cards

A painting by Terry McLean depicting the Burning of Weapons by the Doukhobors

As the reader already knows, the day selected for the burning of weapons was Peter and Paul's day, June 29, 1895. On this day, in all the three guberniias, Doukhobors willing to follow the advice of Pëtr Vasil'evich had to set all their weapons on fire. Not all the Doukhobors knew about the day and where the fire would be started. They were only expected to discuss and decide this matter in earnest, and then they would be notified later. No more than two or three reliable people in every village knew about that day. This was done so that the government would not learn about it in advance, because if they had learned about it, they would have taken all measures to prevent it. Although the weapons did not belong to the government, the officials knew well that the government's power would be undermined by such actions.

The day of the burning of weapons was approaching, and all of the Doukhobors as well as everyone individually were seriously considering their fate and what they should do. On that evening, it was announced to everyone: whoever wanted to burn their weapons should bring them to one specified location. Again, nobody knew where the weapons would be burned except for three or four people who had already prepared the firewood, coal and kerosene beforehand. All was prepared right in front of everyone but nobody noticed. When the weapons were brought together in every village, they were loaded on carts and immediately transported to the place where they were to be burned. All this was done simultaneously and successfully, being conscious of the time, so that the government would not learn about it and would not interfere with this great undertaking. As I had been freed from prison, I also took part in it. Simultaneously, all the villages delivered their firewood, coal, kerosene and all their weapons. First, they put down the firewood, and then about two carts full of coal. Everything was soaked in kerosene, and then they started putting down rifles, revolvers, sabres, daggers, in short, whatever weapon anyone had. All this was done following the guidance of an elderly man, Ivan Ivanovich Usachëv, who was 65 years old and known for his life as a good Christian. The first thing they put on the ground as a foundation was Pëtr Vasil'evich's rifle that he had sent from Shenkursk specifically for this purpose. The rifle had a central precision mechanism and cost 250 roubles. Everything was arranged by midnight and soaked in kerosene. There were 30 gallons[1] of kerosene used. The entire layered pile in its width and height resembled a big building. When the clock struck midnight, the above-mentioned Ivan Ivanovich Usachëv lit up a torch and set ablaze this bonfire of weapons, gigantic as a huge building, with all those weapons invented by evil for the extermination of people. As the flames were kindled, what an awe-inspiring and at the same time joyous site that was! It was located on top of a big mountain, which was close to the river Karsina, and could be seen from a long distance. When the fire was fully ablaze, many Muslims and Armenians from the local auls[2] were frightened, and in the morning, many of them came to see what was going on. They found a heap of melted iron heated to the highest temperature.

On that day, a big sobranie[3] was held attended by brothers and sisters from all the villages. After burning the weapons, after midnight, they all started praying and reading and singing psalms, which lasted until 12 noon. After this, they conversed and discussed the burning at length. Now Doukhobors, as they understood it, were verily passing over to their new life in Christ. Until this time, they at least partly protected themselves from the wild local population and purchased weapons for this purpose. Now all these weapons were thrown into fire and only cinders and a nugget of iron remained from them. At that time, Doukhobors decided to seek salvation and protection from a more mighty being, that is, they placed all their hopes onto God. Of course, hope for this kind of salvation has a more solid foundation, but then one needs to live according to God's will. This kind of discussion continued until the evening, and then they said their good-byes and went to their villages filled with the joy of the Holy Spirit.

This is how the burning of the weapons in the Kars[4] area finished. Soon after this, Doukhobors started giving back their reserve soldier conscription cards. There were no particular incidents while giving back those cards; it was all done with God's help without any fuss. It happened so because the local police officer by the name Baĭrakov, in whose jurisdiction we were, was a person with a good soul. We should remember him in our midst for a long time. Bestow upon him, Oh God, all the good in the world for many years for his exemplary and humane deeds during that time. Whoever wanted to hand back their draft conscription cards approached him, as the closest governmental representative, for returning the cards. He accepted the cards without any fuss or insults; he wrote down all the names and last names and let them all go home. Then he sent the cards to Kars to the military headquarters. He conversed a lot with the first of those who were handing back the cards. He asked them why and for what purpose they were doing this. Doukhobors explained that it was based on the teaching of Christ. Then he said, "You can go home. I will send your cards where they belong. As far as you are concerned, whatever decision they make will be implemented. I personally have no right to condemn or punish you for such a noble action. If you are earnestly considering it, may God bless."

Baĭrakov was a very good person; you could hardly find his like among the police in those days. I will describe here one of his actions that is worthy of attention. In those times, as always, Doukhobors were not afraid of prison, sufferings and exile. All of those who were arrested, faced it with joy, with an exhilarated spirit, as if they were going for a feast on Christ's invitation. One brother from our midst was not eligible for military service and he had no card to return. Those who returned their cards could be put into prison, but he was longing for the suffering, and he wanted to be put into prison by all means. Once he came to Baĭrakov and made a statement, "Sir, I do not want to acknowledge the tsar and all his powers, and will not obey them." Baĭrakov listened to it all, and then asked, "Anything else?"—"Nothing."—"Go back home, God help you." The Doukhobor brother left in the hope that in a week, he would be put into prison, as it had happened with those who returned their conscription cards. One week passed, then another, but he was not summoned anywhere. He appeared again in front of Baĭrakov. This time Baĭrakov remembered him, so he asked, "Why do you come again?"—"I came, sir, to state in front of you that I will not obey the tsar and his powers."—"But you have already told me about it," Baĭrakov laughed and sent him back home, warning him that he should live peacefully. This was the end of his sufferings, and he did not get into prison. This was Semën Chernenkov. All those who returned their conscription cards were arrested and put into Kars prison until further notice.

In the village of Slavianka, Elizavetpol'[5] guberniia, the burning of weapons and the return of the cards occurred in an entirely different manner, since besides the hardened governmental officials, there were also many traitors among our former brothers, such as the three brothers Kotel'nikovs, and others, who without any mercy, reported lies to the government. And the more severe the government's action was, the more they were pleased and filled with Satan's joy.

As the day of the burning of weapons was approaching, those bad people already knew that on a certain day something would happen, although they were not sure what it was exactly. They reported it to the government. By this time, gendarme Colonel Suratov, prosecutor's assistant Strelkov and the local police officer with a few dozen Cossacks and soldiers had arrived in Slavianka from Elizavetpol'.

In Slavianka, the place for the burning of the weapons was selected about two miles away from the village. There was a grove there with some fruit trees planted a long time ago. This grove was well fenced and kept in good order by the Doukhobors. All the Doukhobors went there often in the summertime, performed the divine liturgy and had lunches, so that the grove was kind of a sacred place. The bonfire was placed in the proximity of that grove, over a thousand feet[6] aside from it. This was all done quietly and neatly, despite the fact that there were guards there who were supposed to report to the government if anything happened. The wagons full of firewood, coal, kerosene and weapons passed by these guards and they paid no attention. When everything was ready, also at 12 midnight, the fire burst forth. Immediately, a huge flame sprang up which could be seen from Slavianka. The above-mentioned government representatives there were alarmed. With their cavalry, accompanied by the unscrupulous people, the government representatives rushed to the site of this illumination. On their way they encountered many brothers and sisters who wanted to perform God's liturgy. The gendarme officer and the prosecutor's assistant stopped them and told them to return to their homes. Nobody paid attention, and everybody kept walking. Three people arrested on their way there were Fëdor Golubov, Ivan Aniutushkin and Fëdor Verigin. They were sent with the soldiers to Slavianka and put under arrest. When they arrived at the site of the weapons' burning, Suratov and Strelkov just stood there not knowing what they should do. They had with them about 50 soldiers on horseback and were attended to by the above-mentioned Kotel'nikovs and their followers.

A few people were sent to Slavianka to bring fire irons in order to get the weapons out of the fire. However, it was all in vain. The fire burned so hot that it prevented any approach for about 50 feet around it, not letting anyone interfere with its sacrifice, consuming everything on its way. The government officials were upset that they could not rescue the weapons nobody needed and started discharging their accumulated rage in a more severe form. They started arresting many people and were brutally beating the arrested. Many fell unconscious and others poured water on them so that they would come to. Suratov himself, along with Strelkov, and the police officer participated in this inhuman act. There was also with them a despicable governmental representative Skliarov, who was roaming around like a mad animal in the hope of fixing things. The crueller were their actions, the more passionate became the followers of justice, and they proceeded with their holy course and started returning their military conscription cards. This infuriated the governmental officials even more, as if adding fuel to the flames, and all of them, evil as fierce animals, started a fistfight. The gendarme prosecutor himself was beating people, displaying and maintaining in this way his inhuman nature. Some elders, 23 of them, were also arrested, although they were not eligible for any military service. They were arrested as they were pointed out by the opposite side to be the instigators of this movement. Among them, were four Verigin brothers: Ivan, Fëdor, Luk'ian and Prokofiĭ. There were also Mikhaĭlo Petrovich Popov, Nikolaĭ Potap'evich Malov, Vasiliĭ Nikiforovich Shcherbakov, Vasiliĭ Mikhaĭlovich Konkin, two brothers Fëdor Ivanovich and Vasiliĭ Ivanovich Golubov, two brothers Vasiliĭ Ivanovich and Arefiĭ Ivanovich Arekhov (Verigin), Pëtr Fëdorovich Dymovskiĭ, Nikolaĭ Timofeevich Chernov, Vasiliĭ Fëdorovich Semënov, Mikhail Alekseevich Shishkin and Vasiliĭ Nikolaevich Zybin. From Troitskoe village, there were Osip Fëdorovich Novokshonov, two brothers Nikolaĭ and Ivan Dergousov, and Larion Fëdorovich Terekhov. From Goreloe village, there was Nikolaĭ Timofeevich Goncharov. From Spasskoe village: Fëdor Salykin. About 80 people were arrested for returning their conscription cards. All of them were sent to Elizavetpol' prison.

This was how the burning of the weapons and the return of the military conscription cards ended. Besides Slavianka, three other villages that participated in it were Troitskoe, Goreloe and Novospasskoe.

Notes

1. The text uses the word "funt" (Russian equivalent of the word "pound"), which equals 16.3 kg. Since there is no equivalent unit in the English Imperial system, the word "gallon" was used in the translation. The actual amount of 30 Russian gallons of kerosene equals 30 × 16.3 = 489 kg. Almost half a ton of kerosene was used during the burning of the weapons.
2. "Aul" is a word used to refer to local villages in the Caucasus Mountains.
3. Sobranie (or sobran'e, sobraniia in plural) is a Doukhobor Assembly that typically started with "molenie" (molen'e) (including prayers, psalms and hymns) and continued with the resolution of pertinent matters by the assembly.
4. Kars is a town in Turkey. With its surrounding area, at the time of the narrative, it belonged to the Russian Empire. It was one of the areas of the Transcaucasian exile of the Doukhobors. Since 1921, it has been a part of Turkey.
5. Elizavetpol' (later Kirovabad, since 1989, Ganja) was the capital of Elizavetpol' guberniia in the Russian Empire. Since the separation of Azerbaijan from the Soviet Union, it is one of the largest cities in Azerbaijan.
6. The original text uses "sazhen" (pace), a unit of measurement employed in tsarist Russia, which equals about 2.1 m. Thus, the actual distance from the grove indicated in the text is over 400 m.

CHAPTER 15

The Burning of Weapons in the Akhalkalak Area and the Brutal Massacre by the Government

Now I will pass to the description of the Doukhobors who lived in the Akhalkalak[1] area of Tiflis[2] guberniia.

When Doukhobors were planning to burn the weapons, the traitors' side, the Goreloe dwellers, who knew that they were guilty of taking over the Orphans' Home and the entire capital, became suspicious that the majority of Doukhobors were getting together with the weapons in their arms to take back the Orphans' Home by force and drive them out. They reported this to Governor Nakashidze in Tiflis and asked for immediate protection. The governor believed this to be true and he summoned 200 Cossacks from Kagizman, a regional centre of Kars area,[3] by telegram. He also summoned 200 soldiers from Aleksandropol'[4] and left for the village of Goreloe. The Cossacks and the soldiers arrived on time and on that night, they surrounded the whole of Goreloe with guards, waiting for the assault any minute.

All this turned out for the better. Doukhobors were calmly engaged in their business and nobody interfered with it. All the weapons were taken out to the Caves, and when everything was ready, also at 12 midnight, they set the fire ablaze.

The Doukhobors had a tradition of gathering at those Caves on the day of Peter and Paul. Here they performed God's liturgy and celebrated. On that night as well, brothers and sisters started gathering from all the villages. There were about 2000 people.

When Goreloe inhabitants saw the fire burning, they were perplexed and decided to find out what was going on there. When they learned that weapons were being burned there, in order not to appear liars because of their demands for the governor and soldiers, they deliberately started to lie to the governor that allegedly the friends of Verigin realized how weak and powerless they were against the army, and got scared, and in rage, burned their own weapons. Allegedly, if it were not for the presence of the army, Verigin followers would have killed all the Goreloe dwellers. The governor believed this as well. He sent out the Cossacks with the order that house owners from every village should come to him in Goreloe. Most house owners were in the Caves. This is where the Cossacks went with this command. The Doukhobors explained to them, "when we finish God's liturgy, we will then immediately go to see the governor."

This simple and just answer made the governor explode with rage. Despite the fact that the people were praying to God, as he had the power to do so, he immediately dispatched 200 Cossacks led by a corporal by the name of Praga and ordered them to herd everyone, men and women, towards the village with whips. Praga and all the Cossacks, following this beastly command, hurried to the Caves that were about five miles away. At about 200 yards from the people, they stopped, let their horses rest a little, and then the trumpeter gave a signal for the charge. All the Cossacks attacked this sobranie assembly, where people were humbly standing in their liturgy, reciting and singing psalms. Attempting to split the assembled people into a few groups, the Cossacks advanced with force, but the members of the sobranie assembly were standing so close to each other, that the Cossacks could not do anything.

Praga ordered a retreat, and when the signal was played on the trumpet, all the Cossacks retreated about 100 yards, and then again a signal for the charge was given. The Cossacks became extremely enraged and started hitting their horses so that they would directly attack the people. But the horses were probably more clever than their riders: as soon as they approached the people, the horses stood up on their hind legs and did not get through into the midst of people. After this failure, the Cossacks started using their whips and were mercilessly flogging whoever they could reach, whether men or women. Almost everyone was bleeding, and in this way the Cossacks herded the whole sobranie assembly of 2000 people to the governor. On the way, the Cossacks brutalized women: a Cossack would gallop on horseback towards a woman, grab her by the hair and drag her for a few yards. Women were wearing silk head scarves. Many Cossacks tore them off and stuffed them into their pockets, as it happens after a battle with an enemy. They did this because this enemy was so powerless that they did not even protect themselves from the attackers. Under such circumstances, the Cossacks decided to display all the bravery of a Russian warrior and pushed people like this as far as Bogdanovka village. When the Cossacks saw that the governor was on his way, they stopped the people and ordered all of the men to take their hats off. To this the response was: "There isn't anyone here yet, why should we take the hats off?" The Cossacks persisted and flogged the people with their whips. One elderly man was trampled by a horse and had three ribs broken. Some people from the village of Bogdanovka came out to meet the governor and stood separately. This was the so-called Vorob'ëv group, they did not participate in the burning of the weapons, and consequently they singled themselves out so as not to suffer with everybody else. The governor first addressed them. Then he addressed us and said, "How are you living?" The response was, "As you can see." The governor spoke again, "Will you obey the government like all the people including this Vorob'ëv group do?"—"Why? Because they took away all our possessions, the capital, the Orphans' Home and exiled some of our innocent brothers into severe Siberia without any trial?" And here, as a sign of a refusal to comply, a few young men handed him their military conscription cards. The governor accepted them as he probably thought it was going to be some kind of a petition. Then he unfolded them. Upon realizing that these were conscription cards, he angrily threw them on the ground. Five more people approached him with the cards, but he did not accept them anymore, and they threw the cards at his feet. The governor became agitated and ordered the alarm signal to be played. The Cossacks were signalled to load their rifles and fire. The Cossacks were about to execute the command, and there was just a moment left before the command "Fire" would be given for them to start shooting.

Present at this illegal action of the governor was a government officer, Duke Kospinskiĭ. Seeing the unjust actions of the governor undertaken by him ostensibly in disregard of all the laws, Kospinskiĭ bared his sabre, raised it upwards and shouted so that anyone could hear: "There aren't such laws that would justify firing at these people who do not deserve it!" Then the command was cancelled, and the governor, while getting into his carriage, called corporal Praga and told him, "I am leaving you responsible for these villages, in particular Bogdanovka. You can do whatever you find necessary to make all the Doukhobors obey." He forgot that earlier they had refused to obey even himself. "When they meet governmental officials," said the governor, "they should take their hats off and make a low bow. Whoever disobeys in this, punish them as you will."

Hardly had the governor departed, when Praga solemnly declared everything the governor entrusted him with. Then the Cossacks started the brutal punishments of the Doukhobors again for the refusal of taking their hats off and of bowing. It was certainly not appropriate that Praga was so impudent, and therefore people did not obey him and stood for their dignity despite all the floggings. Of course, from a side, such persistence may seem excessive—why not take a hat off and bow? This is how we show we are human. But this is appropriate in front of another human. However, if a human turned into a beast and demanded undeserved obedience in an impudent way, it would not be good for reasonable people to pamper to the whims and fancies of a madman. Therefore, the people who stood for their dignity did well.

These people will be remembered for generations. Praga in his cold heart and madness did many disgusting things one can only feel abhorred by. He beat many people unconscious. On one night, instigated by the Vorob'ëv group, he even dared to subject women and girls to flogging. Such a horrible act committed by him is the height of any madness and can only be akin to a wild cruel beast, but not to a man. He also killed cattle and subjected many people to military corporal punishments.

Notes

1. Akhalkalak (modern Akhalkalaki) is an administrative district in the country of Georgia. Now an independent state, in Imperial Russia, Georgia constituted Tiflis guberniia.
2. Tiflis is the old name of modern Tbilisi, the capital of the country of Georgia. In the nineteenth century, it was the capital of Tiflis guberniia, which was a part of the Russian Empire.
3. Kars is a town in Turkey. With its surrounding area, at the time of the narrative, it belonged to the Russian Empire. It was one of the areas of Transcaucasian exile of the Doukhobors. Since 1921, it has been a part of Turkey.
4. Aleksandropol' at the time of the narrative was a town in Imperial Russia. After the collapse of the Soviet Union and the independence of Armenia, it was renamed Giymri. Giymri is the second largest city of Armenia.

CHAPTER 16

The Destruction of Livelihood and Possessions; Resettlement Among the Indigenous Peoples

The governor, likely in concert with the commander-in-chief, decided to disperse all those Doukhobors who did not obey the government among the indigenous peoples. The worst locations with a hot climate were selected for this. An order was sent by the governor to depart immediately. The order split the Doukhobors into groups. The first group included five households from each village, who were to depart immediately. The second group had to leave in the same manner three days after the first group, and so on until the last group departed.

It was forbidden to sell the houses. There were no provisions for taking care of the rest of the possessions: horses, cattle, wagons, etc. Many inhabitants of the surrounding villages wanted to buy these, but the Cossacks would not let them. We did not know whether this was the fault of the government or whether it was the vicious purpose of the remaining brothers, who motivated by greed, likely asked the Cossacks not to let in external buyers, so that everything would be left for them. If they did buy anything themselves, it was for the lowest price. For example, they would buy a horse that cost 100 roubles for 50 roubles or even less than that, and the same with other items. Much was left there without being sold. They did not buy it because they knew it would get into their hands anyway. Indeed, when the people were exiled, there would be a new owner found for all the goods left behind.

Those who were exiled were only allowed to take one wagon with four horses per family; people and clothes were in the wagon. Much was left behind. People felt sorry for leaving things behind because they were all accumulated through dozens of years of work. But nothing could be done about it, and most possessions were left behind. The order did not include any details about where they were sent to and whether it was close or far. Thus they set out on their journey without knowing where they were going. There were guides from the government to accompany them to the place which was appointed by the government. They were settled among the Georgians and Imeretins,[1] five households per aul.[2] The districts of settlement were the hottest ones, Gori, Tiganeti and Dusheti,[3] where unaccustomed to such a hot climate, Doukhobors came down with fever and many of them died. There were some cases where only one family member out of ten would remain and all others died.

This is how the burning of the weapons ended in Akhalkalak[4] district of Tiflis[5] guberniia. In the midst of the destruction of their material wealth, the sufferers were rebuked not only by Goreloe dwellers, the Chaldeans so to say, but also by the Vorob'ëv group, who until recently worked together with the exiled Doukhobors. Now, as if they were sorry for their suffering brethren, they started saying, "This is what it led you to—a complete destruction. How do you think of living after all this? You are approaching death while all the people around you live quietly and peacefully, enjoying their life, and obeying the government in everything. You decided to go against the government in such small numbers. You are but a drop in the ocean, and consider what you could achieve with this tiny drop? You are only attracting the destruction upon yourselves. This is what Verigin is advising you, but it is fine for him to give such advice when it is you who have to suffer through all this here." This was how we were rebuked by brothers and sisters who were staying behind in old places including Kholodnoe.

While delivering his free-willing brotherly advice, Pëtr Vasil'evich knew that if the people followed it, they would have to undergo what was described above. He even thought that for the refusal of military service, they would not only be subjected to this punishment, but that about 20 people could be hung or shot via court-martial trial for the sake of preserving the legitimate order and keeping others in fear.

However, if the Doukhobors believe in Christ and want to be Christians, this should not deter or scare them. It would be better for them to make such sacrifices whereas remaining in the same conditions and living as they lived before would be a worse lot for them and their descendants. Christ speaks about it in the following words: "Who sacrifices his life for me, will gain it, and who keeps his life will lose it."[6] Based on this, Pëtr Vasil'evich offered such advice.

Indeed, in the preceding period in their lives, Doukhobors in some cases had diverted from Christ and His teaching. Consequently, if there was a return to Godly life in Christ, there must be sacrifices, since the Doukhobors deserve it themselves and must be accountable for it. Is it plausible to think that someone else from the outside should be sacrificed or that if Christ came again, as he did nineteen centuries ago, he would take all our sins upon himself again? This would be irresponsible for people to expect. Every great act is only done once, and all humanity should feel grateful to Christ for his self-sacrifice, an exemplary act among humankind. If we believe in Christ and that he wished a good and peaceful brotherly life on earth for us, and that through this God's kingdom on earth will be restored as it is in heaven, then we should live according to his teachings. If we sometimes digress from this and then decide to return, which depends on our good will and our reasoning, then we should be ready to make sacrifices. It was good that the government did not conduct worse punishments, maybe this was because the Doukhobors did not digress from God too far and he was watching over them.

Pëtr Vasil'evich also knew that all the possessions accumulated by the Doukhobors had to be stolen. It was partly accumulated through untruths, and now was the return to the Spiritual Godly life, and according to Christ's words: "you cannot serve two masters: God and Mammon," that is, wealth. This sage advice by Pëtr Vasil'evich has a great meaning and foundation in God's eyes and the people who understood Christ. Christ says in a parable, "Neither do people pour new wine into old wineskins. If they do … the wine will run out and the wineskins will be ruined. No, they pour new wine into new wineskins, and both are preserved."[7] The same in our lives. Through material wealth, we lost our relationship with God, and when we returned to God, the wealth had to be sacrificed. Christ said about this: "But seek ye first the kingdom of God, and His righteousness; and all these things shall be added unto you."[8] And this is what we see: material wealth grows fast, we take it as if from God's treasury, applying our labour. We should not become haughty, and we should use it reasonably, where possible for God's cause.

From this short peripheral description, people can understand more about the life of Pëtr Vasil'evich and his importance among the Doukhobors. They can understand that he walks ahead of others, sacrificing himself fully for God's cause, and gives advice to all people who may desire it. If they do not desire it, then according to God's will, nothing is done by force. Almighty God, God of the whole universe, in whose grace we and all the worlds exist, bestows upon everyone complete freedom, just because He is also free in His creation, independent of anyone, and creates whatever He wills. Pëtr Vasil'evich who wishes to be the son of the almighty Creator, just as everyone else, how could he facilitate his advice through force?

If some people think this on occasion, then they are mistaken, and do not understand him. We also have much evidence from modern times that nothing is done by force. Let us take Doukhobors as an example. Nowadays they have split into three groups, and Pëtr Vasil'evich does not force anyone to listen to him, absolutely nobody is forced. Those who diverted from his brotherly advice, if they are sincere, will confirm this.

Notes

1. Imeretins are one of the groups of the indigenous peoples of Georgia.
2. "Aul" is a word used to refer to local villages in the Caucasus Mountains.
3. Gori, Tiganet (modern Tianeti) and Dusheti are three administrative areas in Georgia.
4. Akhalkalak (modern Akhalkalaki) is an administrative district in the country of Georgia. Now an independent state, in Imperial Russia, Georgia constituted Tiflis guberniia.
5. Tiflis is the old name of modern Tbilisi, the capital of the country of Georgia. In the nineteenth century, it was the capital of Tiflis guberniia, which was a part of the Russian Empire.
6. Based on Matthew 16:25.
7. Based on Matthew 9:17.
8. Based on Matthew 6:33.

CHAPTER 17

My Arrest and Life in Prisons

I remained free until September 22, and then an order was issued by the same Astaf'ev and the Assistant Prosecutor for me to appear in front of them in Kars[1] on September 22nd. Upon my arrival there, they arrested me and I was put into prison where Vereshchagin and brother Vasiliĭ were incarcerated. Nikolaĭ Khudiakov, Fëdor Ryl'kov and Larion Taranov were arrested together with me. We were all placed in the same cell where there were 20 prisoners from various groups already: Muslims, Armenians and Kurds. Since we were not yet accustomed to it, our cell seemed to us unpleasant and dismal, cramped, dirty and even lacking in God's air. This prison was located in a fortress. When it was under the jurisdiction of Mukhtar-pasha, the Turkish governor-general of Kars, it housed a gunpowder warehouse, where gunpowder was stored. When this fortress was taken by the Russians, a different warehouse was constructed for gunpowder and the old storage space was converted into a prison. There were earth works around it, much higher than the prison itself, so you could not see anything from it. There was also very little light in the cell, and it was semi-dark there. The yard was tiny and we were let out to walk there for half an hour every day. One could not see anything from the yard, except for the sky. We were almost in a dungeon. Brother Vasiliĭ and Vereshchagin were held in solitary confinement and we had no access to them. We were allowed to wear our own clothes in prison.

Our sole pleasure and entertainment was on each Saturday, when along with other prisoners, naturally with prison guards, we were allowed to go to wash ourselves in the bathhouse. The bathhouse was over one mile away, maybe even farther than that, so it was two miles both ways—a great exercise. Besides, on the way we could have a look at God's world, at peoples' lives, at the fields, and breathe in the fresh air. In addition, as we walked, we looked out for our brothers. If we saw any, we could talk with them, and ask whether all the relatives were in good health and doing well. Although the guards strictly forbade this, they could only forbid it to the prisoners and could not do anything to free people. So if we met a clever person on the way back, he would tell us the whole story while walking on the side about 15 feet apart from us, almost as far as the prison walls. The guards did not see any danger in this, paid no attention to the conversation and did not do anything about it. During this time, the prisoners devoid of freedom could feel as if they had just made a trip to the free world.

At first, we were bored, but with time, we started becoming accustomed to prison life and its routines. Our food was cooked separately. As we did not eat meat, we were allowed to cook our own meals, but only from the groceries we paid for ourselves. And this is how we lived there until November 16th. On November 16, all six of us mentioned here were sent to Tiflis[2] via Dilizhan.[3] We were transported with very strict guards. The guards were soldiers, as it is normally done. However, to transport us, they also appointed additional three cavalry officers with a captain. We passed by our native villages. Our relatives—fathers, mothers, wives, children and all those close to us—could already feel in their hearts that we were going away from our homeland and from our relatives, if not forever, but for a long time. They came out to meet us and saw us off with tears in their eyes. The soldiers shouted at them: "Do not come close!" They also threatened them with guns, "We will shoot!" In the village of Spasskoe, the centre of our villages, about 2000 people, or maybe even more, assembled from all the six villages. They all came out to see us and say good-byes, maybe forever, since nobody knew where and for how long we were being sent away. Bodily death is a normal thing and can happen to anyone, so all of us, as well as the people who came to see us off, said good-byes as if these were our last farewells. Many people cried. At the request of our relatives, the guard officer gave a command for the guards to stop the prisoner convoy. We were ordered to separate from other prisoners and were allowed to say good-byes to our relatives as well as to all brothers and sisters. Everybody admired this noble action of the officer. Following the schedule, the prisoner convoy moved ahead from Spasskoe. We arrived at the station Argeno, where we stayed overnight. In the morning, all the relatives as well as many brothers and sisters arrived to see us off. This was the last good-bye to them. We could only tell them: "Farewell, remain in God's mercy and live in hope of His holy will, do not forget about us." These words moved all our relatives and all of them in tears told us, "God bless you, do not forget about us either." Then the prisoner convoy moved ahead.

Our way on foot as far as Astafa[4] went well, God be praised. On the way, when we passed through the Molokan[5] village Nikitino, Molokans treated us to a lunch in the house of one of their leaders Vasiliĭ Vasil'evich Morozov. He headed a small group of elderly men and asked for permission of the prisoner convoy officer to invite us to his place. The convoy officer gave his permission. We entered Morozov's house together with the group of elders. They received us as brothers in Christ's faith, they replenished our bodily strength, wished us patience and a smooth journey. After this we exchanged our good-byes.

We stayed overnight in Dilizhan, where most Molokans lived. The prisoners' convoy station was about one mile away from the village, and in the evening, upon the invitation of the Molokans, we attended their sobranie assembly. Despite the fact that we were considered state criminals, the convoy officer by the last name of Grishin, allowed us to go, and he even went there with us without bringing any soldiers. There were three of us: Khudiakov, Taranov and I. When we entered the assembly, there were lots of people, our brothers and sisters. In this very sobranie, three young Molokan men, who were selected to do the military service, were saying their good-byes. While they were saying good-byes almost everyone was crying, particularly women. As we watched this, in the presence of the officer, we started talking with them.

Nikolaĭ Khudiakov was the one who spoke the most on the subject of military service. Based on the teachings of Christ, he proved to them in various ways that it is illegal and unfair to leave the company of parents or wives, if they had them, and voluntarily to go serve this unwholesome and murderous cause. When this unexpected question was raised, the whole sobranie assembly became quieter and then completely silent. Almost the whole assembly looked at us and at the officer sitting next to us, who was wearing his signs of distinction, that is, the military uniform. And they did not know what to do: whether they should agree with us or oppose us.

Their leader started opposing us. He said, "Why? Our fathers did this, and God himself allowed Samuel to be a king. This is what the Bible says." We said in response that the time of the Bible was gone, and that the Bible was now an obstacle for human reasoning. "And why did you not yet comprehend the teaching of Christ, declared 19 centuries ago? Christ, as the son of the living God, proclaimed the complete freedom and equality of all people. He cancelled all that Biblical history and He substituted it with the New Testament, the Gospel. The Old Testament said, 'An eye for an eye and a tooth for a tooth. But I tell you: Do not resist the evil, but if anyone slaps you on the right cheek, turn to them the other cheek also'.[6] He also cancelled oaths. You know well that He replaced anything that did not bring people unity and love with peace, harmony and love, so that people could reach God's kingdom within themselves. For this purpose Christ offers the second birth from above through the Holy Spirit. And whoever does not accept this rebirth, will not enter the kingdom of heaven. Consequently all those who believe in Christ by all means need the birth from above that connects the human with the eternal being of the Father of the primeval Spirit. And you are going to do the military service, where a man hardens and gets perverted in body and spirit. Don't you know that during a war, all these people serve as cannon fodder? This is how they get what is their due—whoever lives by the sword, dies by the sword."

This is how our conversation ended. We did not know if it brought any positive results or not, but the officer fully approved our interpretation and understanding and completely agreed with it.

From Astafa, we were put onto railway carriages and taken by railway to Tiflis. We arrived in Tiflis on December 5th. From the railway terminal we were forwarded to the guberniia transport prison, where we were given torn prisoners' clothes, in which we suffered from the cold. Our own clothes were taken away from us and put in the armoury.

On the third day since our arrival, after the evening roll call, we were summoned into the office of the superintendent. There we saw two men in very expensive clothes. One of them was a teacher from a religious seminary, and the other, as he expressed it, was a spiritual father, that is, a priest of the Orthodox people. After usual greetings, they started asking us who we were and why we were in prison. They likely already knew our story and came to talk sense into us. The seminary teacher started to talk first. He spoke about two stalks of grain growing in the same place. One stalk was growing straight, upright, the other was bent over and lower than the first. The first took pride in being above the lower stalk. Later it turned out that the one that was too proud of its height, was empty, and good for nothing except for being burned. The stalk that bent downwards turned out to be full of grain and worthy of saving. We asked him, "What does it mean: the empty stalk and the stalk that is bent down?" He explained, "The empty stalk means pride, know-it-all, haughtiness, greed, hatred, envy and so on. The stalk bent downwards means humility, humbleness, love, patience, kindness, temperance, etc." Then we asked, "Which stalk of grain do you belong to, and what compels you into torturing people who received humility, humbleness and love from the Lord, and not pride and conceit. You are boasting of your learnedness and knowledge, but don't you know that your knowledge comes from the ruler of this century, and the rulers of this century enslave the people? For Jesus said, 'Amongst you, be it different, but whoever wants to be first among you, shall be a servant to all'.[7] Isn't there greed and envy amongst you? If not, where do your accounts of a few hundred thousand come to banks from? Isn't this from greed and envy? Don't you know the words of the Savior, that He told His disciples, 'Freely you have received, freely give'?[8] But in essence, you did not receive this knowledge freely. While you accumulated it, you must have spent a lot of money, and now you are saying that you received your knowledge from God. But in essence, there is nothing Godly here, and your wisdom in front of God is nothing."

The seminary teacher participated in this conversation, but the priest sat in his chair. Gradually the conversation died out. We turned to the priest and asked him, "On what grounds do you call yourself a spiritual father? Don't you know Christ's teachings, written down in the Gospel, in which Christ strictly forbid people to be called fathers or teachers? This is written in Matthew, chapter 23." He became embarrassed by this question and gave an excuse that he did not refer to himself as Father, but this was what other people call him. "Why won't you explain to these people that this title contradicts the teaching of Christ and that you do not match this title?" This was the end of the discussion. Our conversation partners looked at their watches and said, "We have no more time to converse with you." Upon leaving, they promised to visit us again, but this promise remained unfulfilled. During all our stay in Tiflis that lasted for two years, we never saw them again.

We did not stay long in the guberniia prison. On the 13th of the same month we were moved to Tiflis Metekh castle,[9] with the governmental instructions that we should be kept in the castle in solitary confinement. Since there were no unoccupied single cells in the castle, all six of us were placed into common cells, but all of us were placed separately, and the guards strictly watched so that we would not see each other. As newcomers, we were dressed in the same clothes as in the transport prison.

It was customary in prisons everywhere that a newly arrived prisoner received a prison card, on which they wrote the name of the prisoner, who arrested him and what for. We also received these cards on our second day and it was written on the cards that we were arrested for secretly spreading religious-political propaganda. We did not accept these cards and said that we did not acknowledge any such guilt and we did nothing in secret: "We are arrested for following the law of God, and we spoke about it in front of anyone without any embarrassment. If you write it this way, then we will accept the cards." They could not write this and we did not accept their version. Therefore, we spent all the time there without the cards.

At first, life in prison, where a person was deprived of all the pleasures he had enjoyed while living free, seemed unbearable. Gradually, we looked around, got familiarized with how things were and became accustomed to it.

Once I was put into the cell of the prisoners in leg irons who were sentenced to hard labour for 10 to 20 years. There were about 30 people there, and all of them were in leg irons. They were from different ethnicities: Georgians, Imeretins, Armenians and Muslims. There was also one poor Jew by the name of Freedman, a jeweller who was convicted for the murder of another Jew, a seller of diamonds, and for this he was sentenced to 20 years of hard labour.

The cell was small with bunk beds on both sides and an aisle in the middle. When we went to sleep, the aisle was also taken over by people, who lay down not only on bunk beds but on the floor as well. It was very crammed in the cell, sometimes there was not even enough air for breathing. Every prisoner was given a mattress, a pillow and a blanket. The mattress and the pillow were originally stuffed with straw, but now there was only dust in them—the straw had completely worn out.

In the morning, as soon as the sun rose, the guard on duty opened the door, ordered us to take the night pot bucket out and to place all the bedding onto the porch. There they carefully folded the bedding, and the prisoners went to the water taps to wash themselves. Then everyone was herded back into the cell. They gave out hot water and locked the cell. Whoever had enough means could drink tea. Everybody had relatives who took care of them and at least sent enough money for tea. Then at 11 am, bread and lunch were given out. After lunch the prisoners went to the yard for a walk. Prisoners from each cell went separately, in turn, for half an hour or a quarter of an hour, whatever the time permitted. The rest of the time we spent locked up. In the evening, they also gave out hot water. After the bedding was brought in, there was a prisoner roll call, and then we went to bed. Whether we wanted to or not, we had to go to bed. The lamp was not turned off the whole night, and the guard walked along the corridor watching through the window in the door.

Of course, this whole routine was dismal and sad, so there were many cases when a prisoner went mad, or contracted a disease, such as tuberculosis, which would end his life. On the other hand, many prisoners became hardened. They were no longer afraid of anything, and could commit any actions, even worse than the ones that they had been imprisoned for. We spent our time well knowing that we had done nothing wrong. So while undergoing bodily restrictions, we were not tortured by our conscience. God's spirit always triumphed within us, so the flesh could not complain of restrictions. Sometimes we were visited by relatives. In particular, Pavel Vasil'evich Planidin always came to see us when visits were allowed. If there was anything new, he told us about it. In secret, he also corresponded with a guard who was the prison supervisor.

Once we were visited by Georgiĭ Aleksandrovich Dadiani, a former assistant to the Commander-in-Chief Sheremet'ev. After having accepted the life and teaching of Christ, Georgiĭ Aleksandrovich returned all his awards and titles, retired from service and started living as a Christian. Such people serve as a great example and provide a great support to the spiritual life. Georgiĭ Aleksandrovich Dadiani was a very pleasant person and dressed simply. He was not allowed to visit us. But once he saw brother Vasiliĭ in a third floor window. Dadiani was personally acquainted with brother Vasiliĭ, so he raised his voice and said, "Vasiliĭ Vasil'evich! Christ is with you, Christ is with you!" Brother Vasiliĭ thanked him for the visit and Dadiani left.

Soon after our incarceration, our castle prison was visited by Skvortsov. He came from St. Petersburg as an official in order to find out the details about the Doukhobor case. He went to the Doukhobor villages in all the three guberniias and then visited us. Known for being a reasonable person, he was sent from St. Petersburg in order to find out about Doukhobor beliefs in detail, investigate their religion and the basis behind their actions. However, he was not interested in any of it and did not make an effort to find out anything. When he appeared in the Doukhobor villages, he put on the airs of grandeur while talking with the Doukhobors. If he noticed that people were even slightly afraid of him, he started intimidating them and frightening them with an exile to far away Siberia. In the village of

Spasskoe, Kars region, Ivan Vasil'evich Podavinnikov talked with him seriously about the attitude to the tsar and all the administrative powers, but Skvortsov could not give him any satisfactory answers. When Skvortsov was leaving, he took note of Podavinnikov's name, and guess what happened? In a short while, Podavinnikov was exiled to the Zangezur[10] district of Elizavetpol'[11] guberniia, the worst place in Transcaucasia because of its climate.

When Skvortsov called us into the office, he asked in a loud voice, "You do not want to obey the tsar and his powers?" We said, "We will obey, but as long as his orders do not contradict the law of God. The law of God demands a clear pure conscience from every person. What you do not wish for yourself, you should not do to another person."

Then he turned to brother Vasiliĭ advising him, "The way I see it, you are a responsible person and could be useful for the government. Take on the post of a governmental representative and live in peace." The brother answered, "As far as you can understand it, your advice seems to you to be a good one, but it is entirely useless to me. Firstly, I want to be useful to the one who sent me into this life to do his bidding. Secondly, how can one live in peace? And what is the understanding of peace? Is this a clean conscience? Or is this pleasing Mammon, so that to satisfy the desires of my flesh I would destroy thousands of innocent people, whose cries and tears rise up to God, as is done now to the Doukhobors of Kars and Elizavetpol' guberniias? In every village, they have those blood sucking barbarians assigned to them. Doukhobors have to pay them salaries, and if there is not enough money, they assault the Doukhobors right in daylight, they take away milk cows and take away the last grains of their daily bread and sell it all for almost nothing at auctions. These individuals are put in charge of the properties of poor helpless people, who accumulated their belongings not only in sweat of labour, but also in blood. Not so long ago, in the village of Slavianka, Elizavetpol' guberniia six women and about thirty men were put into prison for pleading to protect their belongings, and this was described as mutiny. So do you consider such barbarian action to be 'peaceful life'? Is this the peace and destiny of a person created in God's image?"

After these words, our interlocutor stopped talking with us, gave orders to bring him back his coat that he had taken off while entering the office. As he was leaving, we asked him to explain our case and the reason why we were tortured to the tsar. He promised to do so and left.

While we were in the castle, for some time we did not get any hot meals, as we did not eat meat. We only received 2.5 pounds of bread. We asked to get some butter to go with the bread instead of meat and to cook for ourselves separately, but our request was denied. The prison director was asked about this as well, but he just pointed to the common pot. We remained without hot meals for three months, and then it took a toll, our bodies started weakening. During one visit, we had to talk about this with Pavel Vasil'evich Planidin, who lived mostly in Tiflis. He visited us and also visited the brothers held in the guberniia transport prison, where about 300 of them were held. All of them were from Kars guberniia and arrested for returning their military conscription cards. So Pavel Vasil'evich started filing petitions to allow us to cook hot meals for ourselves. He applied with his petition to the gendarme colonel, who did grant permission for us to cook from our own groceries. We did not receive any governmental food except for bread. After this permission, our brothers appointed me the cook and I cooked for the rest of the time there.

On one occasion our whole cell, that is all the hard penalty prisoners, decided to dig a trench out of the prison so that all 30 people could escape. In secret, they procured various tools: a big knife, a crowbar that was about three and a half feet long, and started working, that is breaking through the wall. I spent almost whole days, from morning till night, in the kitchen. When I came back in the evening, they notified me about it and asked whether I would interfere with this plan, or not. Their plan was already well developed and I knew that I could not interfere with it at all, or else they could immediately throw a blanket on top of my head and kill me. On the other hand, I had no reservations against their escape from prison and from 10 or 20 years of hard labour. This puts people in such horrible conditions that they are ready for anything. I agreed with their plan and said, "If you all agree with it, then I am willing as well, and I will never betray you."

Their plan went as follows. When they broke through the brick wall of the cell, they would get into the corridor leading to the kitchen. In the kitchen, there was a guard at all times, looking after things to prevent a fire or such other accidents. This guard did not pose any great danger as he was almost always asleep. According to their plan, they were supposed to attack him in his sleep and strangle him. Then one of the prisoners was expected to put on his uniform, take the keys, open the door and walk out into the hospital yard. The nights were dark. At the gate, there was also a guard standing, but he would not suspect anything thinking that it was his comrade walking towards him. After approaching that guard, the prisoner was supposed to attack him. Other prisoners would then come to assist in the killing of the guard. Then, from the gates, all the prisoners would walk out to freedom.

It was impossible to break the wall in the night because it was quiet in the cell and the guard often inspected the cell via the window opening in the door. They had to break the wall about two hours prior to the evening call. During this time, the guards fussed around, they pushed the prisoners into cells, locked up the cells and watched out for prisoners who might linger behind somewhere. At this time, the prisoners in shackles started walking around the cell, and the sound of their shackles dampened the sound of the wall being broken. Two people at a time took turns breaking the wall. All the faces bore a peculiar expression, it was hard to tell whether it was joyous or sad. Perhaps, they were all dreaming that they would soon take off these shackles that weighed six pounds. They were so tired of them, it was impossible to describe. At the same time they thought, "What if this does not work out? Then we will lose everything, and the attitude of the chief and all the prisoner guards to us will get much worse." This is exactly what happened. The senior intendant Pil'sekevich, while walking from the kitchen along the corridor, heard some knocking sounds against the wall. He stopped, listened more and realized they were attempting to break the wall. He immediately notified the superintendent, and without waiting for the ordinary time of the evening prisoner roll call, they conducted a call one hour earlier. When the call started, the senior intendant walked into the middle of the yard and shouted for everyone to hear: "Evening call!" This was the signal to prepare and all the cells heard this and started getting ready and lined up.

This untimely call struck our cell as if by lightening. Everybody felt uneasy and scared. Those who were breaking the wall crawled from under the bunkbeds and also lined up. Everybody just looked at each other, but nobody said anything. Everybody felt, however, that their plan was discovered, and nobody knew what they could do next. At last the guard thrust the key into our cell's keyhole, turned it right, removed the key and the door opened. The superintendent, senior intendant and two guards on duty entered the cell in quick pace. Everybody had a troubled expression on their faces, and this was one of the signs that something was wrong. We were quickly counted, and then they moved to other cells. In a strict voice, the guard on duty ordered all to go to bed. When they checked all the cells, they quietly walked back to our cell again, and the door opened instantaneously as if it had not been locked. Again the superintendent, senior intendant, and guards ran into the cell pushing people on the sides. At the door, they had convoy soldiers with rifles. They rushed to the crime scene hoping to catch the criminals in action, right under the bunk beds but there was not anyone there anymore. There was only the crowbar, knife and a few dozen bricks they had broken out.

The intendant roared "Get up!" "All out into the corridor!" There we were completely surrounded by the soldiers who pointed their bayonets at our chests. A cruel retribution started. We were taken back into the cell one after another and interrogated, "Who was the first to come up with the plan? Where did they get the crowbar and knife from?" But under such circumstances the prisoners did not tell on each other. For this, they were mercilessly beaten and sent into the cold dungeon only in underwear. It was winter and it was extremely cold. Four prisoners were subjected to this punishment. Convoy officer Belianskiĭ heard about such tortures and went into the cell and told the intendant that they had no right to do this to prisoners: "The prisoners and the hard labour prisoners are right in what they are doing. It is their job to attempt to run away, and it is our job to guard them and prevent them from escaping. Since they failed to escape, it means we won, so why should the prisoners be beaten? They have already had the misfortune of losing." He ordered the release of everybody from the cold dungeon and to give them their clothes back. In punishment, we were all displaced into other cells, as a squadron that had lost its banner. This is how the escape of the hard labour prisoners ended.

I was placed together with brother Vasiliĭ on the top floor. There were fewer people there, and there was more room in the cell. Despite all these conveniences, I had a hard time readjusting and was missing my company, with whom I lived for a year.

If the reader remembers the circumstances of my arrest, there were six of us here in the Metekh castle, whereas the other 300 people from Kars district were held in the guberniia transport prison, also in Tiflis.

Tiflis transport prison did not have its own hospital, so the sick prisoners were moved from there into Metekh castle for treatment. Three of our brothers died here. The first one was Grigoriĭ A. Dorofeev at the age of 50. He was not liable for military duty and was arrested as an instigator. Two other brothers were liable for military service. The first of them who died was Danila Barabanov and the second was Vasiliĭ Ivanovich Darofeev. All the three of them are buried in Tiflis in the Molokan common cemetery.

Elizavetpol' brothers were first incarcerated in Elizavetpol' prison, and then 24 of them were moved to Nukhin prison. These were the elderly who were accused of being the instigators. The rest—about 200 people—who were arrested for the return of their military conscription cards were sent to the Cossack prison in Astafa. That area had a very hot climate that caused fevers. Almost everybody suffered from fevers there. Some of them were not destined to get out of the prison into God's world and they died there in the flesh, as the martyrs for God's cause. The memory of their exemplary lives will pass over from generation to generation.

After having kept the prisoners from Kars and Elizavetpol' districts in prisons for over two years, the government exiled them dispersing them among the local population. Two people were sent to each aul.[12] Kars Doukhobors were sent to Elizavetpol' guberniia and some of them—to Baku guberniia.[13] Elizavetpol' Doukhobors were exiled to Erivan[14] guberniia, where they passed their days in poverty and suffering. They lived through many misfortunes. Some of them did not even have daily food. They were put into such conditions by the government. The police officers warned village military leaders that Doukhobors should not be let out of auls anywhere, even to seek employment for survival, and this is what was executed. This is why the exiled Doukhobors had to suffer so much there. I will mention a few who died there: Ivan Vasil'evich Konkin, aged 50, Grigoriĭ Astafurov, aged 50, and Pëtr M. Morozov, aged 30. The first two of them did not have military conscription cards and got there as instigators. They lived in the same aul. These were healthy people, not deprived of anything by nature. The time and the surrounding life nurtured heroes in the flesh, and these people were not hesitant or scared of anything, in particular Ivan Vasil'evich. He often, when the circumstances demanded it, went against 10 Muslims with one big wooden staff, and everyone ran away from him, in fear that they could be hit. Until a certain time, he was the hero of the flesh. But when God visited his soul, it caused compassion in him not only towards people but towards all surrounding nature. And he fully gave himself to this God's call, and this is what he was imprisoned and exiled to this aul for. Both of them got sick at the same time and there was no one to look after them. If brothers from the neighbouring auls attempted to come and visit them, they were sent back and often beaten. They were sick for a long time and could not even get out of bed. Besides the illness, they were terribly tortured by bugs, the so-called lice that are very prevalent among Tartars. One of the Doukhobor brothers died. The brothers from the neighbouring auls were allowed to bury him. My nephew Ivan A. Aniutushkin with other brothers came to bury him. They told us what was going on there. They no longer felt sorry for the diseased, his sufferings were over and his body lay senseless. It was painful to look at him. He was covered with all sorts of dirt. Ivan Vasil'evich was still alive but unconscious. They started with him. The Tartars brought a kettle, warmed up some water, took off all the clothing and bedding, washed him in warm water, changed his underwear and brought new bedding. He was placed into bed and then he started regaining consciousness. After this, they also washed the dead body, clad it in fresh clothes, dug a grave and buried the body.

When Ivan Vasil'evich regained consciousness, he spoke a lot about their situation. He said, "We were fine until we both fell ill. We helped each other, giving water, quenching thirst. Sometimes one of us would go to the Tartars and ask them for some bread, and would bring it to his comrade. We took turns serving each other. But it has been about two weeks that we both became bed-ridden, and during this time almost nobody visited us. A few times some Tatars came, but seeing our illness they felt disgusted and went away. We were often thirsty, but there wasn't anyone to give us a glass of water to quench our thirst. During this torture we often thought of our relatives. But these thoughts did not make our condition any easier, and did not make us feel any happier, but upset our hearts and ailing bodies even more. We said to each other, 'It is better not to remember our loved ones and relatives, because they are so far away and cannot help us. We should be alert in spirit and call upon our Lord and with peaceful soul await our destiny'. Oh, my dear brothers, no matter how much I aspire to be firm, the spirit may be alert, but my flesh is weak. Now you have strengthened my soul and my body, and I am joyous and ready to face death. There were only a few happy minutes for us when we became unconscious, when we felt neither pain, nor thirst, no dampness around us. These were happy times. But then we would come to, and again there would be the dark unpleasant dismal hut, dampness and a bad smell around us. At last my friend began dying. He groaned at first. I asked him, 'Why are you groaning, my friend, it must be time for us to get better'. He said, 'I am dying, maybe you will survive and see my relatives, then pass over a poklon[15] greeting to them from me, and tell them not to feel sorry for me. If we had to suffer for the cause of God, this is temporary, and no matter how severe our sufferings are, they are all over, and now I do not feel them at all. I feel sorry for my relatives, but this is also in vain, they are also transient, only God is eternal, and we have to strive towards Him'. After some time he died, and the Tartars went to notify you."

The Doukhobors stayed there for another night, and asked to stay for a while to look after the sick friend. However, the senior village official insisted on sending them away. As they told us later, "We said our final good-byes to Ivan Vasil'evich, as it was obvious he was not going to survive. Upon parting with us, the poor dear cried, and we also cried and tried to comfort him by saying that he was out of danger. He seemed to believe it, but he still asked, 'Please pass over a poklon greeting to my relatives, kiss them for me, and if I die, do not tell them about our difficulties and our poor conditions here, because it would not help, but would make them grieve even more.' This is how we said good-bye to him and left. On the fourth day we were notified: 'your friend is dead.' We went there again, buried the body and left."

It was a cruel deed of the government officials who themselves believed in the teachings of Christ. In the time we lived in, there weren't any more such cruel executions as in the old days. However, according to the stories of these brothers who buried the bodies, while washing the bodies they saw the wounds on them both from lying in bed and from insects. Such a torture is worse and more brutal than any execution, and those people lived through days of this cruel torture. Upon hearing about it, what should the relatives do? Indeed, the people had their belief and the belief saved them. It was the living belief in Christ, the belief in the immortality of soul, in the words of Christ: "Do not be afraid of the ones who kill your body, for they cannot touch your soul." All this taken together saved the relatives, and the relatives even after such a cruel death remained peaceful and bore everything without complaints.

This is how our sufferers and martyrs for God's cause passed away. Let them be remembered by God in the Kingdom of Heaven.

In addition to the list of martyrs for God's cause, I should also mention the ones who died in prisons. Three people died in Elizavetpol' prison. The first man to die was Fëdor Fëdorovich Verigin. The second was Andreĭ Alekseevich Repin. Both of them were subject to military service. The third person who died was Vasiliĭ Eletskiĭ, aged 50. He was arrested as an instigator. They were buried there in the prison cemetery.

Three people died in the Astafa Kazarsk prison. The first one was Mikhail Iakovlevich Polovnikov. The second was Ivan Kalmykov, and the third was Anton Fëdorovich Verigin (Arekhov). They were buried there in the prison cemetery.

Fëdor Ivanovich Golubev, aged 50, died in the Nukhin prison.[16] He was arrested as an instigator. He was buried there in prison.

Remember them, Oh Lord, in your Heavenly Kingdom.

Notes

1. Kars is a town in Turkey. With its surrounding area, at the time of the narrative, it belonged to the Russian Empire. It was one of the areas of the Transcaucasian exile of the Doukhobors. Since 1921, it has been a part of Turkey.
2. Tiflis is the old name of modern Tbilisi, the capital of the country of Georgia. In the nineteenth century, it was the capital of Tiflis guberniia, which was a part of the Russian Empire.
3. Dilizhan (modern spelling is Delijan) is a town in Armenia. At the time of the narrative, it was a part of the Russian Empire.
4. Astafa most likely refers to Astaf, Azerbaijan, a town close to Slavianka village. However, it might also be Aghstafa, another town in Azerbaijan close to the borders with Armenia and Georgia. At the time of the narrative, Azerbaijan was a part of the Russian Empire.
5. Molokans are a sectarian religious group that split off from the Russian Orthodox Church. At present, Doukhobors of Canada and Molokans of the United States retain amicable relationships and send representatives to each other's major events.
6. Matthew 5:39.
7. Mark 10:44.
8. Matthew 10:8.
9. Metekh (Metekhi) castle was a strongly fortified nineteenth-century prison in the Metekhi area of Tiflis (modern Tbilisi), the capital of Georgia (in the nineteenth century it was a part of the Russian Empire).
10. Most likely Zangezursky Uezd, a region of Elizavetpol' guberniia (governatory) of the Russian Empire, which in Soviet Union time became divided between Armenia and Azerbaijan.
11. Elizavetpol' (later Kirovabad, since 1989, Ganja) was the capital of Elizavetpol' guberniia in the Russian Empire. Since the separation of Azerbaijan from the Soviet Union, it is one of the largest cities in Azerbaijan.
12. "Aul" is a word used to refer to local villages in the Caucasus Mountains.
13. Baku guberniia (governatory) with Baku as its capital was one of the administrative units of the Russian Empire. Baku is now the capital and the largest city of Azerbaijan.
14. Erivan guberniia of the Russian Empire had its centre in Erivan, modern day Yerevan, the capital of the Republic of Armenia.
15. Poklon means "a bow" in Russian. To bow in the Doukhobor tradition means to pass over greetings and best wishes. Bowing was a traditional Russian way of greeting. Doukhobors bow to each other during prayer assemblies in recognition of God in another human being.
16. Nukhin prison was located in the Nukha fortress of the town of Shaki, Azerbaijan. At the time of the narrative, the area was a part of the Russian Empire.

CHAPTER 18

Torments in the Ekaterinograd Disciplinary Battalion

I am giving a complete narrative of Ivan Vasil'evich Malakhov below, who was subjected to these tortures.

In 1894, I was drafted into military service. I took the conscription draft in the town of Akhalkalak,[1] where I drew ticket number 6,[2] which required me to attend active military duty. After this, I was called to the reception for a medical examination. I was in perfect health and was conscripted. I was placed into the local Akhalkalak service. The service started in the beginning of October. It was hard at first, as always happened with new soldiers. The commanders gave strict orders and required respect of rank. At three or four in the morning, we had to get up and start cleaning, polish the shoes and clean the uniform, line up for inspection, and they watched very strictly if everything has been properly cleaned. A corporal walked along the line and we could often hear slaps on the face and yelling, "Why isn't it clean?" After the end of the morning inspection, we had to start gymnastics: bending the head, spreading out arms, turning the body, and there were all sorts of bends and twists that were very difficult for new soldiers. All these gymnastic exercises were performed until dawn. At daytime, until lunch, we performed gun exercises and marching. After lunch, there was a literacy class until dinner. After dinner and until the evening line-up, we were put into the literacy class again. At 9 pm, we had the line-up. After the line-up, they asked us officers' names and ranks beginning with the lowest rank up to the general. This lasted until 12 midnight. Next day, we had to get up again at three in the morning and repeat the same, and the same went for all the five months

© The Author(s) 2019
G. V. Verigin, *The Chronicles of Spirit Wrestlers' Immigration to Canada*, https://doi.org/10.1007/978-3-030-18525-1_18

for new soldiers. The whole service was spent in this action that is boring, entirely useless and destructive for the entire humanity.

After the end of the five-month training, they started forcing new soldiers to take the oath. However, since there were only very few Doukhobors in the local forces, the squadron commander did not force us to take the oath. This is how we served until Easter. Shortly after Easter, the squadron commander Nazarov called us all into his office and told us, "Have you heard that your Doukhobors who served in the Elizavetpol'[3] Aslandur reserve battalion refused to perform the military service and discarded their weapons on the first day of Easter?" We answered, "We have not heard about this." Then he started explaining to us that "they were subjected to court-martial for this, and in a court-martial trial, people are tried and sentenced to hanging or shooting within 24 hours, and they have now been sentenced. Eleven people were sentenced to death. They will be taken to Alexander square to be shot there. So this is why I brought you together to warn you. If any one of you may decide to refuse military service, you should know that you would then be liable for a court-martial. I feel sorry for you, as you are young people who should live and enjoy your lives. And your parents, who have already lived their time, started stirring something up and teaching you."

We answered as follows, "Why do you feel sorry for us, if you teach us every day how to kill people more skilfully, and you call people we have not even seen yet, our enemies? The same goes with the other side, those you call enemies, are also taught to kill enemies. During a war, both sides are brought together and they try to kill as many as possible from the opposite side. Is this a way to feel sorry for us? If you taught us how to love our enemies, as Christ teaches, this would mean that you felt sorry for us." He said, "Maybe you won't face a war and serve during peace time." But our minds were set differently from allowing military service. First, it was because when our parents saw us off, they advised us, "Although you are setting off for service, one should not kill people, as a murder is a great sin, and Christ says that the murderers do not inherit life everlasting." Second, we also now understood this whole discipline ourselves, that it did not agree with the laws of God expressed in the teaching of Christ.

And we started looking for an occasion to put down our weapons, the same as our brothers did. On June 28th, there was an inspection. The Brigade General Kishimov arrived and started conducting the inspection. He inspected the squadron and then started oral examination. He came up to the first soldier and asked, "Are you from the Doukhobors?" "Yes, sir!" This was my friend Dmitrĭ Astafurov. The general asked, "When the soldier stands on guard at the door of a prisoners' cell, what should he do?" Astafurov answered, "The soldier on guard has to cautiously and precisely monitor all the movements and to give warnings to prevent disorders." The general asked, "And what if they do not listen, what should the guard do?" Astafurov answered, "The guard has to pass the message over to the senior guard officer by voice, whistle or via passing people." The general: "And what if the senior guard officer does not hear?" Astafurov: "The guard gives one shot directed up." The general: "And if the prisoner attempts to escape, what should the guard do?" Astafurov remained silent. The general repeated a few more times. Astafurov had to say, "The soldier has to fire."—"And will you fire?"—"No, sir!" The general turned to the squadron commander: "Are there any more Doukhobors?" The squadron officer pointed at me. The general asked, "And will you shoot?"—"No, sir!" He repeated his question three times and each time he received the answer "No, sir!" Then the general said to the squadron commander, "Pay special attention to them," and he left without asking anything from our other comrades Chutskov, Ryl'kov and Vasilii Sherstobitov.

After this, all the soldiers, the sub-officers and the sergeant surrounded us and started asking with surprise, "Do you really refuse to serve the monarch?" We responded to this, "You heard it all yourselves." They said, "How did you dare to speak personally to the general?" And we said, "And what is a general?"—"A general can have you shot to death." We said, "It is peace time now, he has no right for shootings." "What do you mean, has no right? You have just breached a very important matter, nobody in the world has done it before, you are the only ones ever found who refuse to serve our monarch."—"How can we serve him, if he teaches to kill people, and the sixth commandment says 'Thou shall not kill?' Besides, Christ also says that whoever raises a sword will die by the sword." This was the end of the conversation. Everybody dispersed.

At 12 midnight there was an order received that the prison guard had to be strengthened. And all five of us were appointed. We finally refused to comply. After this, we were immediately arrested and not allowed to move anywhere until the morning. At 10 in the morning, we were taken to the dining hall where we were surrounded by a convoy. After a while, the lieutenant appeared in a state of great exultation and scolded us abundantly. The convoy was ordered, "If they only stir, you have the right to stab them to death with bayonets. They do not want to serve our monarch, so we will deal with them." He immediately ordered two convoy guards to bring us to his tent one after another for questioning. I was called in there first, and he asked me, "Why don't you want to serve the emperor?" I answered, "I would like to do the emperor's bidding, but he teaches to kill people, and my soul does not wish this."—"And why doesn't your soul wish it?" I answered, "Because the Saviour bequeath so, that is He prohibited to kill people, and I believe in the Saviour and perform the will of God."—"And who are you?"—"I am a Christian."—"Why are you a Christian?"—"In learning the word of Christ. The spirit alive in a Christian cannot and will not participate in your actions." All the others were also interrogated in a similar way. Then under a strict convoy, we were taken into prison where we spent three months. During this time, an investigator came to see us in prison, took detailed notes of questioning and left.

At the end of September, we were sent from Akhalkalak to Tiflis,[4] where we were put into the military prison and subjected to court-martial. We spent four months there and had to undergo two trials. We did not accept the first trial because the witnesses gave false testimony, and they did not appear at the trial, so the trial was dismissed. The witnesses were called in for the second time and the trial occurred. We were sentenced to be sent to Ekaterinograd[5] disciplinary battalion for reforming for two and a half years.

On February 8, 1895, we were all sent from Tiflis to Novorossiĭsk[6] disciplinary battalion via Batum.[7] When we arrived there, we were placed in different squadrons. Ryl'kov and I were appointed to the fourth squadron, Chutskov and Sherstobitov to the third and Astaf'ev to the second. By the order of the colonel, the sergeant led us into the office, where they carefully searched all our belongings, and warned us in a very strict manner that if anyone had any money, we had to turn it in. It was not allowed to have a single kopeck in the fortress. If anyone were found in the possession of five kopecks, he would receive 30 lashes. After this, we were taken to the fortress and placed in the squadrons.

On the same day, after the line-up, we met our brothers who had arrived here earlier from Elizavetpol'[8] for refusing military service. There were 14 of them. According to custom, we greeted them and started asking them about their lives there. They said, "So far, we are alive, thank God, and in the future, let God's mercy be with us."—"And why do you seem to be so exhausted?" They said, "Here we suffer from a great shortage of food. We do not eat meat, and we get no special additions instead. They give us very little bread, and we only eat bread and salt and drink the Holy water. Besides, we are subjected to very severe punishments here, even including corporal ones."

Upon hearing such stories from our brothers, we were afraid. But the faith and God's Spirit living in us did not allow us to waver. Without displaying any fear, we decided to act together, as far as it was in our power. On the second day, that is, on March 7th, at 9 am the sergeant on duty walked through the battalion, opened the building and conducted a line-up. After this, the sub-officers arrived, each to his own squadron, and conducted the inspection and the gymnastics. I was standing last on the left in the second squadron. The squadron sub-officer came up to me and started inspecting. I stopped him and told him, "I have an announcement to make to you:

because of my faith, I cannot follow your orders."—"Don't you want to serve?"—"No, I don't." He left me alone and started performing his duties towards others. In half an hour the sergeant came, he walked up to me and asked, "Why are you not training?"—"Because I do not want to."—"Why don't you want to train?"—"Because what you are teaching us in these exercises leads to murder, and I cannot do this because of my faith."—"Where did you find such faith?" I said, "In the law of God. You also teach us the ten commandments, and it says there in the sixth commandment, 'Thou shall not kill'. So I wish to live and act following the law of God, and consider all the people equal, the children of one God the Father, and our brothers." The sergeant said, "I will report this to the squadron commander and he will punish you. First, you will be given thirty lashes and then you will be put in the cold dungeon. And they will carry on in this manner adding the number of lashes until you give up, take the rifle and start serving." I said to this, "With pleasure, feel free to report and do whatever you will since I am in your hands."

This is exactly what the sergeant did, he reported us to the squadron commander Pokrovskiĭ. Pokrovskiĭ called in Ryl'kov and me. First, he started interrogating us, "When did you start the service?" I replied, "In 1895."—"And when did you refuse to perform the military service?"—"On 29 June, 1895."—"Why are you refusing and why do you not wish to serve the tsar?"—"Because of our faith, we do not wish to follow the orders of the tsar."—"And what does he require from you?"—"First, when a soldier starts his service, he is required to swear an oath, in which he has to swear to serve the monarch and the native land faithfully and wholeheartedly and to obey all the orders of the commanders. We reject the oath based on what is said in the Gospel from Matthew, chapter 5, verse 34th. But when a soldier takes the oath, he has to execute precisely everything that the authorities, like you, are commanding him. In war, he has to kill people, without hesitation, and we consider this a great sin. It is not allowed to kill a human being under any circumstances."—"And how can you defend yourselves, if enemies attack you?"—"We have no enemies, as Christ said 'You have to pray for your enemies.'"—"But I have to tell you that here, in the disciplinary battalion, you will be very strictly punished for it, you won't be able to bear this, the punishment will be very cruel."—"We do not hold our flesh precious, let us be punished, but we will still ask God that he would send His grace into your hearts and make our situation easier thanks to you."

Next, he placed us into the cold dungeon for three days and nights. After the cold dungeon, there was another interrogation after which we were again locked up in the cold dungeon for three days and nights. Then the squadron commander started pleading with us to accept the rifles, "You won't have to kill anyone here, and you have to serve the term, and then do as you will." He referred to the case of our brothers in other squadrons who were punished with 30 lashes and accepted weapons. After this we were forced to accept the weapons under the following condition, "Although you are forcing us to accept the weapons, we are not going to use them." We lived like this for a while, with the rifles, waiting until all our brothers gathered, who were supposed to be sent here. Then we planned to act together, that is hand back the rifles.

During this time, however, our conscience was torturing us, and would not leave us in peace. We were more tormented at heart and in the soul by our weakness than we would have been by a punishment. Again, we gathered all our strength and declared that we would not serve.

On August 15th, almost the whole night through, I prayed to the Lord, in any way I could, pleading to Him to come to my assistance, so that He, all-merciful, would strengthen my flesh, even to receiving death in flesh. After this, I had no more qualms regarding matters of flesh and my future life and fate, and I again proceeded with God's cause.

When the squad arrived in the warehouse to get the ammunition and the rifles, I also went to the warehouse. In five minutes, the squad was ready and lined up in the yard. The squad leader by the name of Bartsov noticed that I did not line up. He immediately went to the warehouse, saw me without ammunition and asked, "What's up with you? Are you sick?"—"No, I am perfectly healthy, but I do not want to serve and will not take the rifle."—"What have you thought up again, Malakhov?"—"I thought up serving God." He asked me, "Do not do this, please, for God's sake!" And he explained, "In a week's time, I will retire from service, and I do not want to see with my own eyes how you will be punished. My heart does not accept it when my friends are punished in front of my eyes." His eyes were filled with tears. Bartsov was truly a person with a good soul. He understood our convictions, and, even if in his heart alone, he was always sympathetic with our situation. I thanked him for his good will but did not agree to his request. He walked out to the squad and reported to the sergeant.

The sergeant came up to me and asked strictly, "Why don't you take the rifle?" I answered, "I do not want to be taught how to kill people."—"I am commanding you, take the rifle, or I will knock all your teeth out."—"I am requesting you most humbly not to do this, but to report it to the squad commander." He started getting even more furious, jumped closer to me, took the sabre and wanted to hit me in the teeth. I was begging him, "Please do not do this, for God's sake, and do not hit me, I would then remember you for this all my life. But I will not serve no matter what, and you cannot make me." He was stomping his feet and yelling, "I am acting according to the discipline protocol and I will force you into the service." I said, "I know your discipline very well, and according to your discipline, you can set me free and report to the Squad commander, and you will be free of sin." He thought about it for a while and then started forcing me again. He called in the squad leader assistant and they started forcing me into taking the rifle—they tried forcing it into my hands, put it against my chest and undertook many other similar efforts. But I agreed to nothing and was not afraid of anything. So he sent me away from the warehouse. Then he brought in Ryl'kov who also refused to take the rifle, and we were both brought to the squad commander. The squad commander started imploring us, "What have you thought up? And why are you drawing shame upon me? In all the other squads, everyone else is serving, and you do not want to, and Colonel Maslov reprimands me for it."—"We do not know anything about it, we just act as our conscience is telling us."—"And I have to tell you: the two of you cannot achieve anything. Let me give you an example: if there is a whole train moving, and you stand in front of it and say that you will stop it, you have to know that the train will crush you. So you go against the whole state and it will crush you." But we said, "This is all until a certain time, when the time comes, this train won't be able to do anything."—"Yes, I know very well your set of mind and your goal, but it is not yet the time. When the time comes, I will not serve either." But we told him, "The time has come." After this Pokrovskiĭ ordered the sergeant, "Put them in the cold dungeon."

On the second day, at 10 in the morning, Pokrovskiĭ came to visit me. I did not expect his visit and was thinking about my fate and what was ahead. Suddenly the doors opened. He said, "Good day, Malakhov." I answered, "Thank God."—"Have you changed your mind perhaps?"—"Yes, I have changed my mind to serve God."—"And what about the monarch?"—"No, not the monarch, because he teaches to kill people and under no circumstances can I comply with this demand."—"And do you know that the monarch has legislation according to which, for insubordination, one can be subjected to cruel punishments, even to death?" Having said this, Pokrovskiĭ walked into the cell and sat on the bed. He invited me to sit down as well. I refused to sit as I had been sitting there for a long time and wanted to stand for a while. Then I told him, "I do not value my flesh highly enough so that I would ruin my soul for it, as the flesh is destined to die in any case, and the soul will return to its fatherland, that is to God." Pokrovskiĭ said, "I am asking you, please give it all up, finish your service, and later, when you are free, you can continue your cause. And I will forgive you for violating the soldiers' protocol and discipline and let you out of the dungeon, just start your service."—"No, I cannot do this. As I told you before, I am telling you again, that I will not do military service, because Christ has opened the door and is calling me towards Him, warning me not to turn away from His path, saying 'they persecuted me, they will persecute you as well for me.'"[9] Pokrovskiĭ thought about this seriously and told me, "Please, tell me,

Malakhov, who taught you all this?" I answered, "Our teacher is Christ."—"But I am begging you, please tell me the truth, who set you up for this?" And he got up from the bed and moved closer to me. I answered, "I am telling you in truth, our teacher is Christ and our mentor is the Holy Spirit." Pokrovskiĭ said, "I understand now that you are not doing this on your own, and I confess to you, I cannot punish you, my heart cannot bear it. So I will pass your case over to the battalion tribunal, and let them deal with you as they will." He walked out of the dungeon and upon saying good-byes, he said, "All the best to you, and let God send you what you desire." He closed the door and left.

The investigation was scheduled for the next day. At ten in the morning Ryl'kov and I were brought for questioning. We were interrogated by Captain Okinches of the first squad and Captain Bugaevskiĭ of the second squad. The questions and the answers were the same as before and we were again sent into the dungeon.

On the third day, that is, on August 17th, we were taken to the hospital to Dr. Preobrazhenskiĭ, who met us sternly and brought an electric apparatus that he immediately set to work. He sat in an armchair and explained to us, "Here, I brought this machine, and I want to find out how much of it you can bear. The apostles, when they were beaten, did not have any marks left on their bodies, but when you are lashed, your body swells up like a mountain." But I responded to him, "It only seems like this to you, because you are doing the punishing, but those people, although they were apostles, also felt pain. But with great faith, they bore it until they were tortured to death. And this is how it is still done today, even if this were done to us." These words disturbed him. He jumped off the armchair, came up close to me and asked, "Do you know God, where is He?" I responded to him, "Nobody has seen God anywhere, but when people love each other, God abides in love." The doctor then got very angry, his whole body was shaking, and having gathered a mouthful of saliva, he spat it right into my face. I thanked him for it, took out a handkerchief from my pocket and wiped my face. He started yelling even louder, stomped his feet and shouted "Get out of here!" We walked out. The guards brought us back into the dungeon and closed the doors. The machine of Preobrazhenskiĭ was left without any operation.

At 9 pm during the evening line-up, the order was sent throughout the battalion and read to all the soldier inmates, as follows: "Yesterday, at ten am, for refusal of military service, Ivan V. Malakhov and Nikolaĭ V. Ryl'kov were put on trial by the battalion tribunal. The tribunal sentenced them to corporal punishment by lashing, with 80 lashes to be given to each." We were notified of this horrible news in the evening. That evening, our brothers came up to our dungeon and in order to strengthen us, they promised, "Next day, we will do the same." And it was truly done, but not by all.

That night passed as if it were the last night of my existence. I was preparing myself for a certain death, as we knew that Doukhobors were punished in a much more severe manner. So I did not think I could remain alive and carry on with my life. I spent the whole night praying to God while standing on my knees, calling onto God for assistance and saying good-byes in my mind to my mother, father, brothers, sisters and all my relatives and friends. That night was long beyond my understanding; I went to sleep a few times so as to make the time pass quicker, but after barely a minute, I would get up again and again ask God not to abandon me. The flesh was trembling, but the spirit was energetic and did not waver.

At last, the morning came. Then the line-up. The sergeant came to get us. First, they took Ryl'kov and executed the punishment. After this he was placed into the dungeon. Then they came back for me, took me to the place of the implementation, told me to take the coat off, bare my body and lie down. But I refused to do any of this of my free will. Then they pulled me down by force and bared my body. Five people sat on top of me, two on my legs, two on my arms, and one on my head, they were pushing me down so hard that I could hardly breathe. At the order, the whips in the hands of the executioners started swirling, first on the right, then on the left and the third time they hit my body as if scorching it with fire. The count could be heard: one, then from the other side, in the same manner, two, and so on. The longer the lashing lasted, the more painful it became. I felt and counted the lashes until fifty. After this, I became unconscious and I did not remember or feel what was happening to me, only my body trembled occasionally. When the executioners finished the punishment, I was raised and as they told me later, a fel'dsher,[10] poured a bucket of cold water over me. I partly came to, opened my eyes and saw the fel'dsher jumping away from me with an empty bucket. I could not immediately determine where I was and what happened to me, and I could not move at all from the pain, as if I was taken out of fire. They shouted at me, "Put your trousers on!" I wanted to follow their command, but my arms could not move, and I remained motionless. Two people came up to me and tried to put my trousers on, but they could not do anything either, as my body already was shaped differently, it swelled, so I could not fit into my trousers any more. Having put the uniform coat on me, they brought me into the cold dungeon, pushed me in and locked the doors.

I stood leaning on the wall, and I do not remember for how long I could stand, then my legs gave out and I fell on the floor. The floor was made of cement, and it was extremely cold. I tried standing up, but I did not have enough strength, not even for turning over to the side. I was thinking of getting help, of who could have helped me. But it was all in vain. It was pointless waiting for help, so I gathered the last of my strength, and on my stomach, I crawled towards the door, where I fumbled for some place I could hold on to, and I started getting up, holding onto the door lock with my hands. In this way I managed to raise myself up, took a little rest, and I wanted to walk along the cell a little to stretch my body. Then I realized that my left leg was motionless, the pain was getting stronger. Blood was oozing from everywhere. The clothes, mixed with blood, were becoming stuck to my body and caused pain that was too terrible to bear. I started thinking: "Why did they leave me alive for such torture? I was close to death, when I did not feel the last thirty lashes, and they should have added just a little on top of it, and the soul would have parted from the body. This would have been the end of my great suffering." My left leg was motionless because, as the squad leader told me later, one executioner, willing to punish me even more brutally, while delivering the lashes, turned the rods upside down, with the thick part at the bottom. The executioner was hitting with them through wounds already cut and injured my leg. The rods contained curara,[11] which was confirmed later, as curara thorns dropped from our wounds.

After eight hours, Colonel Margunov came to threaten me. He yelled at me like a maniac, "I will force you to serve! Do you think I will kill you at once? No, I will first rip the skin off, then the meat, then I will be pulling the ligaments out with hooks until you start serving. I will even make you eat meat. Today you got 80 lashes, tomorrow you will get 90. Your spirit may persevere, but all the skin and the flesh will be ripped off. I will force you to serve and kill." I said, "I will not kill under any circumstances, and if you terminate my life for God's cause, I am ready to accept death." He got very angry and left the cell. After this I was sent to the hospital where I spent 24 days to heal my wounds. I was subjected to such a cruel punishment and so were all my comrades.

Dear readers, it was not enough for the government to torture us so cruelly, we were also greatly annoyed by a priest. He often came to visit us and in all ways possible he tried persuading us, even lured us with all kinds of lies, to discard the teaching of Christ and to comply with the requirements of the government. We spoke a lot with him, even condemned him as the tempter. We are not giving an account of this here since our ancestors separated from priests a long time ago, and this is no news for us, and that priest does not deserve to have his name written down in our history.

After this, all of us, that is all the Doukhobors in the disciplinary battalion, were subjected to interrogations that were repeated up to three times, each questioning round being repeated with one week's interval. During the first two interrogations, as before, they tried to threaten and frighten us. During the third interrogation, we only had to say one word in response to the question, "Will you kill people or not?" There was a total of 41 people, of whom seven people told their officer they would agree, and remained in the battalion. All the other 34 people said, "We will not kill." After this, on November 25, 1896, we were exiled to Iakutsk area for the remaining term of our prescribed service, that is, for 18 years.

Glory be to our God!
Dear readers of this description of such a terrible event, at the end of the nineteenth century from the birth of Jesus Christ, for some of you, this description may seem not to be worthy of much attention since there was both steadfastness and weakness displayed in it. But we have to consider in earnest, the whole essence of the fate they had to face.

When two opposing sides meet, and recognizing one's own strength, they declare a war on each other, even in this force of one hundred thousand, there are advances and retreats. Sometimes one side may decide to retreat on purpose, and selecting the right moment, they win over the attackers. Sometimes, this side may simply not have enough forces, and it retreats waiting for the reinforcement battalions to arrive. The same can be applied to the cause of God. Since a man consists of the body and the soul, there is a terrible struggle inside him: the body demands one thing and the spirit demands another. And who waged a battle against 180 million of the population of the Russian state? These were young lads aged between 21 and 22, who earlier in their lives, had not had even minor trials. These were the sprouts of the tree which is in its twentieth century. These were young children, who knew almost nothing except their mothers and fathers. They were destined to step up to the cause, into the battlefield against such a strong violent mob, as the Russian state, and they had to bear all these tortures. Two hundred years ago, our forefathers, who did not want to worship the creations of a human hand, and acknowledged and worshipped God the Father in the spirit of truth, were also cruelly tortured and punished. There were cases when they were lashed to death and their lives were terminated. The same with these youths. They accomplished a great deed. If those executioners went just a little further following the command of their authorities, and added just a few more lashes, those youths would have also died the same death as our ancestors. Glory be to the God on high, let there be peace on earth and benevolence among humans! Glory be to God of all the universe for His teaching and protection, and an enormous gratitude goes to all these youthful fighters for truth. They breached the doors of hell, set themselves on the path to freedom and left this freedom to all of our subsequent generations. Whoever comprehends God's cause and His calling should not abandon it.

Here is the list of Doukhobors who refused to perform the military service in the disciplinary battalion:

Grigoriĭ Ivanovich Sukharev
Kirila Nikolaevich Chivil'deev
Vasiliĭ Sherstobitov
Grigoriĭ Vanin
Matveĭ Vasil'evich Lebedev
Ivan Vasil'evich Malakhov
Fëdor Akimovich Khaminov
Nikolaĭ Vasil'evich Ryl'kov
Nikifor Nikolaevich Sakhvonov
Fëdor Pavlovich Samorodin
Nikolaĭ Ivanovich Ryl'kov
Grigoriĭ Savel'evich Zibarov
Mikhaĭlo Arishchenkov
Larion Ivanovich Shchukin
Dmitriĭ Astafurov
Grigoriĭ Nikolaevich Verigin-Orekhov
Fëdor Ivanovich Plotnikov
Pëtr Safonov
Pëtr Fëdorovich Salykin
Pëtr Stepanovich Kiniakin
Ivan Chutskov
Stepan Rybalkin
Alekseĭ Makhortov
Fëdor Nikolaevich Malov
Nikolaĭ Sukhachëv
Aleksandr Gratchin
Ivan Kuftinov
Alistrat Baulin
Danilo Zymovskiĭ
Luk'ian Fëdorovich Novokshonov
Kuz'ma Nikolaevich Pugachëv

Semën Semënovich Usachov
Filipp Popov
Mikhaĭlo Shcherbinin
Romanov
Tsybul'kin
Nikolaĭ Kuftinov
Nikolaĭ Fofanov
Shchukin
Podovinnikov
Nikolaĭ Vasil'evich Shcherbakov

Of them, nine died:

The first one to die was Mikhail Shcherbinin, in the disciplinary battalion.
The second one was Fëdor Samorodin, in Moscow prison.
The third one was Aleksandr Gritchin, in Cheliabinsk prison.
The fourth one was Ivan Kuftinov, in Krasnoiarsk prison.
The fifth one was Luk'ian Fëdorovich Novokshonov, in the city of Iakutsk.
The sixth one was Fëdor Akimovich Khaminov, in the city of Iakutsk.
The seventh was Vasiliĭ Sherstobitov, in the city of Iakutsk.
The eighth was Ivan Chutskov, in Notora.
The ninth was Fëdor Nikolaevich Malov, in Notora.

They all died from beatings and other unnatural causes.

Notes

1. Akhalkalak (modern Akhalkalaki) is an administrative district in the country of Georgia. Now an independent state, in Imperial Russia, Georgia constituted Tiflis guberniia.
2. The author is talking about military conscription draft tickets that were drawn like a lottery. Certain numbers indicated that a person who drew this ticket number was drafted into the army.
3. Elizavetpol' (later Kirovabad, since 1989, Ganja) was the capital of Elizavetpol' guberniia in the Russian empire. Since the separation of Azerbaijan from the Soviet Union, it is one of the largest cities in Azerbaijan.
4. Tiflis is the old name of modern Tbilisi, the capital of the country of Georgia. In the nineteenth century, it was the capital of Tiflis guberniia, which was a part of the Russian Empire.

5. Ekaterinograd is modern Ekterinogradskaia or Yekaterinogradskaya village in Kabardino-Balkaria, a republic of the Russian Federation; it is located to the north of Georgia.
6. Novorossiĭsk (Novorossiysk) is a Russian port on the Black Sea coast.
7. Batum (modern name Batumi) is a port city on the Black Sea coast. It is the second largest city of the country of Georgia, which at the time of the narrative, was a part of the Russian Empire.
8. Elizavetpol' (later Kirovabad, since 1989, Ganja) was the capital of Elizavetpol' guberniia in the Russian Empire. Since the separation of Azerbaijan from the Soviet Union, it is one of the largest cities in Azerbaijan.
9. John 15:20.
10. Fel'dsher in Russia was an assistant medical practitioner (below the rank of a full doctor).
11. Curara (kurara) or *dead finish* is one of the sub-species of acacia bush that has very hard and sharp thorn-like growths on its branches.

CHAPTER 19

Exile to Iakutsk Area. The Description of the Prisoner Transport to Nizhneudinsk

We were kept in Kars[1] prison and Metekh castle[2] from June 10, 1895 to July 22, 1897. When Vereshchagin and my brother Vasiliĭ were in the Kars prison, they were visited by a government official from St. Petersburg who conducted an investigation of the Doukhobor movement. The local gendarme rotmistr[3] Astaf'ev and the prosecutor's assistant Stepanov also conducted many interrogations. In Metekh castle, there were no interrogations except for a visitation by Skvortsov.

On July 4, the decision of the Senate[4] was read to us; by the order of Nikolaĭ Aleksandrovich Romanov,[5] we were to be exiled to eastern Siberia, Iakutsk area, to the most remote places, where we were to be settled among the aboriginal population, for our lifetimes, and we were to be under police surveillance.

On July 22nd, we were sent away from Metekh castle by railway in the direction of Baku.[6] At the railway stations of Akstafa,[7] Dzegam[8] and Evlakh,[9] we saw many relatives, brothers and sisters who came to say good-bye to us. There was very little time for seeing them as the train stopped at the stations only for a very short while. Besides, we were under prisoners' convoy and the soldiers kept yelling at us, "Stop looking into the windows!" But we still managed to talk a little and say good-byes perhaps for the last time. In response to our last greetings, we heard dozens of voices of our relatives breaking down with tears who wished us health and a smooth journey far away to Eastern Siberia: "Let God, our Lord, save you. Please, do not forget us!" And the train pulled away.

These last words of good-byes from our relatives moved our hearts, and tears came unnoticed into our eyes, but we looked at each other and without revealing any weakness, we changed the expressions on our faces and started talking, "How fast the train is running!"

We arrived in Baku on the morning of the 23rd. When we got off the train, we were joined by other brothers who were kept in the Nukhin jail[10] of Elizavetpol'[11] guberniia. They were also being taken to Siberia. There was a total of 36 of us there, including our four brothers, Ivan, Fëdor, Luk'ian and Prokofiĭ. So six Verigin brothers got together there.[12] From the railway terminal, we were forwarded into the transport prison. The prison was seven miles away from the terminal. Walking all this way, we got a little tired. It was the peak of July heat and we were very thirsty.

When we got into the prison, it turned out that the director was a good-natured person. He immediately gave an order to place us into separate cells. We occupied three cells. He ordered to have some water boiled and offered us the opportunity to go bathe in the sea, if we wanted. This is exactly what we did. We went to bathe in the sea, and upon return, we had some tea and we cheered up completely.

On August 1st, we were sent from Baku by a steamship via Caspian Sea as far as Astrakhan'.[13] We were all placed in the ship's hold, where the space was very cramped and it was unbearably hot. On the second day of our sea voyage, we arrived in Derbent.[14] It was getting dark already. The ship stayed there a while and then sailed off. As we sailed off, a strong southern wind started to blow. By midnight, there were huge waves, and the ship was tossed from one side onto the other as if it were a tiny boat. The cargo hold was completely quiet, although we were all awake. In our fear, we hid awaiting our fate that was threatening us with death any minute. At dawn, the wind started growing weaker, and by midday, it became tranquil. Since we were unaccustomed to sea travel, and because of this terrible rocking, we all suffered from seasickness. On August 4th, we arrived at the pier known as "12 feet." There we were transferred to a river boat and on August 5th, we safely arrived in Astrakhan', thank God, with the exception of our brother Luk'ian, who was very sea-sick and became ill. In Astrakhan', we were transferred to another ship, and in the evening of the same day, August 5th, we started sailing up the Volga river towards Kazan'.[15] On this ship, we were accommodated very comfortably. Our convoy officer was a very good person and he allowed us to cook for ourselves separately. We were given plenty of ingredients, and we even saved up a little.

Along the banks of the Volga, we often saw Russian peasant villages that reminded us of our homeland and of our relatives, from whom we were being taken farther and farther away. Our dear brother Luk'ian Vasil'evich did not get any better. On the contrary, he was getting worse. He caught a high fever and was delirious. His unlucky fate did not allow him to go with us anymore. The officer, seeing how sick he was, suggested that we should leave him behind in the city of Kamyshin, Saratov guberniia. We asked the officer to allow one of the brothers to stay with him. The officer agreed. When the ship docked at the shore, Luk'ian Vasil'evich was taken off the ship, and we parted with him forever on the bank of the Volga river. The convoy soldiers put him on a wagon, he was already unconscious, and they took him into prison together with brother Prokofiĭ who stayed behind to look after him. This is how fate separated us when we did not expect it and we were separated forever. Our dear sick brother Luk'ian soon died. This was on August 8, 1897. Our brother Prokofiĭ buried him, and then he was sent with another prisoner transport to catch up with us. He caught up with us in Krasnoiarsk.[16] We arrived in Saratov[17] on August 8th, at 10 in the morning. The ship was docked at the pier until 10 pm. Then it sailed off and on August 9th, we arrived at the town of Vol'sk, where some prisoners were taken ashore, and the ship remained at the pier for no more than two hours. In the morning of August 10th, we arrived in Samara,[18] where the ship remained until 2 pm. About 60 miles before Kazan', the river Kama flows into the Volga, so we had to go to Kazan' first and then go back along the river Kama as far as Perm'.[19]

We had a change of transport in Kazan'. We were moved to another ship attached to a barge. As we travelled along the river Kama, the first town on our way was Chistopol'. On the 14th, we passed by Sarapul', in the morning of the 17th, we passed by the regional town Akhansk, and at 12 noon we arrived in Perm'. At 2 pm we were transferred from the ship to a train, and at 5 pm we moved on by rail through the Ural mountain ridge and to Tiumen'.[20] In Perm', due to illness, we left behind one more brother, Nikolaĭ T. Chernov. The convoy officer did not allow anyone to stay behind to look after him and he soon died there.

On the 18th, we crossed the Ural ridge where it was already frosty. On the 19th, we crossed from Russia to Siberia. The border between Russia and Siberia was located between the railway stations Iushala and Tugalym. There was a big pole erected there with inscriptions on the plaque: Russia and Siberia. As we drove into Siberia, the landscape started getting better and better. It seemed that they had very good crops there; there was mostly wheat, rye, oats and buckwheat. The grain grew to medium height, but it was very thick and the stalks were big. Hemp and flax were also cultivated, and they ripened well. As we were travelling through, the residents harvested spring-seeded grain, and the fall-seeded grain was already harvested. The grain was mostly harvested with scythes by women, and one could hardly see any men around. According to the stories of one man from that area, men mostly spent their time in the factories and mines. They became accustomed to this life and did not live at home. Women took care of the household themselves. We saw some villages on the way. It appeared that people there lived neither too poorly nor too richly. In the evening of the 19th, we arrived in Tiumen' where we were taken off the train and escorted into the transport prison. Upon receiving prisoners, the prison guards carefully searched all the prisoners. We were not searched at all, they only asked us, "Are you from the Doukhobors?" We answered, "Yes." The director gave an order to move us away from the rest of the group and to give us a separate cell for the night. The senior guard officer took us to that cell. There was nothing special in this cell. Of course, everything was the same as in other cells, but the difference was that there was no noise and shouting among us, as is common among other prisoners, which meant a lot to us. We were given hot water for tea. We had some tea and went to bed.

I have not explained why they paid special attention to us. Not only here in Tiumen', but everywhere, they were lenient to us in anything possible. It was because we were preceded on our way by 31 of our brothers about whom the readers already know. They were transported from the disciplinary battalion to Iakutsk region. There were 34 of them in the disciplinary battalion, but they already lost three people in hospitals in different places. Some died in transport prison and some from the beatings by soldiers in the disciplinary battalion. There were now 31 of them left, and they spent the winter in Tiumen'. The prison director observed their honesty and kindness. They performed all work without complaints, and over this short period of time, they managed to earn a profound trust of the prison administration not only for themselves but also for the rest of us who followed them.

In the evening of the next day, we were taken from the prison to the ship pier and placed on a barge. The ship remained at the pier until the morning, and at 9 am, we set off on our journey along the Tura river. This was on August 21st. We arrived in Tobol'sk[21] on the 22nd. The ship stayed there for three hours. During this time, we stocked up on food, we bought some bread and potatoes, butter and cereal. We were given pocket money for cooking food. We bought white wheat bread for 1 rouble[22] a bushel,[23] potatoes for 15 kopecks a bushel, good cow milk butter for 20 kopecks a bushel, good buckwheat grain for 1 rouble a bushel, and everything was very inexpensive. We were stocking up on food because between Tobol'sk and Tomsk, there were hardly any towns or even villages. So if we had not stocked up on supplies in Tobol'sk, we would be starving, or even if we could get some food somewhere, it would be very expensive. Along the banks of the river, we saw many Ostiaks[24] who lived in yurts,[25] putting together two, three, or five yurts. A yurt was like a small tent, covered with birch bark. According to the customs of their ancestors, Ostiaks were engaged in fishing and hunting. When the ship stopped to load firewood, Ostiaks were always at the pier. The men brought fish for sale in their boats and women brought eggs, milk and potatoes, although this did not happen very often. They started cultivating potatoes on their own recently, they had not had it before. They are like indigenous people, actually they are indigenous. All the ones we met were good people and many of them spoke Russian.

We arrived safely in Tomsk[26] on the 30th, thank God. On September 1st, we left Tomsk for Krasnoiarsk by railway. We arrived in Krasnoiarsk in the morning of the 4th. From the train, we were escorted into the transport prison, where we had to wait until the prisoner convoy arrived on September 17th. Thanks to this delay, our brother Prokofiĭ who stayed behind in the town of Kamysh to look after brother Luk'ian caught up with us in Krasnoiarsk. On the 17th we were transported to Kansk[27] by rail. We arrived at Kansk in the evening of the 18th. After spending the night there in prisoner transport, in the morning, we set out on our journey to Irkutsk[28] on foot.

Our group consisted of 300 people. The prisoners came from all layers of society. There were carts designated for carrying our belongings, and some carts were provided for the sick and the elderly, who received doctors' recommendations and who needed them. It was easy to walk between the first two stations. The weather was dry and the road was good. We stayed for a day at the second station. It was raining the whole day, and in the night, closer towards the morning, it snowed and the road got extremely muddy. This walk continued until Nizhneudinsk, and it was not devoid of suffering. All sorts of things happened. After staying in prisons for two years, we were not accustomed to walking so much, and the way was very hard. The convoy soldiers followed their rough discipline: they did not allow us to walk on the side of the road, where it would be easier to walk, but forced us to walk along the road which was horrible even to look at, to say nothing of walking. When we got extremely tired, soldiers paid no attention to our requests, on the contrary, they scolded us, and sometimes even pushed us with the firearm stocks, forcing us into walking.

Drained of all strength, we arrived at the prison transport yard. The whole group was stopped at the gate and the convoy started counting the prisoners. We had 325 prisoners in our group. Counting them took an hour, or sometimes more. If there was an error, they would have to count again. After this, the gates opened and we were let into the prisoner transport station. During this time, every prisoner, gathering his last strength, pushed ahead to occupy a place for the night. Sometimes, and this would happen quite often in this tight space with a lot of people, a person would misstep. He would then stumble and fall, and then others would pile on top of him. They could not see anything. Because there was such strong pushing from behind, the ones in the front had to move their feet very quickly. Sometimes, in this stampede, the ones at the back got into the place first. When we entered the station, we could not get to a good sleeping space. It was very damp everywhere and the prisoners also brought in plenty of mud on their feet. One had to settle down, find a place to sleep for the night, but where? All the space was taken already. Besides us, most other prisoners were Russian, so-called Orthodox, and many of them had walked this prisoner transport many times before. So they knew how to handle everything and they managed the prisoner transport as if it were their own household. The soldiers locked up the doors and moved to their own quarters. After some time, the soldiers unlocked the doors and all the prisoners walked out to buy bread or some other food. The village peasant women, knowing when the prisoner transport was coming, brought bread, potatoes and sometimes milk for sale to the station yard. If any prisoners had money, they would buy milk as well, one bottle for about four people. And if there was no money, they went without it. The pocket money given for food was 10 kopecks per person per day, and you could buy whatever you wanted with it. Rye bread was 3 kopecks per pound and wheat bread was 5 and 6 kopecks per pound. It was good when the village women brought enough bread, but sometimes, when the village was very small, there wouldn't be enough bread for sale. If you told the guard that you could not buy bread, he would tell you, "At the next station, there is a bigger village; there will be enough of everything." And this was the end, and he walked away, as if he satisfied you perfectly. But you had to spend the night without eating anything for dinner and walk the entire following day without food. This was how they cared for the prisoners.

The way to the prisoner transport station Biriusa remained in my memory for a particularly long time. It took 34 hours to get to this station. Five miles before the station, there was a big river Biriusa, and the prisoners were taken across the river by ferry. Since the ferry was very small, they had to split us into two groups. We were taken in the first group and had to wait until the second group was transported. We had nowhere to rest and it was wet and extremely dirty everywhere. It was raining heavily, the sun rolled behind the mountains and it was getting dark. It was cold outside, and we were hungry. Then, when the group was set to go ahead, our legs refused to carry us to the destination. We were no longer paying any attention to guards who were shouting at us for lagging behind. Vasiliĭ Grigor'evich Vereshchagin saw how tired both he and all other brothers were and he told me, "Grisha, ask the convoy officer to give us a separate room, if it were possible, so that we could get some rest." The big station building had a small separate room for about 25–30 people. This room was designated for people who were returning from Siberia at the government's expense and did not have their own money. At the station, they were placed into this separate room. The officer told me that this room was too small for us, but I said that it was fine, and that the tight space was not an issue for us, but we did not want any noise and shouting. My request was granted by the officer, and when we got to the station, we were placed into that room, where we had our dinner and went to bed without any noise and shouting. The Lord always protected us, and even in such conditions, He sent us health and well-being. In the morning, we always had to get up early to prepare to move on, but thanks to God's mercy, we did not feel yesterday's weariness and pain too much. Strengthened, we set off on our journey again praising God.

Notes

1. Kars is a town in Turkey. With its surrounding area, at the time of the narrative, it belonged to the Russian Empire. It was one of the areas of the Transcaucasian exile of the Doukhobors. Since 1921, it has been a part of Turkey.
2. Metekh (Metekhi) castle was a strongly fortified nineteenth-century prison in the Metekhi area of Tiflis (modern Tbilisi), the capital of Georgia (in the nineteenth century it was a part of the Russian Empire).

3. Rotmistr was a rank of cavalry officer in the nineteenth-century Russia.
4. The Senate (the Governing Senate) was the highest governing (legislative, judicial and administrative) body of the Russian Empire, which was under the direct jurisdiction of the emperor.
5. Nikolaĭ (Nicolas II) Romanov was the last Russian tsar who succeeded the throne in 1894 and was officially crowned in 1896.
6. Baku is the capital of the modern state of Azerbaijan. At the time of the narrative, it was a part of the Russian Empire.
7. Akstafa refers to Aghstafa, a town in Azerbaijan close to the borders with Armenia and Georgia. At the time of the narrative, Azerbaijan was a part of the Russian Empire.
8. Dzegam most likely refers to modern Dzagam (Dzegam), a town in Azerbaijan. At the time of the narrative, Azerbaijan was a part of the Russian Empire.
9. Evlakh (modern Yevlakh or Yevlax) is a town in Azerbaijan, which at the time of the narrative was a part of the Russian Empire.
10. Nukhin prison was located in the Nukha fortress of the town of Shaki, Azerbaijan. At the time of the narrative, the area was a part of the Russian Empire.
11. Elizavetpol' (later Kirovabad, since 1989, Ganja) was the capital of Elizavetpol' guberniia in the Russian Empire. Since the separation of Azerbaijan from the Soviet Union, it is one of the largest cities in Azerbaijan.
12. Six brothers relate to the author Grigoriĭ and his brother Vasiliĭ plus four more brothers who were brought in with other prisoners.
13. Astrakhan' (or Astrakhan) is a town in southern Russia located in the delta of the Volga river where it flows into the Caspian Sea.
14. Derbent is a town in Dagestan republic, Russian Federation.
15. Kazan' (or Kazan) is the capital of the Republic of Tatarstan, Russia. It is located on the Volga river.
16. Krasnoiarsk (Krasnoyarsk) is one of the major cities in Siberia located on the Eniseĭ (Yenisei) river.
17. Saratov is a Russian city on the Volga river.
18. Samara is a city in the eastern European part of Russia located high up the flow of the Volga river close to the confluence of the Volga and the Samara rivers.
19. Perm' (Perm) is a Russian city on the river Kama located close to the Urals mountains and to Europe/Asia boundary.
20. Tiumen' (Tyumen) is a Russian city on the Tura river, the first major Russian city in Siberia on the Asian side of the Eurasia border and of the Ural Mountains.
21. Tobol'sk is a Russian city on the Tura river in Tiumen' area, western Siberia.

22. Rouble is a monetary unit used in Russia since the thirteenth century till modern times, there were 100 kopecks to a rouble. At the time of the narrative, rouble was comparable to a dollar and kopecks to cents.
23. The original text uses the word "pud" (pronounced "pood"), a unit of measurement in Imperial Russian system. One pud equals about 16 kg (36 pounds). It is close to a Canadian bushel of 15.4 kg, hence we use the word "bushel" here.
24. Ostiak (Ostyak) is an old name for a group of indigenous people of Siberia; they are currently more often referred to as three distinct groups of people: Khanty, Ket and Selkup.
25. Yurt is a traditional round-shaped dwelling supported by a lattice with skins or felt around it. Yurts could be easily assembled and transported to support a nomadic lifestyle. Yurts are found among many other Asian and Siberian peoples.
26. Tomsk is a city in Siberia farther to the south-east from Tobol'sk.
27. Kansk is a town in Siberia to the east of Krasnoiarsk and to the north-east of Nizhneudinsk and Irkutsk.
28. Irkutsk is one of the largest cities in Siberia, located in Southern Siberia close to Lake Baĭkal.

CHAPTER 20

The Continuation of Prisoner Transport. The Last Words and Death of Vasiliĭ G. Vereshchagin

As I said before, our difficult journey continued like this until Nizhneudinsk.[1] Nizhneudinsk is a regional town separated from Kansk[2] by thirty prisoner transport stations. We stayed in Nizhneudinsk for two days and nights. The transport moved ahead on the third day. It was easier and better to walk as it snowed a little and it started freezing. On November 2, we arrived in Aleksandrovsk[3] transport prison safely, thank God. During the prisoner transport, we walked for 45 days (including the days when we stayed at the stations). We walked for over 800 miles. In Aleksandrovsk, we were placed in the central transport prison; we were to be transferred under the jurisdiction of the governor-general of Irkutsk.[4] The Irkutsk governor-general ordered to send us to Iakutsk[5] under the jurisdiction of Iakutsk governor Skripitsin. The transport of prisoners to Iakutsk was suspended in August. Therefore, we were kept in Aleksandrovsk for the winter. The prison director was a good person. For about two weeks, we were kept in the general barrack where 120 people were housed, and then the director placed us in a separate barrack, which had been previously occupied by political convicts, and there we felt free and well, and even conducted sobraniia prayer meetings on Sundays.

Soon after our arrival, all the prisoners were visited by inspector Sipiagin. We explained to him that we did not eat meat because of our beliefs and requested him to allow us to cook our food separately. He promised, "As soon as I come to Irkutsk, I will immediately make a report to the governor-general." And soon we received permission to cook our food separately. We were pointed to a separate kitchen pot, and we appointed two people to supervise the process. We got some money with which we bought butter instead of meat. Since there was little food provided by the government, once a week, we were allowed to go to the market with a guard. There we bought everything we needed with our own money and added it to the kitchen pot. Had we confined ourselves to the governmental food ration only, it would have been very difficult to survive. Here is an example of their food rations. They gave 40 grams of cereal, 2 grams of salt, about 100 grams of potatoes, and 2 grams of onions per person. We also received 4 grams of pepper per 45 people. In addition, every prisoner was given 1.5 kopecks for butter. So what can one cook with this? Besides, some religious fasts were mandated in prison. These were the tricks of the clergy, of the priests. On Wednesdays and Fridays, we had to fast. On those days, we got a hundred grams of peas and 3 grams of vegetable oil per person. We also had to follow this rule, although we explained that we did not follow such fasts and that they were useless and even harmful for us. We told them, "We do not share your convictions that one can achieve salvation through these fasts. Our conviction is that one can only achieve salvation through following God's will." But they responded to this by saying, "Although you are convinced that such fasts should not be observed, you still have to follow the general rules of the prison."

On the day of the great festival of the light of Christ's resurrection (Easter), all the prisoners received paskha[6] and eggs, and the sum for it was forwarded from the prison committee. However, we were excluded from this general rule for some reason. We were not given anything and told, "You are not entitled to any of this as sectarians." It's ridiculous: we were told to follow the "general rule" in fasting, but when it came to getting paskha and eggs, we were told we were not "entitled to this as sectarians." So the moral of the story is "the powerless is always at fault in the eyes of the powerful."[7]

In January of 1898 Ivan E. Konkin, his wife Varvara V. and his sick daughter arrived in our Aleksandrovsk prison from the town of Mezen',[8] Archangel'sk guberniia, along with 11 young men from the disciplinary battalion of Ekaterinograd.[9] Ivan E. Konkin is already mentioned in my notes. He was exiled from Slavianka to the town of Mezen'. His wife and daughter followed him voluntarily to Mezen'. After they had lived there for some time, they were suspected by the government of converting people into sectarianism. A report about this was submitted to the Minister of internal affairs, and he gave an order to exile them to Iakutsk area. His wife Varvara was now forced to follow him. She was accused and tried in Mezen' and she was exiled as a criminal. We were very glad to see them unexpectedly, and from then on, we lived together with them.

Two of our brothers passed away in God's will in Aleksandrovsk prison. The first one was Larion L. Planidin, aged 22 who died on March 28. He was called to the military service, but following the teaching of Christ he refused to serve. Along with all the others, he was exiled to Iakutsk area. The second brother passed away on April 13. This was Vasiliĭ M. Konkin from the village of Slavianka, an elderly person aged 60.

We stayed in Aleksandrovsk until May 3rd when we were sent to Iakutsk. The officer in charge of the convoy was an indigenous Buriat[10] by the name of Orlov. He had a rough heart and a bad temper. He always found faults with prisoners for nothing at all, swore indecently and often ordered soldiers to hit prisoners with the backs of their guns. He did not do this to us, but he still treated us unfairly. The first example of his bad behaviour was when our group was ordered to depart from Aleksandrovsk. He did not want to allow our belongings on horse carts and told us, "A prisoner is only allowed to carry 30 pounds per person, and you can do whatever you want with the rest. If you want, you can hire two carts from the contractor, and he will deliver your things." We told him in response, "We are prisoners and we have already come such a long way and we had no trouble putting our belongings on horse carts anywhere before, and now you are telling us to hire horse carts. We will not hire horse carts by any means, because we have no money for this. And if you have the right not to accept our things—this is up to you." He became a little angry at this, but he finally did accept all our belongings on carts.

We walked on foot to get to the first two stations, and the rest of the way to Kachug,[11] we travelled on horse carts for 200 miles. The transport group consisted of 310 people. It was very cramped at the stations. However, thanks to good dry weather, we always slept outside in the yard in the open air, under the roof of the blue sky.

We arrived at Kachug on May 9th at 12 noon safely, thank God. We were stationed on the bank of the river Lena. The river Lena served as a fence on the eastern side, and on the western side we had a convoy of soldiers on guard. They also added peasants recruited from local villages as guards. Huge bonfires were lit throughout the night and they kept calling out the prisoners so that we would not fall asleep.

From Kachug to Iakutsk we had to travel along the river Lena by boat, but since these boats were not finished by the time of our arrival, we stayed there on the same bank under open skies until May 13th.

Every prisoner got money for food for the stretch of the way to Kachug. In Kachug, Orlov was supposed to stock various food items to get us to Iakutsk: meat, dry bread, cereal and salt, and to give us rations from those. They bought meat for us as well, and there were 46 of us. We told Orlov, "Since we do not eat meat, could you buy butter for us for the sum allocated to us for meat?" He responded, "I cannot do this, because there were no separate instructions about you, and you have to take meat." After this we wrote a telegram to the governor-general of Irkutsk. The content of the telegram was as follows: "To Irkutsk, Governor-general. You already know that because of our convictions, we cannot eat meat, we request you to give us the value of meat in pocket money. The Doukhobors." Orlov did not accept this telegram and started shouting, "I will put you all in shackles!"

On the evening of May 12th, the boats were ready and all the prisoners were put on board. They distributed the food products to ten people at a time. One person from every ten people was appointed in charge, and he had to receive whatever was due, or to be more exact, whatever they gave. There were five people from our group. Orlov himself was present during the distribution of the food products. When the turn of our brothers came, they were also given meat. They did not accept meat and said that they had already informed Orlov about the fact that they would not accept meat. He got angry and started yelling at us and shouted, "Guards, come here!" But for some reason, the guards did not appear when he summoned them. Perhaps he had warned the guards beforehand and just wanted to scare us with his actions. When he saw that we were not afraid of either him or his guards, he gave us butter in the calculated amounts. And as far as Iakutsk, he did not bother us anymore.

On the 13th, in the morning, with God's mercy, we set off on our journey along the flow of the river Lena on boats. The boat was designed so that it looked like a poor hut. It had a firm foundation of logs and the sides consisted of boards nailed together. Inside, on both sides, they had bunk beds, and in the middle there was a very narrow passage to the entry. The roof was covered with thin wooden boards. The prisoners were located under bunk beds, on bunk beds and on the roof. The boat was eleven metres long and five metres wide. And this tight narrow hut accommodated 120 prisoners and the guards. There were no windows on the boat, but there were very big gaps between the boards on the sides of the boat, so through these holes, one could see very well what was happening on the shore. At the bow of the boat, there was a place for cooking the food and making tea. There was always elbowing, noise, shouting and often fights around it because of an accidentally overturned pot. On the roof of the boat, there was a big steering wheel. The coxswain steered the wheel to get the boat wherever it needed to go. The coxswain had to be experienced and know the river channel very well, otherwise the boat would often hit shallow places. At the bow, next to the kitchen there were two big oars, which were operated by six people when the boat was passing through some dangerous places. This was because in rapid flow, the boat could hit a rock and break apart. Prisoners took turns as oarsmen. Each oarsman was paid 70 kopecks a day. There was a total of four boats. Three boats contained the prisoners and the convoy and the fourth boat carried the food products, and Orlov was also there.

In the evening of the same day, we arrived at the regional central town of Verkholensk[12] and docked at the bank there for the night about 1.5 miles past the city, lower along the river bank. There we were visited by six brothers and three sisters including Fedoseev, Lezhava, and others. There was a boy with them as well. They were exiled for a term because of a political case. Orlov did not allow a direct face-to-face meeting, but we still talked a little with them, and explained how many of us were there. After we finished talking, they gave us two cones of sugar and 10 pounds of tea. We thanked them for this. They wished us a safe journey, said their good-byes and left.

We arrived at the regional town of Kirensk[13] on the 26th and stayed there for three days and nights to buy dried bread and other supplies. Three of our brothers were left behind there due to an illness: Vasiliĭ G. Vereshchagin, Pëtr F. Dymovskiĭ and Fëdor A. Ryl'kov. The former two became very sick, and Ryl'kov, as their brother in Christ, stayed behind to look after them. Vasiliĭ G. Vereshchagin passed away there in a hospital on June 8, 1898. Let God remember Vasiliĭ in his heavenly kingdom. Dymovskiĭ got better and together with Ryl'kov they arrived in Iakutsk.

While he was in prison, Vasiliĭ G. Vereshchagin never became ill. He was a man of good health, slender build, with a kind character and a great mind. He always spoke clearly and with conviction. He thought that his actions were right, and he was ready to sacrifice himself for the truth that had been revealed to us by Christ. And he did suffer for it. He walked all the way from Kansk to Aleksandrovsk, without sitting on the horse cart even once. Seeing that he was healthy, the doctor did not give him permission to travel by cart, although Vereschagin was already 60. When we came to Aleksandrovsk, he felt sick, but did not go to a hospital immediately, as he thought that his ailment was caused by the difficult journey and would clear up on its own.

A month later, the pain kept getting stronger, his right side hurt and he had a severe cough. He went to the hospital and spent about a month there. He got bored at the hospital, and one can say there was little medical treatment there, the care was very poor, the doctors treated their jobs carelessly and just wanted to finish off their shifts. Probably, in a customary way, they did not regard the prisoners the same way they regarded free people. This was a great mistake on behalf of the doctors since they were called to help and alleviate the condition of a person, no matter who this person was.

One should not forget that we are all given our lives only once, and every person holds this life precious. And consequently, whenever one can help another person, it is necessary to help. Otherwise a doctor is ignoring the cause that he is destined to serve.

Vereschagin signed out of the hospital, came back uplifted and said, "I am feeling better." Of course, after staying for a month in a hospital, one cannot walk out of it and say that he is feeling worse, and by the force of necessity, the person is trying to cheer oneself up. But the illness was doing its destruction, and after a short while, he started feeling weaker. When our group was ordered to depart, he was already quite ill. While he still had any energy left, he did not want to part with us and finish his life in Aleksandrovsk prison, and he set out on the journey together with us.

He probably thought that he might have enough energy to get to Iakutsk, and there he would be free of prison. There, if death came, it would be easier to accept it knowing that brothers would take care of him and he would die among his own brothers, who would cry for him and bury him where they chose. On the way to Kachuga, he was suffering a lot, although he was given a horse cart for this stretch. But for a sick person, travelling on the prisoners' carts could be even worse than walking. He felt better on the boat and for a while he even cheered up, as it often happens with people when death approaches.

Once we sat with him talking about the move of our people to America. We already received the news that they were allowed to move abroad. He said, "You are young people, perhaps you are still destined to get to America, but I will likely not have a chance to go there. Grisha, I do not feel very comfortable, and I will die soon." Upon hearing these words, tears came to my eyes, but he resumed talking, "It's fine, all of us have to die in the flesh, but the spirit living within us, that we accept via the second birth from above from the Holy Spirit, has to go back to its origin. This origin is the force that contains everything. This is the essence of our earthly life, to join this origin and live eternally. We are born in the flesh, and then we are replaced. This is also a manifestation of the will of God, in the face of which a man should not feel proud and should not distance himself from his origin. So, if I die, and you were to meet my relatives, please pass over to them my spiritual will, and tell them not to lament that I am dying here, and not in another place that I or my relatives would prefer. But we should not forget that we are suffering for the truth. Wherever death finds us, we must obey it without lamentations, and accept it as the messenger of the morning dawn that is followed by the sun. These are only the desires of our flesh when we reject death or feel sorry for it. God knows better than we do, and does what is necessary." He said a lot more, assuring me that no one should be shy in face of this transition. However, I was genuinely very sorry for him; that we were parting and that we were parting forever in this life.

On June 5th, we passed through a regional town Alekma.[14] The boats stayed there for about five hours. Alekma is a small town, and there is almost nothing worth noticing there. However, as compared to other Siberian towns, it stands out slightly in its buildings and cheap prices of bread and other food products. Some Skoptsy[15] live there, they plough the land and also grow various vegetables, partly for themselves and partly for sale.

On June 10th, at 6 pm, we arrived safely in the city of Iakutsk, thank God. When we arrived, we were immediately taken off the boats and forwarded into the transport prison, where the convoy officer delivered us to the director of prison. This delivery took about four hours. All the prisoners were called out following the lists. After this, the director ordered the guards to put us into a separate cell, where we were fairly comfortable and could almost taste freedom.

On the second day, the governor's assistant came to prison, called us following the lists and asked us what skills each of us had. Then the governor Skripitsin arrived in person and announced the location for our settlement. All the brothers with whom we had been transported were settled in the following way: those who came from the disciplinary battalion were to live with the brothers in the mouth of the river Notora, that is, where the Notora river flowed into the river Aldan. The brothers who arrived earlier took the location for settlement six miles away from Aldan, up the river Notora. Both of us, my brother Vasiliĭ and I were ordered to move to another location, the so-called Nel'kan.[16] This was farther up north, 1000 miles away from the mouth of the Notora river. After this a commissioner was appointed to accompany us all. On the third day, in the morning, about ten of us went downtown, on our own, without any guards, to buy whatever was necessary. In the evening, we set out for the appointed place on board a ship. This ship belonged to a famous merchant woman Anna Gromova, and fortunately for us, it was on its way to Nel'kan for a load of tea. The captain of this ship, a Norwegian by the name Fok, took us on board without any payment, but when the sailors were loading wood on board, we assisted them.

Notes

1. Nizhneudinsk is a town in Siberia to the south-east from Kansk, to the north-east of Irkutsk, and about one-third of the distance between Kansk and Irkutsk.
2. Kansk is a town in Siberia to the east of Krasnoiarsk and to the north-east of Nizhneudinsk and Irkutsk.
3. Aleksandrovsk (the official name is Aleksandrovskoe) is a village in Irkutsk area. Aleksandrovskiĭ Tsentral (Aleksanrovsk Central Prison) located in the village was a major transport prison in the area.
4. Irkutsk is one of the largest cities in Siberia, located in Southern Siberia close to the Baĭkal Lake.
5. Iakutsk (Yakutsk) is a sub-Arctic city in Siberia with a harsh continental climate. During winters, it is one of the coldest cities in the world. It is the homeland of the Yakut (Sakha) people, the indigenous population of the area. It was used by the Russian government as a place of exile. Today it is the capital of Sakha republic.
6. The word "paskha" means Easter, but it also refers to a traditional Easter dish of pressed cottage cheese with spices and raisins.
7. "The powerless are always at fault in the eyes of the powerful" is a quote from a fable in verse by a famous Russian poet I. A. Krylov "The wolf and the lamb," in which the wolf condemns the lamb to death on the grounds of the wolf being hungry. This tale originates from Aesop's fable "The Wolf and the Lamb."
8. Mezen' (Mezen) is a town in the Arkhangel'sk (Arkhangelsk) area in the north of the European part of Russia, close to the Arctic Polar Circle.
9. Ekaterinograd is modern Ekterinogradskaia or Yekaterinogradskaya village in Kabardino-Balkaria, a republic of the Russian Federation; it is located to the north of Georgia.
10. Buriat (Buryat) are the largest indigenous group of Siberia.
11. Kachug (Katchoug, Kachuga) is a town north-east of Irkutsk located in the Irkutsk area of Siberia.

12. Verkholensk is a town in Siberia to the north-west of Kachug, located between Irkutsk and Iakutsk.
13. Kirensk is a town in Siberia to the north-east of Irkutsk, located between Irkutsk and Iakutsk.
14. Alekma (Olëkma), modern Olëkminsk, is a town in the Iakut region of Siberia.
15. Skoptsy were a religious sect that originated in Russia in the eighteenth century. The name of the sect comes from the word "oskopit'" (castrate).
16. Nel'kan is a town in Siberia in Iakut (Yakut) Republic, Russia.

CHAPTER 21

Life in Nel'kan

We left Iakutsk on June 13th and started sailing down the river Lena. After 280 miles, we turned into the river Aldan and went up the river. On the 17th, we got to Ust'-Notora,[1] where our brothers stayed behind. They got off the ship, carried all their belongings on shore and said their goodbyes to us. The ship set sail. After sailing for another 180 miles, we went to the Skoptsy[2] village of Petropavlovskoe.[3] The ship stayed there for 10 hours; they were loading flour for the workers. My brother and I also stocked up on everything necessary since it was difficult and expensive to get anything in Nel'kan.[4] From Petropavlovskoe, we sailed up the river Maia and we no longer saw any Russian population. Here and there, one could see Tungus[5] and Yakut[6] yurts and some indigenous people, but these were rare occasions. We safely arrived in Nel'kan on the 26th, thank God. The settlement of Nel'kan served as a warehouse for tea brought from China by steamship. In winter, tea was carried from Aian[7] to Nel'kan on reindeer sleighs. The total amount of tea transported during winter time was 60,000 bushels. The distance between Aian and Nel'kan was 208 miles. There were warehouses built in Nel'kan, and three Russians in charge of them lived there. They had their own families. In the fall, the three warehouse workers came to Nel'kan from Iakutsk[8] by boat, and in winter, they received the tea shipments.

When ice broke on the Maia, this load of tea was put on a boat and the warehouse intendants accompanied it to Iakutsk, where they spent the summer. It was the first time that the ship we took embarked in Nel'kan.

We had to stay in the quarters of one of the warehouse attendants by the last name of Filipov. His family consisted of three people, his dignified elderly mother Mar'ia Iakovlevna, his son Pëtr Dmitrievich and his wife. They were very good people. Before leaving for Iakutsk on the same ship, they offered us their house with all the house utensils and told us, "You are welcome to live here until we come back, and then we shall see. Do not worry, we will not leave you without accommodation." These words were extremely precious to us and we will never forget them.

Besides the warehouse attendants, the inhabitants of Nel'kan included a police officer, an elderly 60-year-old man, Nikolaĭ N. Bol'shov, to whom the executive Popov handed us over. There was also a man named Fakter who was in charge of the governmental gunpowder warehouse. He lived in Nel'kan with his wife. There was also a small chapel, and a deacon with his wife lived next to it. The priest came only for the winter, and in summer, he left back for Iakutsk. This was the whole population of Nel'kan.

Life in such a desolate remote place is extremely boring, but our life was fine, and the time passed quickly. The only serious drawback was that there was no postal service in Nel'kan, and we could only get letters from our relatives twice a year.

First, we engaged ourselves in haymaking, a job allocated to us by the executive. After haymaking, we started building a bathhouse that Filipov had asked us to build before he left. Filipov had already prepared the wood for the building, as well as for the roof and the floor. On weekdays, we always worked. On Sundays, we rested and often went to the woods to gather various berries that grew there in abundance: wild strawberries, bog bilberries and the so-called procumbent red currants.

By September 20th, the Filipovs returned from Iakutsk. The bathhouse was finished; it came out very nicely with two compartments. The Filipovs were very happy with it. Besides, this bathhouse helped us to get to know all the Nel'kans. Every Saturday, everyone came to wash themselves there and in addition to the payment for our labour, everybody said, "Thank you so much for building the bathhouse."

Together with Filipov, our older brother Ivan came to Nel'kan. By mistake, the government left him in Notora, but then they saw that by the special dispatch of the minister, he was to be sent to more remote places in Siberia, the same as us. We were very glad to have this unexpected reunion. He brought with him lots of news, a story of life in Notora, and a few letters from the relatives, where they said that all our people, that is, all the Doukhobors, were beginning to resettle to America. All this was a great novelty for us. We were thinking that perhaps soon we should also be freed to go to America, where all our relatives were moving. We stayed in the same house, and we built a new house for the Filipovs and they moved there.

In winter, we did not work at all, as it is extremely cold there in winter and the frosts reach minus 50 degrees. In March, we suggested adding a porch to the new house for the price of 200 roubles, and by the beginning of June, this work was finished and we received the payment.

On June 24, 1899, a ship arrived in Nel'kan to get the tea. Iakutsk governor-general Skripitsin and a doctor came on it. Skripitsin was somewhat sick and the doctors recommended him to go to Nel'kan and bathe in the waters of the Maia river, as much as possible. The water in the Maia was very therapeutic. Upon his arrival in Nel'kan, the governor invited brother Vasiliĭ to see him on board the ship in his cabin and discussed some matters with him. Then the governor was invited for tea by Filipov, and after this visit the governor and the doctor dropped by our house, where the governor spent about an hour with us. We talked in detail about such things as, "How do you live here? What are you doing? Why aren't you ploughing the land?" We replied that first, there was no suitable land here. Second, to clear off the taiga one needs young healthy people. There were only three of us there, and the third one was already elderly. He fully understood our situation and asked, "What could I do?" We told him, "If you want to ease our difficult situation, let us go to Notor to our brothers, where we will work as hard as we can." The governor was a good person after all; he understood the difficulty of our situation and said, "Then take the same ship back." We thanked him for treating us so nicely. They left. The ship was supposed to be docked for three days and nights in order to load the tea. We started getting ready for the departure.

This news soon reached the Filipovs. Pëtr Dmitrievich came to visit us and said, "Is it true that you are leaving us?" We said, "Yes, the governor is letting us go." "It can't be, I will go and ask the governor not to let you leave." Of course, he said this jokingly, but they in earnest felt sorry to let us go. Firstly, we became well acquainted, secondly, when leaving for Iakutsk they did not worry about their household and trusted us with it. Thus, we lived at the Filipovs' as if they were our close relatives, they did us lots of good, and we will keep good memories of them forever. We lived with them exactly for a year. On the 26th, the loading of tea was finished. We boarded the ship, said good-bye to Nel'kan and left for Notor.

Notes

1. Ust'-Notora (Notora/Notor) was a small village in the Iakut (Yakut) region of Siberia in the delta of the Notora river where it is joined by the Aldan river. The village's name means "Mouth (Delta) of the Notora river." Two versions of the name of the river and the village are found not only in this book, but in other Russian sources as well: Notor and Notora.
2. Skoptsy were a religious sect that originated in Russia in the eighteenth century. The name of the sect comes from the word "oskopit'" (castrate).
3. Petropavlovsk(oe) is a village on the bank of Aldan river in Iakut (Yakut) region founded by Skoptsy in the late eighteenth century. It is located to the south-east of Iakutsk (over 300 km distance).
4. Nel'kan is a town in Siberia in Iakut (Yakut) Republic, Russia.
5. Tungusic people are a group of indigenous people of eastern Siberia who speak Tungusic languages.
6. Iakuts (Yakuts or Sakha people) are the indigenous population of the Republic of Saha, a subject of the Russian Federation. Iakutiia is located in north-eastern Siberia. Iakuts (Yakuts) speak the Yakut language.
7. Aian is a small Russian port town in Khabarovsk region on the Okhotsk Sea.
8. Iakutsk (Yakutsk) is a sub-Arctic city in Siberia with a harsh continental climate. During winters, it is one of the coldest cities in the world. It is the homeland of the Yakut (Sakha) people, the indigenous population of the area. It was used by the Russian government as a place of exile. Today it is the capital of Sakha republic.

CHAPTER 22

Life in Notor, Iakutsk and Other Areas

We arrived at Notor[1] on June 29th. We were greeted by Doukhobor brothers, and also by a few sisters who had just arrived from the Caucasus about two weeks earlier and had visited our relatives there. The meeting was a very happy one; there was no end to questions and stories. We asked them how our relatives were doing, whether they were all healthy and well. They told us about everything. Then we switched to talking about their journey, how it was, and whether it was safe.

Such a journey from the Caucasus to Iakutsk[2] is not an easy or safe one for women to make, but with help from good people, their entire journey went safely. Golitsyn, the commander-in-chief, appointed a guide to accompany them from Tiflis[3] to Irkutsk.[4] That guide helped them with everything, particularly where they had to change transportation. He addressed the senior ticket collector, and all was taken care of in the best way. Also on behalf of our community, one elderly man, Nikolasha Chevel'deev, was delegated to go with them. In addition, following a request by Lev N. Tolstoy, they were also accompanied by Prokofiĭ N. Sokol'nikov, a resident of Iakutsk. He became acquainted with Tolstoy in Moscow, and since he had to travel from Moscow to Iakutsk, he respected the request of Lev Nikolaevich. He joined the sisters in Rĭazhsk.

Anna I. Gromova took an active role in transporting the sisters from Irkutsk. There was a total of 29 sisters and 9 children. Everybody travelled on horse carts as far as Kachug.[5] From there they travelled by boat on the Lena river as far as Zhigalov. In Zhigalov,[6] they changed from boats to a ship sailing to Iakutsk. Thirteen sisters stayed in Iakutsk because their husbands were there, and twelve sisters arrived at Notor on board the same Gromova's ship that went to Nel'kan for the load of tea. All this was a charity by Anna Ivanovna Gromova; she paid for the whole journey from Irkutsk to Notora. Such a great act of charity merits full gratitude not only from the sisters but also from all the Doukhobors.

When we arrived at Notor, some Notor brothers were in Iakutsk. First, they were not allowed to live in Iakutsk, even for temporary employment. However, when the governor's house was being built, they were allowed to live in Iakutsk because they were hired as construction workers. The construction of the whole house was contracted for the lowest price, and they were promised that when they finished this house, they would be able to stay in Iakutsk, and would even be given a plot for their own housing. With those promises, they started constructing the house. Every worker was paid 50 kopecks with no extra expenses covered. When they finished the house, they were given one lot of land 12 miles away from the city and another one 150 miles away from the city close to Amga.[7] When they were leaving Notor, they promised to live helping each other. But this did not last long. The circumstances were against it. Since they were allowed to stay there and were even given lots, they had to settle with their own individual households. Thus they were done with Notor and never came back there. However, they did do lots of work in Notor, they lived there the whole summer, together they put up a large house and they also cleared the land from wood for farming. All this was left for the benefit of the Doukhobors remaining in Notor.

In Notor, brothers started getting their household together. They all lived in that one house. In addition to the house, they built a small grain barn and a roofed shed. They had 12 horses and about 15 cattle. They developed some land where they sowed rye, the spring type, similar to wheat, it is sewn in the spring. Our own family—brothers Fedia and Pronia—were in Notor. No elders got to Iakutsk either. The elderly were Vania Usachëv, Misha Popov, Nikolasha Malov, Vasia Shcherbakov and Nikolasha Goncharov, and the rest were young married and single men. There were up to 50 people and they all lived together as a commune and as one family.

Soon after our arrival, it was time for haymaking. Many brothers were making hay, and about six people started adding to the structures. They built a good mill, a smithy, a bath house and added a small shed for the cattle.

When they started harvesting, the rye did not come out very well. It was slightly touched by frost, and there was little of it. Since there was not enough bread for the winter, they had to go seek employment in the Skoptsy[8] villages of Petropavlovskoe[9] and Troitskoe.[10] We decided to go there by boat. There were seven of us. We took two small boats, on which we loaded our clothes and food supplies. On the 20th of September, we said good-byes to our brothers and sisters and set out on the journey. First we had to go down the Notora river as far as the Aldan river and then go up the Aldan. We pulled the boats up the current. During this journey, we suffered a lot and instead of five to six days, as the local people normally make it, it took us 10 days of suffering until we arrived in the Skoptsy village of Petropavlovskoe, where we were greeted by our brother (by birth[11]) Prokofiĭ Vasil'evich.

He invited all of us to his dwelling and treated us with whatever God sent him. He was living in one old Skopets's house. As Prokofiĭ said, that old man was 100 years old, had a small decrepit house, lived alone and nobody was looking after him. The old Skopets did not attend to any business, he saved some money in his time and was now spending it in his old age. Because of this old man's situation, Prokofiĭ offered to live with him in order to serve and help him. The old man was incredibly happy about it, and this was how they came to live together. When I arrived, I also stayed in their house, and the three of us lived together.

My mates found employment and worked as hired help. I was destined not to work the whole winter, as in Notor I caught a fever, and when we travelled down the river, I developed a full-blown illness. I was so sick the whole winter that I felt barely alive. Brother Prokofiĭ worked and earned our sustenance. Our nephew Fëdor G. Aniutushkin also lived in this village. He lived at a Skopets man's house and got hired for a year. He often came to visit us, and if we needed anything, he always helped out. In spring, I fully recovered from my illness, and I also started working.

The Skoptsy are Russian people and they are very good. They had lived there for about 30 years. They were all exiled from Russia for their convictions and their belief in Christ, that is, for Skoptsy beliefs. From the beginning of their settlement, they suffered a lot and had to undergo severe trials. The place where they were forced to live was totally deserted, there were no villages and the town was too far away. Rye flour in those days could cost as much as seven roubles per bushel, and everything else was also very expensive there. According to the stories of the old man Dorofeĭ Il'ich about the past, they had lived through so many sufferings and tortures that one's heart shivers with fear and tears come to eyes. Merciful Lord, people had to survive through so much and they had already survived a lot.

From the first year of their settlement, they started to develop the land so that they could grow wheat. The forest there was huge and very thick, so they spent a lot of effort in developing the land. Many of them died having caught a cold. They toiled so much developing the land, but nothing came out of their ploughing. For seven years all the grain was destroyed by frost. They were exhausted, exasperated by this long hard toil and they decided to leave these lands and move somewhere to a different place. However, the government persuaded them to stay for at least one more year, and gave them free grain for eating and for sowing. They stayed, and in the eighth year, they had a bountiful harvest, without frost damage. This gladdened their hearts and gave them hope for a better future. Gathering their remaining strength, they resumed the toil. Now, thanks to that toil, they all lived well, and they all, without exception, had enough not only for oneself, but also for sale to others.

They were very good people and were ready to die for their convictions. They did not eat any meat, except for fish. They did not drink alcohol, did not smoke tobacco, one could not hear a single swear word from them. In everything, they followed a great modesty and fairness. Those brothers and sisters were all hard working, one could say even to an excess, and they were frugal. They all had been saving up, as they say, for the rainy day, that is, when they got old. This is because following their religious convictions, they did not leave an inheritance behind them. They took their understanding from the Gospel and from the teaching of Christ where Christ says, "There are some eunuchs, who were so born from their mother's womb; and there are some eunuchs, who were made eunuchs of men: and there be eunuchs, who have made themselves eunuchs for the kingdom of heaven's sake."[12] They paid attention to this text and spent their lives according to it, and therefore, they procured means for their old age. Because of this, they displayed thriftiness and excessive labour. This was a manifestation of their free will, and nobody could condemn them for it, even for their thriftiness.

The summer passed, and from November, I started threshing for Semën Ivanovich Domashchenko. I was getting a monthly salary of 12 roubles. Semën Ivanovich was a well-to-do man; he had lots of grain fields, a horse-powered mill, six horses and four cows. He lived together with his sister, and hired help yearly. His help was my nephew Fedia. First, we were delivering the grain from the fields, and then there was threshing. The threshing was done by horses with rollers. First, the threshing floor is poured with water, so that it becomes one whole slab of ice. While threshing during severe frosts one gets frostbites on the cheeks and nose. When the threshing was over, we carried hay, and then firewood from the forest. I lived with Domashchenko for three and a half months. Semën Ivanovich was a good person; he did not even consider us as his workers, he simply called us his friends and brothers. When he was paying us for the work, he always tried to pay even more than what was due, and tried to bargain about it. Because of the way he treated us, Semën Ivanovich deserves a good memory for eternity.

In the last days of February, I went to Notor to visit my brothers by birth and also all my brothers and sisters in spirit. On my way, I made a stop in the village of Ust'-Maĭskoe[13] to see the police officer Aleksandr Il'ich Aslamov. He had just arrived from Amga and brought many letters from relatives in Canada. He gave me all the letters that were to be sent to Notor. I arrived in Notor where everybody was glad to see me and to get the letters I brought. While we were talking, I took out the letters and gave them to everyone present. Everybody started reading. My brothers (by birth) and I received a total of six letters from our mother and relatives. From these letters we could see that they were all healthy and well, but our mother was very worried about us, and in a few lines she expressed her maternal feelings. She wrote as follows, "We live well in Canada, thank God, brothers and sisters support me and my family, and for this, I am extremely grateful to them all, God save them. All this is well, but my dear children whom I carried in my womb and nourished with my breast are far away somewhere. I thought that they would pay me due respect in my old age. Even now I am not giving up, but I keep aspiring and hoping that God our Lord will not forsake me and at least in the end of my life of suffering will send me a consolation, and lift my burden. But sometimes an unwanted thought comes and it tells me: there is no way you can see your sons again. You are already old, your years are coming to an end, and you are getting closer to death, and your sons, as they say it in fairytales, are across 27 lands in the 30th kingdom.[14] But I chase away this thought and tell myself the opposite. Even if I am not destined to see all of them again, at least I have to see the younger ones by all means before passing into eternity." This same evening we decided to write a letter with a request to the empress on behalf of our mother. This letter should go to Canada and there our mother should read it, copy it, sign her name and send it to the empress to St. Petersburg.[15] The text of this letter will be given here in full.

After staying as a guest in Notora for a while, I went back to Petropavlovskoe. I spent another summer and winter there. We received a letter from our mother, who wrote that she received the letter to the empress, read it, signed and was sending it to St. Petersburg along with this letter to us. The letter was sent via Vladimir Grigor'evich Chertkov, who even rewrote this letter in English and sent it to its destination.

Although I was expecting a positive answer to that letter, at the same time, the opposite thought appeared, that although the empress would read this letter, she would not find it possible to grant this request, as she had never experienced anything like this in her own life that could make her focus a little on this request and consider it rationally. "How come that old woman had seven sons, and all of them by the order of the empress's husband were taken away and exiled a few thousand miles apart, so how can she live through the last days of her life, and what impact does it have on her maternal heart? Since the empress is the mother to her own children, she should be able to understand this situation." Another thought arising in connection with the previous one was, "What happens if the empress does not do this, if she does not let you go to your mother? You are free to find an opportunity and go without asking the government at all, and through this, you will prove your love to your mother, as well as prove to the empress that she has no power, and consequently, it is useless to approach her with such a request. If she is proud of her power because of confusion and lack of understanding, then the action will prove her powerless."

I tried to object to this thought, that maybe this was wrong. Wouldn't I be considered a fugitive? But a voice responded to this objection, "Can't you see that you are not committing any criminal offence for which your conscience could reproach or punish you later. You only want to go to your mother, find her alive, quench her heart's desire, and at least during her last days pay her your debt of a son, for coming to this life thanks to her. Knowing all this, knowing your duty that one should consider necessary, would you really stay in Iakutsk Siberian taiga and would you justify your actions by the fact that some empress did not let you go? Don't you feel you are free in spirit and in body? You came into this life independently of all those empresses, and you have an equal share with the same very empress for a particular existence. You understand that the one who sent you into this life never left you entrusted to other people, and consequently there is no need to ask them about this noble action, whether you should stay in Iakutsk or go to your mother. And regarding your fear that other people would consider you a fugitive, your conscience should not in the least suffer because of this, and reasonable people who feel the mother's love to her children and who know the child's debt to the mother, would say nothing to you except for good wishes and a happy journey."

This is what I decided, that is I decided to wait for permission, and in the worst case, leave without asking anyone. I wrote about this decision to brother Pëtr Verigin in Obdorsk[16] and got a response. He wrote as follows, "About going to see the mother, I fully share your opinion." All the letters to Pëtr Vasil'evich, as the reader already knows, were looked through by the government, and one had to write skillfully about such a secret as a person under surveillance going abroad.

The month of April came and I decided to leave Petropavlovskoe for Notor and live there until the end of May. When the boats loaded with tea were to leave from Nel'kan, I would take one to get to Iakutsk. It was already the mud season. During other times, one could always find company among the Iakuts[17] also going to Notor. But because of the mud season, there weren't any, so I had to walk all the way on foot alone.

On April 10th, I said good-bye to my brothers and set off on the road. I took food with me that according to my calculations should be enough to last me until Notor because one could not find bread among the Iakuts. The Iakuts only consumed very little bread, if any at all, they mostly ate animal meat, and in summer, they caught fish abundant in rivers and lakes.

I knew the way and was accustomed to staying overnight in yurts[18] because I already made this way twice, although before, I travelled on horses and not on foot. I had to walk the same distance as we covered on horses earlier, otherwise there would be no place to stay for the night. It was a little difficult to walk, but I persevered. I got up early in the morning and arrived at the place to spend the night when it was already dusk. When one entered a yurt, there would be firewood burning in the fireplace at full flame, the whole family would be assembled together getting ready for tea drinking. They were very curious and immediately started asking questions, "Where are you from? Where are you going to?"

For example, they asked, "kapse dogor," which means, "Tell us, friend!" "Khantan kellia" means "where are you going from?" "Tokh chukhaĭ bar" means "what's your news?" Then they invited me to take off my coat and gave me the place closest to the fire, and then we all proceeded to tea drinking. They used brick pressed tea; a three-pound tea brick cost

30 or 40 kopecks. They drank tea without sugar, but with milk, if it was available, if there was none, then without milk. After this, they brought a bundle of rye into the yurt, spread some leather and started threshing. Then they cleaned the grains, poured them into a frying pan and put it close to the fireplace. The grains dried immediately and then the Iakuts started grinding them. In the corner of the yurt, there were two small stones. The top stone had a handle attached to it to turn the stone, and they started grinding. This lasted for about half an hour. The dough was made very thick and it was spread into long stretched pieces. This dough was pasted onto a thin splinter of wood, which was stuck with one side into the ground next to the fireplace. And this was how they baked their bread. When it was ready, it was served with dinner, one chunk of bread for the whole family of ten people. Besides bread, for dinner they cooked a big pot of meat of domestic cattle or very often bear, deer, moose or any other possible kind of animal. A Iakut has no mercy for any animal, he kills and eats it. The living conditions did not allow much cleanliness, and the Iakut people were therefore frequented by contagious diseases, such as smallpox and others. They were friendly, hospitable and did not hurt people and they had no barbarian customs. However, alcoholism, smoking tobacco and card play were spread among them to the highest degree. They said that they had not had these things in the old days because there was nowhere to get them from. However, when they started to be visited by priests who tried to convert them to Christianity, for their personal gain, the priests started bringing in this devastating poison. Now wherever the priests had been to, one could say all the Iakuts, women being no exception, were corrupted beyond turning back. They prayed to God, bowed in front of the man-made icons, that the priests supplied them with, but at the same time for a bottle of alcohol or vodka, a Iakut would give you whatever you may want. Iakuts had no money but they had various expensive furs such as foxes, beavers, etc. There were also silver foxes, but they were rare, and priced at 100 roubles or higher. And a Iakut would give away this fox for a bottle of alcohol. Such a profit led the priests to a temptation and they corrupted the whole tribe. I described here very briefly the life of these two peoples who lived close to one another: Skoptsy and Iakuts.

I arrived at Notor at midday on the 14th. Everybody was well and healthy and they were surprised to see me. They were probably thinking, "Why is this unexpected guest here?" It was the first day of Easter, of the luminous resurrection of Christ. Everybody was cheerful and dressed in their best

Sunday clothes. They asked me whether there was any news. The elderly were asking whether we were allowed to go to America to join our relatives, as this was their cherished dream. I said that I had not heard anything.

This is how I stayed in Notor waiting for the boats. During this time, we talked everything through. We decided to go to our mother by all means. There was no point in waiting for the response to the letter. On May 29, 1902, when the boats started sailing, I said good-bye to everyone, even to Notor. Brother Vasiliĭ accompanied me as far as Aldan along the river Notora on a small boat. He gave me a ride closer to the ship, and I changed quickly from the boat onto the ship and from the ship I shouted: "Farewell, brother, maybe we are not destined to see each other again!" and tears started flowing down my face. He took his hat off and shouted something to me, but I could not discern what it was. We were already far apart. The ship was quickly carried by the water down the Aldan river. This is how my journey to America and to my mother began.

Notes

1. Ust'-Notora (Notora/Notor) was a small village in the Iakut (Yakut) region of Siberia in the delta of the Notora river where it is joined by the Aldan river. The village's name means "Mouth (Delta) of the Notora river." Two versions of the name of the river and the village are found not only in this book, but in other Russian sources as well: Notor and Notora.
2. Iakutsk (Yakutsk) is a sub-Arctic city in Siberia with a harsh continental climate. During winters, it is one of the coldest cities in the world. It is the homeland of the Yakut (Sakha) people, the indigenous population of the area. It was used by the Russian government as a place of exile. Today it is the capital of Sakha republic.
3. Tiflis is the old name of modern Tbilisi, the capital of the country of Georgia. In the nineteenth century, it was the capital of Tiflis guberniia, which was a part of the Russian Empire.
4. Irkutsk is one of the largest cities in Siberia, located in Southern Siberia close to the Baĭkal Lake.
5. Kachug (Katchoug, Kachuga) is a town north-east of Irkutsk located in the Irkutsk area of Siberia.
6. Zhygalov (Zhigalovo) is a town in the Irkutsk region of Siberia.
7. Amga is a village in Amga area of the Sakha (Iakut) Republic, Russian Federation.
8. Skoptsy were a religious sect that originated in Russia in the eighteenth century. The name of the sect comes from the word "oskopit'" (castrate).

9. Petropavlovsk(oe) is a village on the bank of Aldan river in Iakut (Yakut) region founded by Skoptsy in the late eighteenth century. It is located to the south-east of Iakutsk (over 300 km distance).
10. Troitskoe was a village in Iakutiia (Republic of Saha), which was a settlement of Skoptsy.
11. In some places in the text, the author specifies whether a brother he refers to was an actual family member (brother by birth), as opposed to a Doukhobor or Molokan brother (as a generic way of reference within the group).
12. Matthew 19:12.
13. Ust'-Maĭskoe (modern—Ust'-Maia) is a town in the Republic of Saha (Iakutiia, a subject of the Russian Federation) located on the bank of the Aldan river at its confluence with the Maia river, about 400 km away from Iakutsk.
14. "za trideviat' zemel' v tridesiatom gosudarstve" (across 27 lands in the 30th kingdom) is a Russian folk expression meaning "very far away."
15. St. Petersburg was the capital of Imperial Russia in 1713–1728 and 1732–1918. It was also called Petrograd and Leningrad during some periods in the twentieth century. Now, it is the second largest city in Russia with a population of over 5 million people. It is known for its museums, architecture, music, theatre and other cultural attractions. Its historic centre is a UNESCO World Heritage Site.
16. Obdorsk (now Salekhard) is a town in north-western Siberia on the Ob' river. It was often used as a place of exile in Imperial Russia.
17. Iakuts (Yakuts or Sakha people) are the indigenous population of the Republic of Saha, a subject of the Russian Federation. Iakutiia is located in north-eastern Siberia. Iakuts (Yakuts) speak the Yakut language.
18. Yurt is a traditional round-shaped dwelling supported by a lattice with skins or felt around it. Yurts could be easily assembled and transported to support a nomadic lifestyle. Yurts are found among many other Asian and Siberian peoples.

CHAPTER 23

A Trip to Russia

I arrived in Iakutsk[1] and stayed with my close friend, Pëtr I. Shchukin. Before I was put into prison, we had always treated each other with warmth and sincerity. When the arrests began, he was arrested and put into jail as well. He was not liable for military duty, but he was arrested for his trip to Ordagan, where eight Doukhobors including his brother Larion were doing military service. A week after his visit there, all eight Doukhobors in Ordagan turned in their guns. The interrogation and questioning started, and some other soldiers reported that a week ago there was one Doukhobor visitor who spoke with the soldiers. He was arrested for this as the principal criminal and thrown into jail.

God's cause drew us so much closer together that now we were willing to sacrifice our lives for each other. When we met, he gave up all his work assignments, and we went to the city. I saw many brothers who lived there. All were glad that I came to visit. On the second day, Shchukin asked me, "Wouldn't you like to go to America to your relatives?" I said, "Of course, I want to go, but I need a passport." He said, "I will get the passports, but the police are watching carefully when the passenger ships go up the Lena river." We decided to leave. Since in Iakutsk the authorities watched the ships about to sail off very strictly, we decided to go via Nel'kan[2] to the port of Aian.[3] There we planned to take a Chinese ship to make our way to America in secret. I knew Nel'kan, and from there to Aian, one only had to walk for 208 miles. These 208 miles, however, were very difficult to traverse in summer because of the tundra and the marshes.

© The Author(s) 2019
G. V. Verigin, *The Chronicles of Spirit Wrestlers' Immigration to Canada*, https://doi.org/10.1007/978-3-030-18525-1_23

Shchukin did not object to this plan, and on the third day of my stay in Iakutsk, Gromova's ship was setting off to Nel'kan for a load of tea. Both of us boarded this ship and we left Iakutsk on it. In the Skoptsy[4] village of Petropavlovskoe,[5] I met an Aian policeman Vladimir F. Popoff. He was a Tolstoyan,[6] and I already knew him from before. When I saw him, I told him without hesitation that my friend and I wanted to get through his port on a Chinese ship to go to America. He considered this plan and concluded that it would be better for us to go via Iakutsk than Nel'kan. He said, "This route is too perilous, and you can get lost forever without achieving your goal." We totally agreed with him. The ship went to Nel'kan and we stayed in Petropavlovskoe.

When the ship returned, we boarded it and went to Iakutsk again. Since the police inspection was too strict there, we decided not to take the ship in Iakutsk but to walk the length of one prisoner transport station as far as Tapaga on foot. Here in Iakutsk, we asked one acquaintance to board the ship and take all our luggage, and watch out for policemen, who could have been sent somewhere by the government and in whose hands we could fall while boarding the ship. We agreed with that man that when the ship was approaching Tapaga, he would give us a secret sign. If the police were on board the ship, he would waive a red handkerchief, and then we would not get on board. If there were no police, then he would waive a white handkerchief, this was the sign that it was safe.

At midnight, we walked out from Iakutsk on the way to Tapaga, where we expected to arrive by 9 am. We got there safely and still had about an hour to wait until the arrival of the ship. Then, we saw steam rising up from about two miles ahead, which was the steamship approaching! This time span seemed very long, we were both sad and happy, as our thoughts galloped around when the moment of our happiness or misery was coming closer.

At last, the ship approached and we started to look at the bow, where the man who agreed to inform us of our joy or sorrow was supposed to be, and we waited for the verdict to be delivered any minute. One more minute, and all will be resolved. We saw him waving a white handkerchief. He waived again, and we also waived back with a handkerchief. The captain slowed down the ship and three sailors quickly picked us up in a boat. After the boat picked us up and took us to the ship, we climbed up the ladder. Almost all the people gathered to watch us. At this time, we ourselves thought that we were suspicious individuals. However, the public did not suspect anything and just watched us climbing up the ladder. Only one half-drunk priest clung up to Shchukin with questions about why we did not board the ship in Iakutsk. Shchukin answered something clever and the priest left us alone.

We looked for a place for ourselves, but all the cabins were already occupied, and we stayed on deck. It was on July 7, 1902. We bought the tickets as far as Alekma[7] because we were afraid that the captain might become suspicious. There we met one man we knew whose name was Andreiashinko. He was a good person. When we saw each other, I recognized him immediately and he looked at me in disbelief. I stretched my hand for a handshake and said, "Be nice to your neighbor." He answered, "No worries, but are you leaving?"—"Yes, as you see."—"God help you to reach your desired goal." With these words, he took the kettle, brought hot water, brewed tea and treated us to it to celebrate our happy departure.

In the afternoon of the 10th, we arrived at Alekma. My brother-in-law Ivan E. Konkin and my sister Varvara lived there. I wanted to see them very much. When they threw down the ladder, I got off the ship. It was the day of a market fair, and there were many people around. I met a Skopets there who showed me the way to Konkin's house. I went there and Konkin came out to greet me in the yard. He was just beginning to recover from an illness. My sister was busy in the kitchen cooking dinner. We entered the room. My sister heard my voice, dropped what she was doing, approached us and started kissing me. She had tears in her eyes. They thought we were dead. A month ago, Vasiliĭ I. Golubov passed by along the same route. He met Konkin and told him that Grisha and Shchukin also left for America, but they went from Nel'kan to Aian and China. Konkin knew very well that we did not know a word in any language save our own, and they thought that if we went to China, we would not ever get out of there. They only had one hope that the police would detain us in Aian and then we would be saved.

I stayed with them for about two hours, and they treated me to everything they had. When the captain blew his second whistle, I said good-bye to them and left. Good-byes were indescribable. On the one hand, there was solemn joy in them. My sister even talked about how I would come to Canada, how I would see my elderly mother and how glad she would be to see me. I replied to her, "All this would be great, but if I am detained somewhere by police, what would happen then?" But they told me with some conviction that this would not happen, "Firstly, the dangers are almost behind, and the farther away you go, the safer it will be. Secondly, we are sure that in this good deed, the Lord will assist you and you will reach your goal safely."

I went back to the ship where my friend was already waiting for me. We bought some food for the road. Soon, there came the third whistle, the ladder was taken in and the ship sailed off. We continued our journey, Thank God. We bought the tickets to Kirensk.[8] We arrived at Kirensk on the 17th and at Iskut[9] on the 19th. From there we travelled by post horses in a carriage. This is how we arrived in Irkutsk[10] on July 27. We stayed there overnight, and on the second day around 2 pm, we set out for Russia on a post-passenger train. Here we were completely safe. We bought the tickets to Samara,[11] 4000 miles ahead. We arrived in Samara on August 4, and at 12 noon we left Samara for Astrakhan'. We went down the river Volga on board a post-passenger steamship "The Empress." We arrived in Astrakhan'[12] on August 7. On the 8th, we went from Astrakhan' to Petrovsk[13] over the Caspian Sea. From Petrovsk we bought direct railway tickets to Batum.[14] And thus we went there by railway passing by Elizavetpol',[15] Dzegam[16] and Akstafa.[17]

This area was our home, where we knew everything. We hoped to run into some Doukhobors travelling to Tiflis[18] by rail, but we did not meet anyone. We arrived in Tiflis, where we had to change trains, and then we set off for Batum. We arrived in Batum at 10 pm. We were not in the least familiar with Batum, and did not know where we could stay overnight. We were afraid of staying in a hotel, as they would look at our passports there. We walked out of the terminal building into the street. There we saw a street sign "Tavern," where they cooked food for anyone. We walked into it. The keepers were Georgian. We asked them, "Can we spend the night here?" They said, "Yes, you can." We had some tea and went to bed. We could not fall asleep for a long time as we were facing very serious business the next day that could end with success, or not. Until Batum, all we had to do was to get new tickets, where necessary. Now we had to prepare to cross the state border, where there was strict surveillance by the police.

Notes

1. Iakutsk (Yakutsk) is a sub-Arctic city in Siberia with a harsh continental climate. During winters, it is one of the coldest cities in the world. It is the homeland of the Yakut (Sakha) people, the indigenous population of the area. It was used by the Russian government as a place of exile. Today it is the capital of Sakha republic.
2. Nel'kan is a town in Siberia in Iakut (Yakut) Republic, Russia.
3. Aian is a small Russian port town in Khabarovsk region on the Okhotsk Sea.

4. Skoptsy were a religious sect that originated in Russia in the eighteenth century. The name of the sect comes from the word "oskopit'" (castrate).
5. Petropavlovsk(oe) is a village on the bank of Aldan river in Iakut (Yakut) region founded by Skoptsy in the late eighteenth century. It is located to the south-east of Iakutsk (over 300 km distance).
6. "Tolstoyan" means a follower of Tolstoy's teachings.
7. Alekma (Olëkma), modern Olëkminsk, is a town in the Iakut region of Siberia.
8. Kirensk is a town in Siberia to the north-east of Irkutsk, located between Irkutsk and Iakutsk.
9. Iskut is probably "Ust'-Kut," a town in Irkutsk region, eastern Siberia.
10. Irkutsk is one of the largest cities in Siberia, located in Southern Siberia close to the Baĭkal Lake.
11. Samara is a city in the eastern European part of Russia located high up the flow of the Volga river close to the confluence of the Volga and the Samara rivers.
12. Astrakhan' (or Astrakhan) is a town in southern Russia located in the delta of the Volga river where it flows into the Caspian Sea.
13. Petrovsk is modern city of Makhachkala, the capital of Dagestan Republic, Russian Federation. The city is located on the western shore of the Caspian Sea.
14. Batum (modern name Batumi) is a port city on the Black sea coast. It is the second largest city of the country of Georgia, which at the time of the narrative, was a part of the Russian Empire.
15. Elizavetpol' (later Kirovabad, since 1989, Ganja) was the capital of Elizavetpol' guberniia in the Russian Empire. Since the separation of Azerbaijan from the Soviet Union, it is one of the largest cities in Azerbaijan.
16. Dzegam most likely refers to modern Dzagam (Dzegam), a town in Azerbaijan. At the time of the narrative, Azerbaijan was a part of the Russian Empire.
17. Akstafa refers to Aghstafa, a town in Azerbaijan close to the borders with Armenia and Georgia. At the time of the narrative, Azerbaijan was a part of the Russian Empire.
18. Tiflis is the old name of modern Tbilisi, the capital of the country of Georgia. In the nineteenth century, it was the capital of Tiflis guberniia, which was a part of the Russian Empire.

CHAPTER 24

A Trip Abroad

I have not yet explained that when I was just considering leaving Iakutsk,[1] I wrote to Canada to my close friend Pavel V. Planidin, and I asked him whether he had any close acquaintances in Batum[2] who could assist me with going abroad. He, indeed, knew such people and he sent me their first and last names. The next day, we would have to find them. We slept for no more than two hours. At dawn, we got up, and when people started to walk along the city attending to their own business, we also left the tavern and walked ahead.

First, we had to find Tret'iakov. It turned out he was not in the city. He had been gone somewhere for a long time. We decided that only one of us should go to see the next person on our list. I went to see him, and my friend went back to our quarters. I came up to the house and rang the doorbell. A servant came out. I asked, "Is your master at home?" She said, "Yes."—"I would like to see him." She left and then came back out and said, "He does not receive anyone here at home, you have to go to his office," and she added, "He will be there soon." I did not know where his office was and decided to spend the time there so that I could see him when he walked out of the house. In half an hour, he walked out of the door. I approached him and said, "Are you Mr. Stephens, the English consul?" He said, "Yes."—"I have some business with you."—"What is it?"—"I want to move to Canada, but I do not know how to arrange this."—"You have to come to the office," and he made an appointment and gave me the address where to find the office.

I went back to my friend and told him everything and we cheered up a little since things seemed to be on track. It was time to go to the office. I went there and knocked on the door. He opened the door and said, "Come in" and locked the door. There was no one else in the office. He started asking me who I was, where from and why I wanted to go there [to Canada]. I only met him for the first time and I did not know his attitude to people. And yet I had to approach him with this very important, honest and at the same time brave undertaking with which only honesty could help, from both my side, and from the side of the person I approached with my story. I decided to tell him the whole truth, as it was the only way a person could understand my situation.

I started explaining, "I am a Doukhobor from Transcaucasia,[3] Elizavetpol'[4] guberniia. My name is Grigoriĭ Verigin. In 1897, for our Doukhobor cause, along with others, I was exiled by the government for an indefinite term to Iakutsk district under police supervision. After having lived there for about 6 years, without notifying the government, I decided to go to Canada, where I have an elderly mother, wife and two children. I managed to travel safely so far, but I do not know what the outcome of my risk is going to be. I have always put my hopes in God, and I now trust in Him. I also ask you to understand my situation and to help me with granting my request, which now only depends on your good will. My earlier mentioned relatives already moved together with other Doukhobors to Canada. I personally do not know you, as you do not know me, but Pavel Planidin wrote to me about you. You hopefully still remember him, and he assured me that you are a kind-hearted person and that you may do all this."

My last name "Verigin" seemed to interest him. After my explanations, he looked at me and asked, "Are you a relative of Pëtr Verigin who is now residing in Obdorsk,[5] Tobol'sk guberniia?" I said, "He is my brother."—"And do you have a passport?"—"Yes, I do." I gave it to him, he looked at it and said, "The passport is not verified anywhere, and the name here is different than the one you say."—"I did not verify my passport, because we did not stop anywhere to show it to the police, and this is a different name, because as I explained to you, I did not receive this passport from the government, but from a person to whom I paid 15 roubles for it, and it could not contain my real name."—"Are you alone?"—"No, there are two of us."—"It's a pity a British steamship has just left from here, and you would have to wait for about five or six days."—"This is fine, if you could only arrange our business."—"All right, I will try, but you will have to come by my office every day for an update: the steamship might arrive earlier." I thanked him for his kindness, and went back to our quarters.

I went back and explained everything to my friend. We were both very glad that our matter seemed to be positively resolved. We had to change the accommodation, as the policemen on duty often checked it. We found a more convenient place and moved there. I went to the office every day to check up on things. On the sixth day, I went to the office and found a captain of a ship there. Stephens saw me and said, "At last your waiting time is over, the ship docked yesterday." He pointed at the captain and explained, "This is the captain of the ship that you should take." And right there in front of me, he discussed how much the captain would charge us. The Captain said, "150 roubles for the two people to take you to the British town of Goole." The captain was British and he did not know a word in Russian.

After Stephens discussed everything with the captain, he turned to me and said, "You have to get on board the ship tonight, as the ship sails off tomorrow afternoon. Be careful, the police watch very strictly. In the worst case, if the police detain you, then you are on your own, and do not mix anyone else in." He meant himself. I said, "Oh, no, God be with you, you are doing such a good deed for us, and we would never pay you back in such a terrible way." He explained again, "You only need to get to the ship, and there the captain will receive you, and you will be safe. But I am warning you: do not give the money to the captain until the ship sails off, because if the police find you on the ship, the captain will deny having anything to do with you, and your money will all be lost. When the ship sails a long distance away from the pier, then you can give him the full amount of 150 roubles." I thanked him sincerely for this entire good deed that he undertook for our benefit, we said our good-byes and we left for our quarters.

On that day, we went to the pier to find out where the ship was docked. The ship was a cargo ship transporting kerosene. When we returned from the pier, we wrote letters to Iakutsk. We wrote to our relatives there as follows, "The long journey from Iakutsk to Batum went safely, thank God. Now we only have to live through this evening, during which our task will be resolved. What awaits us? Will our long journey result in happiness and success, and give lots of joy to our relatives? Or will our fate cast a different lot and perhaps tomorrow we will be on the way back to Iakutsk accompanied by guards? But we put our hopes with God, and leave our destiny to His will."

Merciful Lord! How can one express on paper everything that we felt in our souls? Everything in our souls was in turmoil. One thought or feeling quickly followed and replaced another. One cannot explain it. Such moments cannot be rendered in any description. We were calm all the time until that day. But when we learned that on that day we had to replace our dreams with reality, the closer the time came, the more worried we became in our hearts. We packed and tied up our belongings. We had three pieces of luggage. We called in the owner of our accommodation, thanked him and offered him money for the stay, but he did not take it. He said that we would need the money for our journey. He was a Muslim. Then he told us that we should not appear on the pier with the luggage because we could be arrested. —"And what should we do then?" —"I will call in a man who will carry your luggage, but you have to walk separately from him." We trusted him and agreed to his offer. He called in a man who took our luggage. He was a working man who made his living by transporting luggage and other things. We took a separate way. My friend and I split up: he went along one street and I went along another. On my way, I dropped the letters into a mailbox. As I approached the pier, electric lights were on everywhere and it was as light as in daytime. I passed by the first control booth. The officer on duty was busy with something and only after I walked a few metres past the booth he called after me: "Where are you going, mate?" I was a little perplexed by this unexpected call, and I immediately answered, "Right there," without stopping. He called out again raising his voice, "Where are you going, mate?" I also raised my voice, "Right there," but I did not stop. He did not say anything else to me and I went up to the ship. My friend was already there and I asked him, "Have you been on board the ship already?" He said, "No." We went up to the ladder on board the ship. I asked a sailor, "Where is the captain?" The sailor was English and did not know a word in Russian. Two more of them came up to us. I insisted, "Where is the captain?" One sailor went away and brought along a Russian sailor who served on the same ship.

The sailor asked, "What do you want?"—"Where is the captain?"— "The captain went to the city early in the morning, and he has not come back yet."—"And where is the Second-in-command?"—"The Second-in-command is standing right here."—"Ask him to take us on board." He responded, "Without the captain's permission, I cannot take you on board," and he ordered us to leave the ship immediately. I tried to plead with him, but he did not want to listen to anything and insisted that we should get off the ship. When we got off, the man brought our luggage, we gave him 20 kopecks, and he left. We had only one thing left to do: wait for the captain.

About ten minutes later, a policeman came up to us and asked, "Who are you and what are these things?" We answered, "We want to see the captain to ask him whether he will hire us as sailors." He did not say anything about this, but he paid attention to our luggage and said that it needed to be carefully inspected. "Please, do us the honour." "I will bring my friend and we will inspect your luggage." Close to us, there was a Russian man who was looking after the kerosene tap. He told us: "It won't work well for you, there will soon be an officer on duty with patrol here, and he can arrest you." We were wondering what we should do.

Fortunately for us, at this time, the captain of this ship came in a boat and he asked whether there were two Russian men around. The sailors answered that they were standing by the ship. He immediately ordered two sailors to take our luggage and invited us on board. They immediately went down the ladders, took our luggage and we went on board with them. There they received us and placed us in the ship's hold in a secret compartment, and this is where we stayed until the ship sailed off.

At 3 pm, the ship blew a whistle, then the second one and the third, and it sailed off. The captain sent a sailor to invite us to come on deck. We walked out, the weather was beautiful, there was not a single cloud in the skies and the sea was perfectly calm. The ship was gaining speed, it left behind huge waves that were disappearing in the sea at a distance. We were happy and joyful: "Thank you, merciful God, that everything worked out so wonderfully, and that all our worries are banished." Our hope of achieving the desired goal to see our relatives and all the brothers and sisters was revived. This is how we parted with the country where we were born and grew up. This was on August 20, 1902. We arrived in Constantinople on August 23. We stayed there for a short while and then sailed forth. We went through the Marble Sea, Archipelago islands, the Mediterranean Sea and proceeded onto the Atlantic Ocean. So far, we travelled safely. Although the ship was rocked at times, there was no danger. We sailed to the West all the time.

The ship slowed down: it turned out that the boilers broke and they had to be repaired on the way. While one boiler was working, the other was being repaired, and on the way to Goole, each of them had to be fixed twice. Other ships passed us by. Upon entering the Atlantic Ocean, we soon turned to the North. From midnight, a strong wind from the opposite direction started blowing, the sea was highly turbulent, our ship dropped down and then was raised high above, and every giant wave poured over the deck. There was no time for the water on the deck to drain through the pipes before a new wave poured over. The wind blew for two days and nights and was getting stronger and stronger. The ship first resisted the waves, but in the end, it got tired and became their playtoy. It was tossed around like a tiny boat; the sailors were scared and did not know what to do. They were all wearing waterproofs, and the life boats were prepared and lowered. We thought, "Merciful Lord, is this the end of our existence, and the fishes of the sea are going to get our bodies?" We were giving up hope for salvation, and with every tilt of the ship, we expected death, and when the ship rose again on a wave, we thought, "Maybe it is not all over yet." I thought about my elderly mother, wife, children and all the relatives and said good-byes to all of them over the distance. What a tragedy it would be for them if we died at sea. However, the Almighty God did not will us to die such a terrible death. After two days, the wind started becoming weaker, but the sea still did not calm down and formed peaks and troughs. At last, the wind stopped completely, the sea started calming down, and our hope that we were all safe revived in us. Praise be to the Lord every day of our lives!

Notes

1. Iakutsk (Yakutsk) is a sub-Arctic city in Siberia with a harsh continental climate. During winters, it is one of the coldest cities in the world. It is the homeland of the Yakut (Sakha) people, the indigenous population of the area. It was used by the Russian government as a place of exile. Today it is the capital of Sakha republic.
2. Batum (modern name Batumi) is a port city on the Black sea coast. It is the second largest city of the country of Georgia, which at the time of the narrative, was a part of the Russian Empire.
3. Transcaucasia is an area in and around the Caucasus mountains (located between the Caspian and the Black Sea). It is comprised mostly of the territories of the modern states of Russia, Georgia, Armenia and Azerbaijan. At the time of the narrative, it was the territory of the Russian Empire.
4. Elizavetpol' (later Kirovabad, since 1989, Ganja) was the capital of Elizavetpol' guberniia in the Russian Empire. Since the separation of Azerbaijan from the Soviet Union, it is one of the largest cities in Azerbaijan.
5. Obdorsk (now Salekhard) is a town in north-western Siberia on the Ob' river, which was often used as a place of exile in Imperial Russia.

CHAPTER 25

Arrival in England. Meeting the Chertkovs

Vladimir Grigor'evich Chertkov (the first person on the left) with members of the migration committee who assisted with organizing the move of the Doukhobors to Canada

On September 10, we arrived in the town of Goole, the first English town we saw. We went downtown and bought some food and fruit. Everything was very expensive. We spent the night on the ship and at 9 am, we left to visit the Chertkovs by railway. We got their address in Batum[1] from Stephens, the English consul. Unfortunately, this turned out to be their old address, and over a year ago, they had moved 250 miles away. We went to their old address, and people explained this to us. We had to stay overnight there, and in the morning at 8 am, one Englishman took us to the railway station to put us on the train to the Chertkovs.

We had to walk over a mile to get to the station. While passing by one house, the Englishman who was showing us the way pointed at it and said, "This is Russian, Russian." We knocked on the door. A Jewish lady opened the door and said with joy, "You are Russian people, come in, come in!" We entered the room. A certain person named Zhukov lived there. He left Russia because of persecutions by the Russian government, and he lived there, wrote foreign newsletters and sent them to Russia. He was upstairs and was busy. She notified him about our arrival and he came downstairs to meet us. He received us very cordially since we were Russian, and took an interest in our successful move from Russia to England, and asked us many detailed questions. After this conversation, he asked us, "Where are you going now and how are you planning to get to Canada?" We explained that we were now on our way to the Chertkovs, and we were going to them because we did not have enough money to get to Canada, and we hoped that they would help us with it. He said that this trip was going to be very expensive, because it took 250 miles to get there, and then we would have to get back to Goole in order to take a ship to Liverpool. He asked, "Do you have any other business with them?" We said that we didn't. "If you have no other business with them, then we could probably find enough money here as well." We agreed to this. Then he asked his wife to cook a nice lunch.

After lunch he invited us to go together to an Englishman named Maude,[2] who lived seven miles away from him. Maude was closely acquainted with Tolstoy, he had a Russian wife,[3] and Zhukov was sure they would help us. They harnessed a horse and the three of us went to see Maude. This was in the evening. We walked into the room. Maude's wife greeted us and was very glad to see Russian people and received us very cordially. Soon, a samovar was brought in and she treated us to tea. We explained to her that we came to see her husband on business and explained the nature of our business. She said that her husband was away in London, but she was waiting for his return soon. In about half an hour, there was a train which he was supposed to return on. In the worst case, if he did not return on that train, she could gratify our request herself. We were very grateful. We still had not finished drinking tea when Maude entered the room and looked at the unexpected visitors with surprise. We got up and explained who we were and how we got there. He, as well as his wife, was very glad and happy to meet us, and thanked Zhukov for bringing us there. The matter was resolved and he promised to send a telegram to London to a shipping company to find out when a passenger ship was leaving from Liverpool to Quebec City. The sister of Maude's wife who came to visit them from Moscow promised to send a telegram to the Chertkovs to inform them about us, and she explained that if nobody notified them, they could get upset.

We returned back to Zhukov to spend the night there and to wait for the news about the ship. The next day Maude informed us that there were three days until the departure of the ship. The Chertkovs sent a telegram, saying that without any further delay, we should go to see them, and they would cover all the railway travel expenses. Upon Maude's invitation, we went with him to London, where in the office of a shipping company he bought us two direct tickets from Liverpool to Quebec City, and from Quebec City, a railway ticket to Yorkton for me, and to Saskatoon, for my friend. He paid a total of 190 dollars. With gratitude, we promised Maude to pay him back this money when we got to our families, but he categorically refused and explained that he was giving this money to us and it was not to be paid back. We thanked him sincerely for this charitable deed and said our good-byes cordially. He went back home and we went to the Chertkovs.

The Chertkovs, Vladimir Grigor'evich and Anna Konstantinovna, greeted us very cordially at a great distance from their house. When we saw each other, they kissed us, as it happens with a close family, and received us as if we were family to them.

Vladmir Grigor'evich was a son of a rich landlord and he himself owned 40,000 sheep of the shlënka breed and a plot of land that was 70 miles in length. When the common Doukhobor movement began, as it was described in this book, he took a big part in it, advocating for us before the government officials and even personally before the monarch. He maintained that the handling of the Doukhobors by the government was unfair and cruel. He was a Tolstoyan, one can simply say, he was a great supporter and protector of God's cause via the teaching of Jesus Christ; and for this interference, with his whole family, he was exiled to England for an indefinite period of time. We walked to their house, and on the way, they asked a lot about how we got away from Iakutsk, whether the government allowed us, or whether we went on our own. We said that we left without any permission. —"And you were not detained anywhere?" We said, "No. There were some dangerous situations, but we survived. Thank God!"—"And how glad your families will be now, particularly your mother!"—"Yes, if God grants us to get there safely, there will be no end to joy, we have not seen each other for seven years. Our mother must have aged a lot by now."—"And how old is she?"—"80."—"Yes, this is the time when people age. Are all your brothers in Iakutsk in good health?"—"Thank God."—"Aren't they missing their families?"—"Of course they do, all sorts of things happen, but it is still bearable for the young people. But there are many elderly brethren, and of course, it would be better for them to live with their families."—"It is such a pity that the government keeps them there, but the time will come, they will be liberated, and those elderly who survive, will see their families."

Engaged in such conversations, we came to their house. In the house, they immediately treated us to tea, and in an hour, dinner was served. All the time, there was no end to questions and conversation. Anna Konstantinovna asked even more questions.

After staying with them for two days, we said good-byes to them as if they were family. Vladimir Grigor'evich and his son Dima went for three stations with us on the railway to see us off. We went to Liverpool. We arrived in Liverpool on September 17, and in the evening of the same day, we left for Quebec City on board a passenger ship.

On the way, there was turbulence for two days, but there was no great danger. On September 27, at 10 am we arrived safely in Quebec City, thank God. On October 3, we arrived in Winnipeg, where my friend Pëtr I. Shchukin and I said our brotherly good-byes. He went to Saskatoon, and I waited for two days in Winnipeg for the departure of the train.

On October 5, in the evening, I arrived at Yorkton, where a wagon was already waiting for me, and two hours later we went on it to our village, which was located 40 miles away from Yorkton. By the evening of the 6th, I was approaching my village that I had never been to, but my dear family and my spiritual brothers and sisters were there. Something extraordinary was happening to me and my heart was beating fast. When I was about half a mile away from home, they saw us and recognized me. When I approached the house where my mother lived, all the brothers and sisters from the village, including even the smallest child, were in the yard and greeted me with the singing of the psalms. My mother also came out of the room. First, I came up to her and with the son's love I bowed to the ground in front of her. Then I kissed her tenderly. She was crying with joy and could hardly talk, and I comforted her. Then I kissed my wife, children and everybody who was there. Everyone was immensely rejoiced to see my return to the family, with whom I parted on September 22, 1895, and it was now October 6, 1902. In a common prayer, we all raised our praise and gratitude to God for His merciful vision and my safe arrival, and then everybody went to their homes.

Notes

1. Batum (modern name Batumi) is a port city on the Black sea coast. It is the second largest city of the country of Georgia, which at the time of the narrative, was a part of the Russian Empire.
2. Maude, Aylmer (1858–1938) was a British translator of Leo Tolstoy's writings as well as Tolstoy's friend and biographer. He also wrote a book about the Doukhobors called "A Peculiar People: the Doukhobors" (1904, New York: Funk and Wagnalls).
3. Maude's wife Louise was British but was born and raised in Moscow, Russia. Since she spoke Russian as a native speaker, G. Verigin probably assumed she was Russian.

CHAPTER 26

A Request for Relocation. A Letter by Pëtr Vasil'evich to the Empress Aleksandra Fëdorovna Romanova

From the beginning of the movement and until resettlement in America, Doukhobors suffered a lot for their beliefs in the teaching of Jesus Christ and for not resisting evil with evil.[1] Many died in separation from their families and many lost their material wealth. I can say that the total loss was about ten million roubles. Particularly affected by such sufferings were the so-called Kholodensk group, who lived in Tiflis guberniia,[2] Akhalkalak[3] district. Earlier, they had all been quite well off, but when the Tiflis governor Shervashidze dispersed them with their wives and children among the indigenous population in the mountains, where the climate was very hot, they carried the cross of their sufferings. Many of them died there, and many did not have enough to eat on a daily basis, whereas shortly before, they had their own properties, houses and everything else in abundance to support their lives. All this made them leave their Motherland Russia and move to the distant country of Canada. They did not know what was awaiting them there, perhaps even a worse destiny, and they only wished to liberate themselves from the slavery and oppression of the Russian government.

Empress Aleksandra, the wife of Nikolaĭ,[4] received a request letter from Pëtr Vasil'evich Verigin as well as a separate one from the Doukhobors. I give the exact text of this letter in the book. Because of this letter, Doukhobors were allowed to move abroad.

A great role in this resettlement was played by the late grandfather Lev Nikolaevich Tolstoy,[5] who was very close to this entire God's cause. Together with his friends, V. G. Chertkov, P. I. Biriukov and I. M. Tregubov, he wrote long appeals to the people to assist in the resettlement of the Doukhobors. We remain very grateful to him and revere him as one of the prophets of our time. Based on the teachings of Jesus Christ, he revealed and condemned the unfairness of the social order of humanity, particularly the deceptive clergy, the absolute monarchy of the emperor and the kings, as rough and violent enslavement of the people, as it was in the old times. Let him enter the Kingdom of heaven, eternal peace.[6] Let his name and his deeds forever remain a treasured memory among us and our descendants.

A Letter of Pëtr Vasil'evich Verigin to the Empress Aleksandra Fëdorovna Romanova.

May God protect your soul in this life as well as in the future one, sister Aleksandra. I am a servant of the Lord Jesus Christ, I live bearing and announcing the benevolent tidings of His truth. Since 1885, I have been in exile from the Transcaucasian community of Doukhobortsy. The word Doukhoborets (Spirit Wrestler) means that we live in spirit and in our soul, we believe in God (see the Gospel, the meeting of Christ with a Samaritan woman at a well).

I implore you, Aleksandra, my sister in Lord Christ, request your spouse Nikolaĭ to spare the Christians in the Caucasus from persecutions. I appeal to you because I think that your heart is more turned towards our Lord, God. Women and children suffer the most: hundreds of their husbands and fathers are incarcerated and thousands of families are scattered among mountainous auls, where the authorities are encouraging the local population to treat them roughly. This is particularly hard on Christian women. Recently, they started locking up women and children in jails as well. Our fault is that we are trying as far as possible to be Christians. Perhaps, some of our actions may need more understanding.

You are probably familiar with the teachings of vegetarianism; we are followers of these humane beliefs. We recently stopped eating meat, drinking wine and doing other things that lead to a sinful life and darken the light of the human soul. Not killing animals, we consider it impossible to take the life of a human under any circumstances. Killing an ordinary man, even if he were a robber, seems to us to be like a consent to kill Christ, and this is the major reason. The state requires our brethren to learn how to handle guns in order to get a good training in murder. As Christians, we do not agree to this, and we are thrown into prisons, beaten and starved. Our sisters and mothers are being rudely mistreated as women, the perpetrators often ask with ridicule, "Where is your God? Why isn't He saving you?" Our God is in heaven and on earth, and He creates anything he wills (Psalms of David 113–114). And it makes it even more sad that all this is happening in a Christian country. Our community in the Caucasus is about 20 thousand people. Can this small number of people cause any harm to the governmental body if they were not taken as soldiers? They are being taken now, but it is pointless: 30 people are in Ekaterinograd[7] prison in the disciplinary battalion, where they are being tortured. We consider a human a temple of the living God, and we cannot get ready to murder Him, not under any circumstances, even if we were threatened with death. The most convenient solution would be to relocate us to one place, where we could live peacefully and work. We will pay all the government's dues in the form of taxes, but we cannot be soldiers.

If the government cannot agree to this, let it give us the right to move to one of the European countries. We would gladly move to England or, even more conveniently, to America, where we have many brethren in the Lord Jesus Christ.

From the depth of my soul, I request the Lord to bestow well-being on your family.

The servant of Jesus, Pëtr, living in exile in Obdorsk, Tobol'sk guberniia.

Notes

1. "Not resisting evil with violence" often translated into English as "peaceful non-resistance" is an idea expressed by Leo Tolstoy, the great Russian writer and a supporter of the Doukhobors. The author, however, refers here to "not resisting evil with evil."
2. Tiflis is the old name of modern Tbilisi, the capital of the country of Georgia. In the nineteenth century, it was the capital of Tiflis guberniia, which was a part of the Russian Empire.
3. Akhalkalak (modern Akhalkalaki) is an administrative district in the country of Georgia. Now an independent state, in Imperial Russia, Georgia constituted Tiflis guberniia.
4. Nikolaĭ (Nicolas II) Romanov was the last Russian tsar who succeeded the throne in 1894 and was officially crowned in 1896.
5. Leo Tolstoy (Lev Nikolaevich Tolstoĭ) (1828–1910) was a famous Russian writer, the author of "War and Peace," "Anna Karenina" and of multiple other novels. He also was a philosopher and thinker who developed the concept of not resisting evil with violence (non-violent resistance). He was

a great sympathizer and supporter of the Doukhobors and assisted them in their resettlement to Canada.
6. Tsarstvie nebesnoe, vechnyĭ pokoĭ means "[let him/her enter] the Kingdom of heaven, eternal peace." These are Russian and Doukhobor expressions of respect used about the dead.
7. Ekaterinograd is modern Ekterinogradskaia or Yekaterinogradskaya village in Kabardino-Balkaria, a republic of the Russian Federation; it is located to the north of Georgia.

CHAPTER 27

The Relocation

A group of Doukhobors upon their arrival in Canada in 1899

The 2140 exiles from Tiflis[1] guberniia departed on board the first ship from Batum[2] on December 10, 1898. Delayed by a severe storm, the trip took 32 days. The ship arrived in Saint John on January 11, 1899. Ten people died on board during the trip. L. Sulerzhitskiĭ[3] accompanied the passengers of this ship.

The second ship departed from Batum on December 17, 1898. There were 1600 Elizavetpol'[4] and 700 Kars[5] Doukhobors on board, a total of 2300. The ship was at sea for 27 days. On January 15, 1899, the ship arrived in Saint John, where it was kept under quarantine for 27 days due to a disease. Six people died during the trip. Sergeĭ L'vovich Tolstoĭ[6] was the accompanying person on this trip. The third group sailed off from the island of Cyprus on April 15, 1899. The ship had 1010 people on board. After a 26-day trip, it arrived in Quebec City on May 10, 1899. These were the Doukhobors who were the first to depart from Batum, who temporarily stayed in Cyprus and then later moved to Canada. P. I. Biriukov lived with them in Cyprus and assisted them in various ways. At the end of April 1899, the last (fourth) group set off on the journey from Batum. There were 2300 people from Kars. The ship was at sea for 27 days. Upon its arrival in Quebec City, it was kept under quarantine for 27 days because of a disease. Seven people died on the way. The accompanying persons were Aleksandr N. Konshin and Vladimir Dmitrievich Bonch-Bruevich.[7] All of the accompanying persons were on board following a request by Lev Nikolaevich Tolstoy.

In Quebec City and in Saint John, Doukhobors were greeted by a thousand people who gave them presents and treats. The Minister of the Interior, Sifton, addressed them with the following words: "It is known to us that you have suffered a lot in Russia for your religious beliefs. But now you are free from Egyptian slavery and came to the country of utmost freedom, where you can maintain your faith as it allows you to, i.e., practise your belief as you understand it."

These words by Minister Sifton gladdened the Doukhobors; they rejoiced and thanked the Lord and also sincerely expressed their gratitude to the minister, as the country's representative, for his welcome. Doukhobors came to Canada not like immigrants seeking material benefits. They moved and were accepted by the people of Canada as martyrs and sufferers for Christ's faith. Both sides understood and knew this—the Doukhobors and all of the Canadian people, otherwise Canada would not have accepted them.

Before the relocation, some trusted individuals were sent here in order to find some land: Pëtr Makhortov and Ivan Ivin, as well as Prince Khilkov,[8] who had a good command of the English language. Besides, Khilkov was well aware of the government order in Russia, and here it was also necessary to learn everything in minute detail and to make an agreement so that the Doukhobors would not fall under the government power in Canada, as they did in Russia.

Before the arrival of the first group, the trusted individuals had already been shown the lands by the government where these individuals started directing people. The first allotment was in the area of Yorkton. This area was deserted; it had primeval forest, shrubs and marshes. This area did not suit the relocation of the Doukhobors, and its severe climate was alien to them. Because of their vegetarianism, they needed a warm climate where they could grow vegetables and consume them. However, following the government orders, out of necessity, they had to settle there. On the other hand, taking into consideration the minister's announcement of complete freedom of beliefs and religious practice, they were glad to get even this land. As was pointed out earlier, the reason for their relocation from Russia to Canada was not the search for good land or wealth but the promised freedom of their religious beliefs. This is the whole purpose of the Doukhobor resettlement, and the land was not part of the picture.

Another land plot was allocated near Prince Albert. The land there was dryer and there was plenty of cultivated land. Doukhobors also started settling there. However, most Doukhobors settled in the Yorkton area. They were allocated the so-called Doukhobor reserve of about 40 square miles. They were allowed to settle in villages and cultivate the land communally. For accepting the land, that is, for a farm, one had to pay 10 dollars, and the land became one's property. They also had to pay two dollars per farm yearly for the settlers' roads.

An announcement was made that conscription, that is serving in the military was cancelled for them forever, and this was reflected in a document which I quote here verbatim.

The Office of the Immigration Commissioner in Winnipeg
I, John Obed Smith, of the town of Winnipeg, province of Manitoba, Canada, an Immigration Commissioner and Notary Public for the province of Manitoba, hereby testify to the following: by the power of the decree given to the private councils of Canadian lands by the Honorable Minister of the Interior and approved by his Excellency Governor-General of Canada

on December 6, 1898, in accordance with the third paragraph, section 21, chapter 41 of the revised Act of Canada, Doukhobors who due to their religious teachings, refuse to carry weapons, are completely excluded from militia and army service upon providing a proof that they belong to the Community of Doukhobors. Signed and sealed in the town of Winnipeg, as above mentioned on 25th of June, year 1901 AD.
Immigration Commissioner and Notary Public.

Following this explanation, Doukhobors started building houses, acquiring domestic animals, horses, buying agricultural tools and ploughing the land through arduous toil. In the beginning of their settlement, because they had no oxen or horses, women pulled the plough and ploughed the land for vegetable gardens. Men went to earn money to support their fathers, mothers, wives and children. They had to do this of necessity and great poverty as Doukhobors arrived from Russia penniless, one must say, and it was very difficult for them here because everything was new and they did not know the English language. So here as well, in the beginning, Doukhobors experienced a lot of suffering as well as hard and even unbearable toil.

Notes

1. Tiflis is the old name of modern Tbilisi, the capital of the country of Georgia. In the nineteenth century, it was the capital of Tiflis guberniia, which was a part of the Russian Empire.
2. Batum (modern name Batumi) is a port city on the Black sea coast. It is the second largest city of the country of Georgia, which at the time of the narrative, was a part of the Russian Empire.
3. Leopold Sulerzhitsky (1872–1916) was a theatre director, artist, a man of letters and a Tolstoyan who accompanied Doukhobors on their way to Canada and wrote a book "To America with the Doukhobors" documenting this experience. Sulerzhitsky was born in the Ukraine in a family of Polish descent. He studied and worked mostly in Moscow. The author uses the Russian version of his name "Sulerzhitskiĭ."
4. Elizavetpol' (later Kirovabad, since 1989, Ganja) was the capital of Elizavetpol' guberniia in the Russian Empire. Since the separation of Azerbaijan from the Soviet Union, it is one of the largest cities in Azerbaijan.
5. Kars is a town in Turkey. With its surrounding area, at the time of the narrative, it belonged to the Russian Empire. It was one of the areas of the Transcaucasian exile of the Doukhobors. Since 1921, it has been a part of Turkey.

6. Sergeĭ L'vovich Tolstoĭ (Tolstoy), a Russian musicologist and composer, was the oldest son of Leo Tolstoy and a Tolstoyan. He accompanied the Doukhobors during their resettlement to Canada and wrote memoirs about the experience (Sergej Tolstoy and the Doukhobors: A Journey to Canada (Diary and Correspondence) / Trans. J. Woodsworth; Ed. by A. Donskov // Slavic and East European Journal. 2001. Vol. 45).
7. Bonch-Bruevich, Vladimir Dmitrievich (1873–1955) was a Russian anthropologist who was actively involved with the Bolshevik party and became a member of the Soviet government. He accompanied Doukhobors during their resettlement to Canada, and compiled Doukhobor psalms in "The Living book of the Doukhobors" published in St. Petersburg in 1909. He also wrote some memoirs and archival materials about the Doukhobors.
8. Khilkov, Dmitriĭ Aleksandrovich (1857–1914) was a Russian Duke and a military officer who became a Tolstoyan and a revolutionary. He assisted in organizing the resettlement of Doukhobors to Canada.

CHAPTER 28

A Letter of Anastasiia Vasil'evna Verigina to Empress Aleksandra Fëdorovna Romanova

We are providing below the letter of the mother of Pëtr Vasil'evich which she wrote to empress Aleksandra Fëdorovna Romanova.

Honoured with all my heart, kindest Sovereign Empress Aleksandra Fëdorovna, in a passionate prayer from my broken heart I call upon peace and blessing of God, our Lord, to descend upon your life, may God grant your wishes.

With all my soul, I beseech you, sister in Lord, Aleksandra, to find a place for my pitiful plea in the treasury of your kind heart.

I am a petitioner from the Doukhobortsy Community, a Christian, Anastasiia Verigina, who in 1899, relocated together with other brothers from the Caucasus to North America, Canada, the Dominion of the state of Great Britain. I am the mother of seven children who are currently in exile in the remote parts of the Russian Empire in Western and North-Eastern Siberia, and of whom the first one, Pëtr, was exiled in connection with a social issue originally to Arhkangel'sk, and then in 1894, moved to Tobol'sk guberniia, Berëzov region, the village of Obdorsk. It has been 14 years since his exile. And five of my sons have been exiled to Iakutsk region: Ivan, Fëdor, Prokofiĭ, Vasiliĭ and Grigoriĭ Verigin. Excluding their incarceration time, it has been six years since their exile. My seventh son, Luk'ian, in accordance with God's will, passed away on his tragic journey in Saratovsk guberniia, in the town of Kamyshov, on August 8, 1897, in the dungeon.

Kindest Lady Sovereign, you probably know of the movement of Transcaucasian Doukhobortsy, who disagreed with carrying arms and doing the military service. Over the past years, my sons were never conscripted as soldiers, but during the governmental inquiry, they testified to their beliefs, their faith in Christ, non-resistance to evil with violence, not reciprocating evil with evil, as the Old Testament of mankind says 'an eye for an eye and a tooth for a tooth'. Having accepted the spiritual baptism in the Faith of Christ, they promised to serve Him, according to the Testament, with love and self-sacrifice, remembering the words of the Saviour: 'Whosoever therefore shall confess me before men, him will I confess also before my Father who is in heaven'.[1] There was no reason for my sons to hide anything from the interrogators. But in their reports, the local authorities began calling my sons anarchists, falsely saying that they were disseminating the propaganda of Anarchism. I did not even understand the meaning of this word, and I only learned its meaning from some knowledgeable people later. I can assure you, kindest Aleksandra Fëdorovna that my sons did not know anything like this, and it was only due to their faith in Christ that they were exiled for life in the land with a harsh climate, where they are struggling to support meagre existence, are short of nutrition and separated from the world and from their kin.

My precious children have been taken away from me. Affection, mother's love and longing for my children do not leave my heart in peace. My dear sister, as the mother of your own children, you know and can easily understand a mother's affection and love. Probably, there is no difference in the hearts of the rich, the educated, and of the lower classes of people: love is the same. Therefore, I turn to you with a heart-felt plea to take part in my destiny, to convince your spouse Nikolaĭ to let my sons come to me. I am elderly, around 80 years old; I want to see them and peacefully pass into the netherworld's eternal life, blessing the world's rulers. I hope I can rely on your kind heart filled with love.

You are active in disseminating the teaching, through the true life of Christ, you will turn many to the best deeds, those of mercy and love. And if my petition to you does not result with the desired return of all my children, then please consider the possibility of releasing to me at least my two younger sons, Pëtr and Grigoriĭ, who will pay me the last duty as sons, as is necessary among humankind. This is my whole request to you, please be so kind, do not forget my great plea, make me rejoice with the desired answer. Please, do not judge me for lack of sophistication and for faulty grammar, I related my request to you in a simple and heart-felt way. My sons' wives and children, like me, are living here in Canada, the wives who are like widows, and the children who are like orphans. From my whole family we will send solemn heart-felt prayers to God the King for your spouse and for your whole family wishing that you would live happily for many years and have all your wishes gratified by the Lord. Yours truly in the Christian love, widow Anastasiia Vasil'evna Verigina.

Note

1. Matthew 10:32.

CHAPTER 29

The March of Brothers and Sisters for God's Cause

The march of brothers and sisters for God's cause

At the time of my arrival in Canada, there was a terrible turmoil between the Doukhobors and the government. This discord arose because of the land issue since the land in Canada was being distributed through signing up with agents. Every person accepting a land plot had to register his name, patronymic and last name. This registry happened in an agent's office, where it was required to make a promise of sort, like a pledge, in particular for a three-year lease and living on the land. The land had to become the property of the owner, and a document was provided by the government certifying that the land, indeed, had become the property of the owner.

To receive this document, a full oath of allegiance[1] to King Edward was required that included acknowledging him as the supreme power and a commitment to indubitable execution of all his orders and decrees. This caused a commotion among the Doukhobors, and based on these illegal actions of the government, they refused to accept the land. They began to understand that the government had fooled them with its treats at the arrival so that they would trust the government, and so they did, and now the government started gradually pulling them into its net. And what happened to Minister Sifton's promise of complete freedom for Doukhobors to practise Christ's faith that the Minister expressed while greeting them? It must have been only words, and the reality assumed a completely different form. After this, all the Doukhobors decided not to accept the land, otherwise the same history as in Russia would repeat itself.

The villages had been already built, and the Doukhobors started purchasing everything required for cultivating the land, but they did not accept the land. The government did not press them too hard, and gave them some leeway in the hope that the Doukhobors would come to a decision to accept the land through the oath of allegiance on their own. In the worst case, the land could be taken away and given to others, and the Doukhobors could leave and go wherever they wanted. And then the government through its agents again started coercing the Doukhobors either to accept the land in accordance to their law or vacate the land so that it could be settled by others.

Then a part of the Doukhobors of over 2000 people, in fear of falling victim to the governmental demand that did not agree with the teaching of Christ, followed the second scenario: to give everything away and follow their destiny, relying on the will of the almighty creator of all the worlds. This was very risky, however, since winter was approaching already and it was getting cold. They set all the horses free and other domestic animals they had and left behind their houses and all their possessions. All of them, the old and the children, the sick and the disabled, went on the way to Yorkton. In Yorkton, they were met by the government representatives, since the government officials realized that they were to blame for this entire movement and for the terrible situation of a 2000-person group, who were deprived of everything, even their daily food. Then the government officials decided to correct their cruel mistake and began asking the Doukhobors to return to their homes.

When the Doukhobors did not agree, the government tormented them in various ways, even trampled them with horses, but all this was to no avail. Then women and children were separated by force from the men and incarcerated in the Immigration house, where they were given small portions of food. Men were allowed to go wherever they wanted, but the locals were forbidden to give them as much as a piece of bread, even if they asked in the name of the greatest teacher of truth, Jesus Christ. Thus the Doukhobor men left their wives, children and the sick in Yorkton. Hungry, freezing and exhausted near death, the men walked for 100 miles to the town of Minnedosa. There the government thought of stopping them but nothing worked.

The government realized that many of the Doukhobor men were extremely exhausted, and some even stayed behind by the road where they would be doomed by imminent death, which would cast a shadow of sin over the whole civilized world of the British and their free country. So the Doukhobor men were forced into railway carriages and sent to their homes. They were brought to Yorkton, women and children were released, and they went to their villages together.

I did not describe this part of the history in a very detailed way, but the readers must understand how cruel and out of place it was. It happened in the beginning of the twentieth century since the birth, teaching and death of the great teacher Jesus Christ, who called upon the entire human race to carry out the will of the Heavenly Father. And this was exactly what Doukhobors were trying to do. Was this the right way to treat these people, particularly by the English, who also consider themselves to be believers in Christ as the son of God?

Note

1. Please refer to "Appendix 2: Oath of Allegiance (the Early Twentieth Century)."

CHAPTER 30

The Release of Pëtr Vasil'evich Verigin by the Russian Government and His Journey to Canada to the Doukhobors

Pëtr Verigin in England on his way to Canada

On December 10, 1902, we received a telegram from Anna and Vladimir Chertkov from England, which said, "Pëtr Verigin has safely arrived and is staying with us. We will inform you about his departure to Canada with a telegram. The Chertkovs."

This joyful tiding instantly flew over all the Doukhobor villages, and everybody learned that our great sufferer was on his way to us. Merciful Lord, what an indescribable joy it was, and it was expressed everywhere: when people met or attended sobraniia,[1] everywhere one could hear "Praise and Glory be to God that the Lord has returned to us our sufferer, who has endured a lot for the truth and our common cause. His separation from the Doukhobors was like a stormy dark night that lasted for sixteen years. Yet, despite this lengthy period of time, Doukhobors remained hopeful for his return. Now it was happening, and this joyful news coming from the Chertkovs was the advent of dawn after which the true sunrise should manifest." All the Doukhobors were unspeakably happy, but even more so, the joy came to the heart of our dear mother, who during that time became really old and tormented. I do not undertake here the description of her maternal joy, and I would not be able to express it precisely either.

The next telegram was addressed to our mother. When I started reading it to her, tears dropped from her eyes, but her face was beaming, and she looked young. She praised and glorified God, since at least in the last days of her life, God heard her prayer and returned to her the undefeated hero and a dear son close to her heart, who fought for a long time for God's faith and truth and remained true to God. She made me read that telegram a few more times and asked me in detail, how long it would take for him to get here. I planned out the whole journey in my mind and told her how many more days it would take. She objected and said, "Could it really take so many more days? This is terribly long, and I will be completely exhausted waiting." I comforted her and told her, "Dear mother, do not worry about it, and the time will pass on its own, as those long 16 years have passed, of which nothing is left now except for the memory."

Following this telegram, the Doukhobors decided to have a congress with representatives from all villages; the day was appointed and two people from every village came for the congress. At this congress, it was decided to delegate two people to go to Quebec City or Saint John depending on where the ship would dock. These two individuals should go on behalf of all the Doukhobors to meet Pëtr Vasil'evich. The first person, Pavel Vasil'evich Planidin, now in his middle age, in his youth was closely acquainted with Pëtr Vasil'evich, and due to his behaviour throughout his life fully deserved this trust and respect of the society. The second person, Semën Fëdorovich Rybin, was a young man of a good character and heart, who had already learned to speak English well.

When the second telegram was received from the Chertkovs, "Pëtr Verigin on such and such date left London for Canada," then, in accordance with the schedule, Planidin and Rybin left for the indicated place. Not only the Doukhobors knew about the arrival of Pëtr Vasil'evich in England, all the English knew about it too. It was covered in newspapers, and the Canadian government in particular was glad to learn that Pëtr Vasil'evich was on his way to the Doukhobors in Canada, since around that time a big turmoil had started among them. As mentioned above, the government tried to handle it in various ways, but nothing helped and they were hoping that the arrival of Pëtr Vasil'evich would calm down the Doukhobors.

When the ship docked at the pier, Pëtr Vasil'evich was on the deck and was watching the shore, and he recognized Pavel Vasil'evich. Their meeting was very joyous. After being in separation for such a lengthy period of time as 16 years and meeting on the other hemisphere of the earth, where everything was new and unknown to Pëtr Vasil'evich, there came the people who were like the locals of this country, and yet they were so well known to him! How could that meeting not be full of joy?

On the way, in the city of Montreal, where the train stopped for half an hour, the Minister of the Interior had a personal meeting with Pëtr Vasil'evich, and after meeting him and talking about his safe arrival, the minister addressed Pëtr Vasil'evich with a speech requesting him to quiet down the Doukhobor unrest. Pëtr Vasil'evich responded to the minister: "I am now travelling as a guest, and I have here an elderly mother whom I have a duty to visit. Consequently, I have yet nothing in common with the matter between the Doukhobors and the government. I may even return back to Russia. And if I stay here, I can let them know my opinion, but I cannot force anything, even if it were for a good cause." After this they said good-bye to each other, shook hands, and their meeting was over.

They arrived in Yorkton safely. Horses to take them home were already waiting. It was about 40 miles from Yorkton to home. Halfway, they had to let the horses rest and stopped at Jacob Burtsev's who lived in that area. He was German, married, and his wife's name was Sarah. She had a true Christian's heart. They had three sons and a few daughters. They were settled here before the Doukhobors, and were relatively well off, not rich, but they had all the necessities.

In the beginning of their settlement, Doukhobors were buying everything in town, and on the way there and back, got to know the Burtsevs. Jacob and his wife were so kind-hearted that they did not charge anything for guests and their horses staying at their place, as other people did. Moreover, if the guests were short of any food, they would always give it to them without charging anything at all. I considered it necessary to mention their kindness here, even if very briefly, since they fully deserve it.

My mother did not allow me to go to Yorkton to meet my brother, but told me to go to Jacob's, so that I could meet him there, pass over the mother's greetings and learn about his health and well-being. When he was to stop for rest at Jacob's, I was supposed to go back and notify her that everything was in order. I came to Jacob's in the evening, stayed overnight, and in the morning, set off for the meeting. After riding for about two miles, I met my brother. He was very glad to see me and invited me to sit in his sleigh. I got in his sleigh and we started talking. First, he asked me, "How is our dear mother doing, she must have aged?" I said, "Yes. She is waiting for you very eagerly, and she sent me to see you, to pass over her mother's love and go back to let her know ahead of your well being." Engaged in this conversation, we got to Jacob's. My dear brother stayed there, and I went back to mother. When I arrived, she started asking me whether everything was in order, and how soon her dear son would arrive. I said, "Everything is fine, Thank God, and in about three hours, he should be home." The whole village became excited and started getting ready for the meeting.

At seven in the evening, Pëtr Vasil'evich arrived in Otradnoe, where he was greeted with great joy by the singing of the psalm "Our Dear Guests." Everybody was so joyous that I cannot even describe it. It was a remarkable day for all of us, and particularly for our mother. She forgot her old age, forgot her sufferings and grief, all that was left behind, and she was happy now. She rejoiced and thanked God for His great mercy to her. And we lived happy and joyous lives.

Pëtr Vasil'evich was separated from the family and all the Doukhobors and was exiled to suffer on February 2, 1887. And now it was December 24, 1902.

Note

1. Sobranie (or sobran'e, sobraniia in plural) is a Doukhobor assembly that typically started with "molenie" (molen'e) (including prayers, psalms and hymns) and continued with the resolution of pertinent matters by the assembly.

CHAPTER 31

Pëtr Vasil'evich Travels Around All the Villages. His Speeches and His Advice to the People

First temporary houses that Doukhobors built in Saskatchewan

When Pëtr Vasil'evich arrived, there were severe frosts, and riding or walking from villages to meet him was very difficult, so he decided to go to all the villages himself to meet all the brothers and sisters who wanted to see him.

When Pëtr Vasil'evich was visiting the Doukhobors, everybody greeted and met him with great joy and sincere love, as a dear guest and a sufferer for our common cause. Everywhere, a lot was said about the past, that is, about the incurred sufferings, persecutions and how they endured everything in the hope for a better future.

He said, "Yes, brothers and sisters, we had to suffer through the catastrophe, as Jerusalem, from which not a single stone was left. This is how the Russian government treated us. But I tell you, brothers and sisters, verily, we should not be horrified or grieved by the past sufferings. We should solemnly remember them with a great joy and glorify God, as He participated with us in those sufferings and sent us the Spirit of Truth, that touched our souls and hearts, that inspired us to forget for a while all the earthly matters, and trust ourselves to the providence and the will of God and pursue only what He reveals to every person in the mind. In those times, we had to pursue not the will of the flesh, but the will of the spirit, the boundless Eternal Spirit, that had no beginning and will have no end. We suffered in the name of Jesus Christ. One only needs to sincerely remember His birth, His earthly life, His teaching that He carried forth with great difficulties. He broke the eternal chaos of the darkness of ignorance, pride and haughtiness. He lived in the time of worse ignorance as compared to our time, and thus to accomplish what He achieved, He required spiritual efforts. A person needs a great physical strength and a huge hammer to break an eternally standing rock of precious stone, that would not yield to anything but a great physical strength and a big hammer. Likewise, Christ possessed a great power of His mind and carried out God's cause entrusted upon Him by His Father.

We see that in this great struggle, He also weakened. We see this when He was in the desert. He spent forty days and nights there, in fasting and prayers. And when He got hungry, then the Enemy of Mankind started offering Him all the world's bounties on the condition that Christ would worship him. But He solemnly rejected all these world's bounties and said, 'Away from me, Satan! For it is written: Worship the Lord, your God, and serve Him only'.[1] After this Christ had no more doubts or obstacles, and He faced a painful mortal death, trusting His spirit to His heavenly father. And His testament is: as I was persecuted, so will you be, and everyone who has left father or mother, wife and children, brother or sister, or lands, and houses and all the possessions, for My sake, will receive many times as much, and will inherit eternal life.

We are the descendants of the kin of sufferers. Our ancestors suffered from the clergy, from the priests who falsely present the worship of God to the people through the creations of human hands, through icons, that they made people worship as God. Our ancestors, seeing this sacrilege, started openly denying these icons and calling them idols, for which we were tortured even more severely. They were incarcerated, walled inside stone pillars, had long strips of skin cut off their backs, they were whipped to death and exiled into the worst parts of Siberia, to Kamchatka, Sakhalin and Kola. Now we, their descendants, are free from such abuse and we should remember them with kind words, because their sufferings liberated us from that deceit [by the clergy].

In our time, we had to suffer as our ancestors did, because in front of our eyes, there unfold terrible wars, bloodshed, murder of a human by a human, all sorts of violence, deprivation of freedom, whereas Christ taught that all people are children of the same God Father and should live with each other as brothers. The first commandment is to love God with all your heart and soul, and the second one is similarly, love thy neighbour as yourself. And do not wish upon the other what you do not wish upon yourself, and this is God's Law and the Prophets.[2] If we had not engaged in the open struggle against the Russian government because of their lives contradicting the teaching of Christ, we would have been condemned by Jesus Christ, and it would have been also upsetting for our ancestors. Also among our future generations who will live after us, we would not have deserved good memories. Our struggle was not only for the Doukhobors and their generations, but the whole world received the signal for the termination of wars, bloodshed and of everything that contradicts the teaching of Jesus Christ. While finishing this speech, brothers and sisters, from the bottom of my heart, I thank you for not turning away from God's cause that I suggested to you. Let us remember with kind words all those who before their due time perished in this struggle. Their deeds are honourable, and let them enter the kingdom of heaven, eternal peace be upon them. And let God help us to perfect ourselves and live according to the teaching of Christ, which is the conduit for the will of God."

After this conversation, he passed over to the discussion of accepting land. Pëtr Vasil'evich asked, "What do you think about accepting the land?" Almost all villages provided the same answer, "We have not made the final decision yet, and do not know whether we are going to accept or not." Pëtr Vasil'evich said that this matter should be seriously considered and one common conclusion should be arrived at. If the decision is to accept the land, then it would have to be accepted, and if not—then a serious consideration should be given to the questions of how to secure nourishment since there were families and many children involved. Each village should consider this individually, and then a congress with representatives from all the villages should be held, which would make the final decision on what to do.

When we arrived in the village of Terpenie, so many people came out to meet him that Pëtr Vasil'evich was surprised. The village was not very large, but there were many people there. It turned out that this whole village was Svobodniki.[3] When the government turned them back, many Svobodniki from other villages settled there for the winter. They explained to the government, "Since you turned us back, we consider ourselves under arrest, and you have to provide for us." In their villages, they all had their own grain, but now the government brought them everything they needed from Yorkton, and took their grain in exchange for the delivered goods. The government did not lose anything in these arrangements, but it was not advantageous for the Doukhobors, as much of their labour was wasted.

Pëtr Vasil'evich stayed in that village for two days, and conversed a lot about everything. He advised them to inform the government not to deliver anything to them from the next day, and that instead they would procure their own supplies to the best of their abilities. And in tasks that were beyond their abilities because they had no horses, for example to deliver firewood from the forest, or to take the grain to a mill, other Doukhobors who had not set their domestic animals free would help them, and the government would not be involved in any way. They all accepted this advice and immediately sent two people to Yorkton who informed the agent to cease the supplies from that day on. The agent was glad about it and said "good."

Then Pëtr Vasil'evich suggested to those who were from other villages to go back to their villages and resettle in their own homes, explaining to them that an outbreak of a disease and even death could occur from high concentration of people in houses, and therefore they should go back to their own homes. They accepted this as well, and all went back to their villages and homes.

And this is how Pëtr Vasil'evich went around all the villages. He discussed everything necessary with the people and they started seriously considering how to live in the future.

Notes

1. Matthew 4.
2. The Law and the Prophets are two parts of the Bible (the Torah that describes the laws of Moses, and the Prophets that relate to the other books of the Bible).
3. Svobodnik, Svobodniki in plural (otherwise known as Freedomite, or the Sons of Freedom), from the Russian word "svoboda" (freedom), are a radical group who split from Doukhobors during the Yorkton march of protest in 1902 and subsequent events in Saskatchewan. After the resettlement of most Doukhobors to BC in the early twentieth century, Svobodniki were active in BC with protest actions against the government and other Doukhobor groups until the late 1960s. The Canadian government reacted to their protests by building two prisons for Svobodniki and incarcerating them in these prisons, initiating raids on Svobodniki villages and taking away children who did not attend schools from their families and placing them in juvenile detention facilities or reform schools.

CHAPTER 32

The Congress for the Discussion of the Land Issue. Acceptance of Land

Doukhobors building a village in Saskatchewan

The congress to discuss the land issue was called on April 10, 1903. The congress was to be attended by two representatives from each village. The agents responsible for these allotments were also invited from Yorkton and Swan river to provide detailed explanations about the conditions on which the land was provided and what was required. These were their explanations.

"Each individual between 18 and 60 years of age willing to accept the land can accept it. One has to find a vacant farm, whichever one likes, and write down its number, come to the agent's office and declare that he wants to accept that particular farm. The agent checks in his books whether the farm is vacant, and offers to write down in his book that the land is accepted by this particular person, as well as his name and last name. It costs 10 dollars, but these 10 dollars are taken for land measurements, whereas the land itself is free. While this person lives on the land for three years, the government is watching him: if he is lazy and does not cultivate the land, it can be taken away and given to a different person. If the person works on the farm, in three years, it is transferred into his property, and a document confirming this is issued by the government, condition of the person signing off the fact that he has sworn allegiance to King Edward." The agents explained that this oath was not obligatory, and only those who wanted to do so could swear the oath, and those who did not want to were not forced. They also explained that school had to be accepted; children had to go to school and parents had to pay their expenses. Also, civil records were obligatory. The village roads had to be maintained, and if they were not, each farm should pay 2 dollars a year, and this was it. This was the end of the agents' presentation and they left for their regions.

Doukhobors started discussing the issue. However, they did not arrive at a decision. Some spoke in favour of accepting the land, while others were against it. They asked Pëtr Vasil'evich for advice. He took into consideration the whole discussion and expressed his opinion in the following way:

> I think that the land should be accepted. The land is necessary and vital for us to cultivate it and feed our families. You say that the land comes from God and people come from God too, so it is not necessary to accept the land from the agents, and everyone should be able to use it without any records. I agree with this and it is good that Doukhobors are ahead of others in their thinking. A few more centuries or millennia will pass, and the entire mankind will arrive at the same conclusion. There will be no land surveying any more, and they will use the land together, like children of one Father, because all people will understand that land should not be purchased as private property or taken by force and then resold. This is illegal before God who created it. He created it not for exploiting one's own brother on it, but

to gain necessary nutrition from it, that is, apply to it one's labour as much as possible and feed off it. And the land remains untouchable by anyone save God. This is what we see: over centuries, nations come and go, but the land remains. Now, while land surveying is still in place and most people follow it, I think that this is good enough for the time being. Here, everyone, rich or poor, can receive an equal share, as it is ordained by God. I do not see any danger in the record books. This is a simple record to denote which land is free and which is occupied. You are afraid of taking the oath, but there is still a long way to it, three more years, and we have to live now. In three years from now, maybe it will not be required, and if it is required, you can oppose it then. Let me say it again: in our time, there is nothing criminal in land surveying or accepting land through agents. If you sincerely wish to live like Christians and follow the teaching of Christ, then after accepting the land, you can prove it in practice: after you accept the land, nobody will consider it one's own farm, but you can use it together, as children of one Father.

Everybody who attended the congress agreed with this, and all gave their honest Christian word that after accepting the land, nobody had the right to use it individually. The free word of the Doukhobors was their law, which could not be changed under any circumstances, and if somebody did, then this person was not a Doukhobor any more. Land acceptance had to be recorded in agents' offices. Going there individually would be a big waste of time, and therefore three people were appointed to accept all the land allotments. The individuals entrusted with this were Pëtr Vasil'evich, Pavel Planidin and Nikolaĭ Zibarov. They were supposed to get the land blank forms from the government, and then travel around all the villages, write down the first and last name of each person, and then go to the agent's office for land acceptance. Among the participants in the meeting, there were Svobodniki,[1] who also agreed to accept the land. They had some money left from the sale of their cattle and horses by the government—7000 dollars, which they decided to use to pay for the farms. This would be the beginning of the voluntary communal life. The Svobodniki had neither cattle nor horses. At the same congress it was decided to give them horses, cows and whatever necessary gathered from other villages, that other villages could spare.

The above-mentioned was decided only by those who attended the congress, with two representatives per village who were the trusted individuals from the villages. Upon their return to their villages, these trusted individuals had to call a meeting not only of men but of women as well and explain in detail everything that was decided at the congress. Next, everybody individually had to seriously consider the matter and voluntarily arrive at some decision. When the blank forms with the requirement of filling in the name and family name of everyone willing to accept the land would arrive from the government, they would have to write their names in the forms. Those who were opposed to these arrangements should not write anything in these forms, but should go to an agent on their own and accept a farm on their own accord.

It took at least a month for these blank forms to be delivered. For the convenience of signing up, all the villages were split into three districts: the southern, the northern and the so-called Liman.[2]

Pëtr Vasil'evich did not go to his district but designated this task to me, and I followed it through. I went to each village, explained the reason for my trip there and invited everyone to a meeting if they wanted to fill in their name and last name in the form for accepting the land. When all assembled, I explained: "I came to your village on request of Pëtr Vasil'evich in order to identify all individuals willing to accept the land following the conditions that were determined at the general congress and to enter all their names and last names in the blank forms. This land will be taken from the Doukhobor reserve, and will be mostly accepted as a bulk, without considering the good and not so good farm quality, since all the land will be in communal use: the better lands will be used for grain farming, and worse lands will be used for pastures."

Filling in the forms was voluntary; literate individuals wrote down their names and last names on their own, and I filled in the names for illiterate individuals, following their requests. In this manner, I travelled around all the villages. In Pokrovka village, one person did not want to accept the land following the common conditions. In Goreloe village, five individuals did not sign up, but the rest signed up, and also gave their word not to demand to know which individual farm was assigned to them.

When signing the forms was completed in all the villages, the trusted representatives went to Yorkton and accepted the land. A total of 2025 farms were accepted. After this, the Doukhobors started proper cultivation of the land, they bought ploughs, harrows, mowers, harvesters and everything else needed for agricultural work.

Notes

1. Svobodnik, Svobodniki in plural (otherwise known as Freedomite, or the Sons of Freedom), from the Russian word "svoboda" (freedom), are a radical group who split from Doukhobors during the Yorkton march of protest in 1902 and subsequent events in Saskatchewan. After the resettlement of most Doukhobors to BC in the early twentieth century, Svobodniki were active in BC with protest actions against the government and other Doukhobor groups until the late 1960s. The Canadian government reacted to their protests by building two prisons for Svobodniki and incarcerating them in these prisons, initiating raids on Svobodniki villages and taking away children who did not attend schools from their families and placing them in juvenile detention facilities or reform schools.
2. Liman means "a river delta." It was the name of one of the Doukhobor villages in the Molochnaia river settlement (before the events described in this book). There is no record of "Liman" village in Saskatchewan, but besides the north and the south regions of Doukhobor settlements, there was also Devil's Lake and Saskatchewan colonies (ref. http://www.doukhobor.org/settlements.html). The author probably refers to what is now known as "Saskatchewan" group of Doukhobor colonies in Saskatchewan.

CHAPTER 33

Starting the Communal Household. The Life of Pëtr Vasil'evich in Otradnoe

A communal house in the National Doukhobor Heritage Village. The first floor served as a prayer home and a gathering place, the second floor was the residence of P. Verigin

When the spring came, we needed to seek external employment. It was decided that two-thirds of adult workers from every village should look for external employment and one-third should stay back in the village and attend to the household. There were no mills in the villages, and the grain was taken to the towns for grinding. Pëtr Vasil'evich put the question of establishing four steam mills in the districts on the agenda. Everyone agreed and the construction of the mills followed immediately. Four steam threshing machines were ordered and promptly delivered. The mills were also constructed very quickly as they were built communally by a few villages. From then on, grain was ground at our own mills.

When all the grain was harvested, and the threshing time arrived, these mills and steam machines threshed all the grain successfully. At the general congress in summer, it was decided to increase the number of horses for ploughing the land. The horses were purchased in the south about 500 miles away. The individuals responsible for purchasing the horses were Pavel Planidin, Semën Negreev and Fëdor Sukhachëv. Pëtr Vasil'evich participated too since a large number of horses were purchased, and it had to be done very carefully taking into account first, the price, in order not to overpay, and second, horse quality. They bought 320 horses, each at the price of 75 dollars. All the horses were untrained, and they had to be herded across the steppes to the villages. This took 22 days, they were delivered successfully and in the fall, these horses were distributed across the villages. All the horses were counted, both already available and the newly bought, and by a common decision, each village was allotted 9 pairs of horses. One village comprised 40 farms. The villages that already had 18 horses did not take the newly purchased ones, and those villages short of the established number, took some horses. In this way, all the horses were distributed.

Since then, all the purchases were done together. Everything necessary for agriculture as well as clothes and footwear—all this was bought in Winnipeg from the warehouses, where everything was much cheaper than in the neighbouring towns. A common warehouse was established at the Verigin[1] train station where both household goods and agricultural implements were stored, and from there, everything necessary was delivered to the villages. At the warehouse, there was an office where all the incoming and outgoing goods were handled. A detailed record of incoming and outgoing goods was kept. At the annual congress attended by two to three representatives from each village, the records were verified. These debit and credit record reports were printed at the office and sent to all the villages. This was a way of notifying all the commune members about all the affairs of the communal life. This is how the Doukhobors settled in. With great effort, they started tilling the land and acquiring all the necessary household goods.

When Pëtr Vasil'evich arrived in the village of Otradnoe, a small house had already been constructed for him with two compartments: one was a dining room with an attached kitchen and the other was a bedroom. He took his mother to live with him in order to pay her his last respect as a son. Both his mother and he required some care, so he invited in some girls who were immediate relatives. The first of them was invited in on the second day after his arrival. She was Nastas'ia F. Golubova, the 17-year-old daughter of his niece Mariia. Two sisters were also brought in, Avdot'ia and Fedos'ia, who were his nieces. They were orphans: their father Luk'ian, brother of Pëtr Vasil'evich, passed away in prison in the town of Kamyshov, Saratov[2] guberniia, on the way to Iakutsk.[3] Their mother died here in Canada. There were also Varvara and Pelageia, two nieces once removed. Each one of these helpers was responsible for a particular part of the household, looking after Pëtr Vasil'evich and his mother. Their household duties included doing the laundry and cooking.

Pëtr Vasil'evich had many visitors from the villages who came to consult about communal household matters, and this disturbed his mother who needed peace and quiet. In order to provide her with peace, Pëtr Vasil'evich moved out to live close by with his nephew Ivan A. Aniutushkin, where it was more convenient for him to receive the visitors and discuss communal business. That room was also his bedroom. The dining room was at his mother's place. He visited her at breakfast, lunch and dinner, in order to see her, spend some time with her, converse with her, pity her and to make her smile, as she once did for him.

After moving to the other accommodation, he invited me and my wife to live with our mother. I did all the household work along with the communal work in the field. My wife looked after my mother and cooked for everyone, assisted by all the girls, and we all lived as one family.

The government did not forget about Pëtr Vasil'evich's case and conducted strict surveillance over him. They appointed some policemen of Russian ethnic origin to the northern district, and on business and without any business, these policemen visited the villages. They would stop in a village, order lunch and feed for the horse and pretend to be English-born. Pëtr Vasil'evich was often invited to the villages. Knowing that he was under surveillance, he would take the girls who lived in his mother's house, and also add a few more from the village that he was visiting. When there was a policeman around, he would ask the girls to sing and entertain. The policemen were required to submit reports to the central government about the behaviour and life of Pëtr Vasil'evich, and they reported what they saw. They reported that Verigin was not a dangerous man, he travelled around with young girls and that was that.

Our mother lived for about two more years and then died. The girls married and left when their time came. Only Nastas'ia and Fedos'ia stayed with Pëtr Vasil'evich until his death.

Notes

1. Verigin (Veregin) is a village in south-eastern Saskatchewan founded by the Doukhobors in the early twentieth century and named in honour of Pëtr Verigin. At some point, the name of the village was incorrectly recorded by the government officials as "Veregin" instead of "Verigin." Nowadays Veregin houses the National Doukhobor Heritage Village http://www.ndhv.ca/.
2. Saratov is a Russian city on the Volga river.
3. Iakutsk (Yakutsk) is a sub-Arctic city in Siberia with a harsh continental climate. During winters, it is one of the coldest cities in the world. It is the homeland of the Yakut (Sakha) people, the indigenous population of the area. It was used by the Russian government as a place of exile. Today it is the capital of the Sakha republic.

CHAPTER 34

Cancellation of Land Entries by the Government for Non-acceptance of Allegiance to the British King Edward

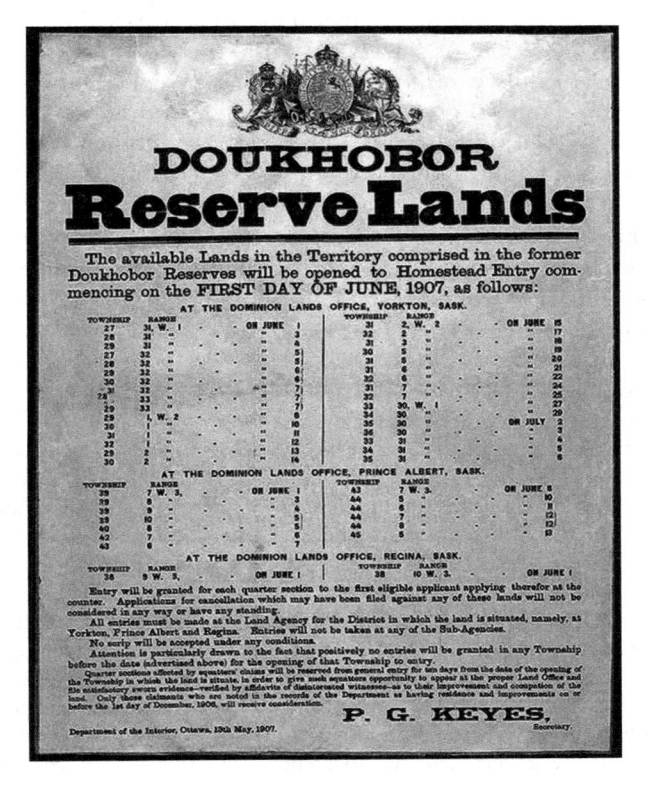

Doukhobor reserve lands cancellation poster

© The Author(s) 2019
G. V. Verigin, *The Chronicles of Spirit Wrestlers' Immigration to Canada*, https://doi.org/10.1007/978-3-030-18525-1_34

January 28, 1907. During this time, Pëtr Vasil'evich became acquainted with many government officials, with whom he seriously addressed the issue of citizenship. For example, he got to know Governor Spears quite well. He discussed this matter with him and asked in detail whether citizenship is required in Canada. [Spears responded,] "I can tell you that I have not met a single person in this country who did not accept citizenship, but this is not required. If you do not want to, you do not have to accept it. I repeat that I have never met a person who would not accept citizenship, so I do not know how the government would handle such a person. All of the newly arrived people want and demand citizenship, because after a person accepts citizenship, the land becomes this person's property, and this person can vote at the elections of the new government and such other affairs." Of course, while explaining this, Spears thought that we would want citizenship. As already known to the reader, citizenship could be accepted after three years of working on the land. During these last three years we built 40 giant Russian villages, good houses, warehouses and stables; we cleared and cultivated a lot of land; grain was no longer bought as we had done in the past, but we began selling grain. Therefore, when the commissioner for special affairs MacDougall[1] came to bestow citizenship, all the villages refused to accept it. He then left three legal forms in each village and left for another village. In this manner, he travelled around all the villages.

I provide here the contents of these forms:

> The government is pleased to see that some Doukhobors have been cultivating their own land and have already become or are planning to become Canadian citizens and British subjects. However, the government is sad to see that after having lived in Canada for seven years, the majority of Doukhobors are still cultivating their lands communally and are refusing to become citizens of this country. They left large plots of land allocated to them by the government without development and cultivation. According to the law, a settler has to cultivate his own land, otherwise he has no right to keep it. People who are not Doukhobors are now demanding that the Doukhobors should not be allowed to keep the land if they are not cultivating it and are not accepting citizenship of this country. The government of Canada has to answer to the majority of the Canadian people, and if the majority says that the Doukhobors should not be allowed to keep the land any longer, the government has to comply with this. The documents for farmsteads should be destroyed in case of illegal possession by the owners, so that these farmsteads could be passed over to other people who would own them in accordance with the legislation.

Doukhobor farmstead documents are legal only if the land is owned by a person who either lives on this farm, or lives in a village no farther than three miles away from this farm, and who cultivates the land for his own household and who already accepted Canadian citizenship or who has the intention to accept it. If a person lives in a village and cultivates his farm which is farther away than three miles from the village where he lives, he will retain his right to the land for six months, to give him an opportunity to build a house on his farmstead and move there ... If he does not build a house and move to his farm within six months, his claim to land ownership will be cancelled.

Although the government wishes that every person cultivates the land for himself and becomes a citizen of the country, it has no intention to force the Doukhobors into either. As before, the government will continue to protect the freedom of religious practice among the Doukhobors, but it can no longer give them the privileges for land ownership that it gives to other people. If the land or a part of the land on which a village is located is signed off to one individual, all this land or its part will be confiscated from this individual so that the government is able to protect homesteads. The assignment of land to a commune when the land is located close to a village is 15 acres per person, but if the land is communally cultivated it will no longer be allowed, and such land will be repossessed by the government to protect the Doukhobor commune for as long as the government wills. All the land registries signed off to the Doukhobor communes will be cancelled.

Doukhobors whose land registries are cancelled will be allowed a three month period since the receipt of this notification to sign off unoccupied farms to themselves. They have to submit an application, but they will not be charged the farm possession fees for the second time. Doukhobors who will sign off a farm within three month period either through a commissioner who will attend their village or through a government's agent, if they want to live on a farm or in a village, upon signing off a farm, have to declare their intent to accept British citizenship. If the land is located no farther away than three miles from their village, they will have the right to own the land and cultivate it while living in the village. However, if this farm is located farther than three miles away from the village, they have to live on their farm and have to settle there within a six month period after signing off on the allotment. If somebody wants to keep the land in his possession and signs off a new farm, this registry will not be legal unless it satisfies these legal requirements. If there is any communal field or communal cultivation of land on a farm that some person wants to keep via this second registry, this land will be left in communal use until the end of the year 1907. After this, it transfers into the ownership of a person who signed off on it.[2]

Notes

1. Reverend John MacDougall was the chief architect of Doukhobor land foreclosure. On December 28, 1906, he was appointed the Commissioner of Investigation and Adjuster of Land Claims for the Doukhobor lands. He was empowered to recommend the cancellation of homestead entries to the local Land Agents, who would make the actual cancellation. He was also empowered to receive applications for re-entry, to issue receipts if homestead fees were paid and to administer the naturalization oath.
2. For a more complete picture of the Canadian government's reversal regarding land ownership and the Hamlet Clause, see: http://www.larrysdesk.com/sklandseizure.html

CHAPTER 35

A Letter to the Government and the People of Canada Regarding Cancellation of Land Entries

After the above announcement by the government, a congress comprising two representatives from each village was scheduled to discuss this matter. Pëtr Vasil'evich was away in Russia at this time. He visited Lev Nikolaevich Tolstoy[1] and all the friends who assisted the Doukhobors during their resettlement to Canada. He thanked all of them and also met minister Pobedonostsev[2] who graciously received him.

It was decided at the Congress to send three representatives from the whole commune to the Prime Minister[3] of Canada and the Minister of the Interior to explain our convictions verbally. A letter of explanation was also written which was translated into English and submitted to the Prime Minister of Canada and the Minister of the Interior, and which was also printed in three venues for all the people of Canada. Two publishers accepted this letter and printed it, and one governmental publisher demanded 140 dollars for printing. The representatives paid the fees and the letter was printed. The representatives were Ivan Konkin, Fëdor Markin and Semën Rybin, the latter was a representative and interpreter into English. I quote this letter here.

The Christian Community of Universal Brotherhood. Doukhobors Residing in Canada. An Appeal to the Government and All the People of Canada.

On January 28, 1907, John MacDougall[4] visited our villages and announced that the land that Doukhobors had accepted and had in their possession for three years from that day onwards was no longer theirs, but was repossessed by the government. He left forms in each village in which there were explanations for Doukhobors why their lands were being confiscated. Although the forms did not contain any information about it, John MacDougall declared that in three months he would again visit our villages and the land would be redistributed again on entirely different principles.

First: if any Doukhobors are willing to swear allegiance to the British government but do not change their convictions in regard to communal cultivation of land, they will be given a reserve of 15 acres per person, not excluding women and children. The rest of the land is declared free, and whoever wants it, can accept it.

Second: Whoever does not swear allegiance to the British government and does not change convictions about communal cultivation of land, they will be given a reserve of 15 acres per person, not excluding women and children. The rest of the land is declared free, and whoever wants it, can accept it.[5]

The form says, "The government of Canada represents the majority of the Canadian people. And if the majority of people say that the Doukhobors should not be any longer allowed to have the land they have been cultivating, then the government should listen to the majority and should destroy the records for these farms that are held by the owners incorrectly, so that the farms could be given over to other people who would repossess them in compliance with the law."

As John MacDougall explains, the government and the people of Canada find that the main reason for this action is that we are not cultivating the land. However, we are in doubt that he was sent from the government with this message. This is why we would like to bring it to the attention of the government and the people. It is said that we are not cultivating the land. What can justify this unfairness? A commission which arrived last year and measured the cultivated farm land, determined that we have more homesteads of cultivated land than is required by your legislation. The second piece of evidence that we are cultivating the land is our sales of grain. This year our community sent 250,000 bushels of wheat and 500,000 bushels of oats for sale, and we had enough left over for the summer and for the following winter. You can check these records at the elevators. If we are not cultivating the land, where did we get this grain from? We would also like to tell the government and all the people of Canada in all sincerity that we are farmers and we prefer this kind of labour since it is the most honest, correct, legal and primary occupation in our lives, and we have earlier tried and will keep trying full-heartedly to cultivate the land.

When we arrived here not having either horses or oxen, our women pulled the ploughs and ploughed the land. We think you have not forgotten this as newspapers wrote about it. From the side, it may seem ridiculous and humiliating, but there was no other way we could handle it, considering farming honest and legal work. Please, men and women, consider it seriously, if there is no honest interest in agriculture, which woman can be made to pull a plough? This is not common among people, particularly among women, we know and understand it, but we had no other way out. Our earnest disposition towards agriculture motivated us to do this. And if based on such false reports our land is taken away, this would be illegal and inhuman.

It is true that the population of the town of Yorkton, which is the closest to us, who are not land owners, but merchants (for example, Buchanan and McKenzie) regard our lives with hatred, and with all their might are trying to destroy it themselves and call upon others to destroy it. But each sensible person on the outside who does not know our lives well should not believe this because these instigations can only originate from an evil dark spirit that hates the union and communion of people, despite the fact that this is the foundation of the law of God and of the teaching of Christ.

Isn't it known to all that Jesus in His teachings called and is still calling upon a unity of all people, as one father and children? And such a life, as written in the New Testament, was carried out in the times of Christ. This was 19 centuries ago. In those days, people who accepted the faith and the teachings of Christ proved them through their deeds. The riches and material possessions were brought to the apostles and became the communal goods. This is the foundation of our lives as well.

People who believe in Christ should accept this way of life because much time has passed from His call, but they are not following it, moreover they are trying to destroy the life of those who follow it. How can these people justify their actions before Christ on the day of his second advent that people are waiting for? Who can positively say that that day is not coming any time soon? That day may be approaching, but people like those merchants are still living carelessly. Are they waiting for that day, or are they seeking profit by hook and by crook?

When the Doukhobors came to those merchants for anything they needed, Doukhobors were good. Now when the Doukhobors have built their own warehouse and are buying everything in bulk from warehouses and even from factories, they are seen as bad. Those untruthful people wish that the land will be taken away from the Doukhobors, as if this would make their lives any better. However, we hope that the majority of the people supported by the government will not agree with this and take into consideration that this land is God's creation. It was created for people, and for all that live on it. The land is our common mother, it feeds us, gives us shelter, makes us happy and keeps us warm; it loves us from the minute of our birth until we fall into eternal sleep on its maternal bosom. And people still have not figured it out that we can live on the land and use it without separations and measurements, but they decided to divide the land with each adult being allocated 160 acres.

In a way, this is fair and lawful, but if there were an increase in population it would result with a shortage of land. They would have to again redistribute the land according to the number of people. Then, instead of 160 acres, it could be perhaps 100 acres, and this would be lawful. In our times, there is still plenty of empty lands in Canada. And if among people living in the same neighbourhood, one may take 160 acres and another—15 acres, would it be then lawful and fair?

John MacDougall assures us, and it is also what the forms say, that the government will keep protecting our religious freedom, as it has done up to now. But the government says that we have to swear an oath of allegiance and citizenship. We tried to explain it to MacDougall and asked him whether he believes in Christ. He said that he did. Then we asked him again, "Do you know the teaching of Christ?" He replied, "Yes, I do."—"Does Christ in his teaching forbid to swear oaths, and allegiance would be one of them?" He says, "No, He does not forbid it." Then we told him that he did not know the teaching of Christ. He became confused and with his face turning red, he said, "The Gospel says 'yes, yes or no, no, and what is above this is from the evil one.'" We said, "Just based on this fact alone, we cannot swear any oaths, and if the people's government of Canada wants to protect our freedom of religion and its practice, then this is our faith to live according to the teachings of Christ. We cannot accept Christ's faith, believe in Him and consider Him the Son of God, but live contrary to His teachings. What kind of faith is it then, one can ask?"

Then after this conversation, MacDougall said, "I don't know anything. I am leaving the forms with you, and it is all explained there. There are two options identified, and you can chose whichever you want." And he again repeated that the majority of the people demand this.

Then either the people of Canada do not understand us and do not wish to consider the specific features of our situation because of our faith, or we cannot understand these people. If the land is taken away from us because we are not cultivating it, then we explained it earlier. If the land is taken away from us because of our refusal to swear the oath of allegiance, then we can say that we considered this issue resolved already when we left Russia and moved to Canada. Please consider our words not to be rude, but to be a brotherly explanation. Did you not know why there were some problems between us and the Russian government, and why we left the motherland and moved here to Canada? It was only because we did not swear an allegiance to Nikolaĭ Aleksandrovich Romanov, and refused to be soldiers afterwards. Our reason for this is because Christ forbade us to swear allegiance. The Russian government did not take into account the teachings of Christ and treated us very cruelly, and now if the Canadian government and the Canadian people want to raise this question and start persecuting us by taking away our lands, then it would be like the same ox having its skin ripped off for the second time but by different people. Do not these people see that the old skin has already been ripped off, and the new one has not grown yet? If you start taking the land away from us, even if not all the land, it means that the teaching of Christ is not taken into account in deed, and if it is, then only in words. And this would force us to prepare for the sufferings that we already experienced in Russia.

We sincerely say that we are very grateful to the government and people of Canada for accepting us, giving us shelter and making exceptions for us in some general rules that are against our convictions and our spiritual understanding. We were excluded from the military duty, we were allowed to settle in villages and cultivate the land together for which we have a document from the government. If it were not for these concessions, we would not have stayed here and we would not have invested so much work, particularly over the last three-four years, when you returned us to our places of residence by force.

We worked so hard, not only men who are more accustomed to labour, but also women and children worked extremely hard. We obtained steam mills, we purchased steam thrashers, we built brick factories where the work is done with steam engines, we are building a large flour mill that together with its equipment would cost about 70 thousand dollars. So despite having lived here for eight years, we have not enjoyed our lives, because the life itself did not allow it, because we had nothing, and we had to work, often excessively hard. Now, thank God, we have a little bit of everything, and we could live in a freer way, as everyone wants, right? However, there come some unexpected misunderstandings, like this announcement that can lead to persecutions, and persecutions lead to sufferings and becoming destitute.

In these times people should have more compassion rather than a desire to cause sufferings. We are requesting you to consider all this seriously and act as your heart suggests. If you can consider our brotherly explanations and acquire some understanding of our faith, then the land will not be taken away from us, the announcement will not have any consequence, and we would be extremely grateful to you all for this.

All our efforts and the fair proofs of cultivating the land and settling in did not work, and all our land was taken away. But all this was only the deceit by priests, the communion to the body of Christ via bread and wine, and the essence was in the oath. After a while, the same governmental official came to us again and started asking if anybody wanted to swear allegiance, then such a person would get the full allotment of 160 acres. Whoever did not want to, would only get 15 acres per person, and this land would not be considered their own, but the property of the government until further notice. When new land allocations were finished, over half of our land was taken away from us and given over to whoever wanted it. Some of our Doukhobors were also tempted and started accepting the farms. We were not taken aback by this, but we started consulting with each other about what we could do so that the government would not take away our last remaining land and would not leave us and our children without a piece of bread.

Notes

1. Leo Tolstoy (Lev Nikolaevich Tolstoĭ) (1828–1910) was a famous Russian writer and the author of *War and Peace, Anna Karenina* and of multiple other novels. He also was a philosopher and thinker who developed the concept of not resisting evil with violence (non-violent resistance). He was a great sympathizer and supporter of the Doukhobors and assisted them in resettlement to Canada.
2. Pobedonostsev, Konstantin Petrovich (1827–1907), a highly conservative statesman, the Ober-Procurator of the Most Holy Synod (the chief government official overviewing the operations of the Russian Orthodox Church) as well as a member of the State Council (the Supreme legislative body of the Russian Empire).
3. The author erroneously refers to the "President" of Canada.
4. Reverend John MacDougall was the chief architect of Doukhobor land foreclosure. On December 28, 1906, he was appointed the Commissioner of Investigation and Adjuster of Land Claims for the Doukhobor lands. He was empowered to recommend the cancellation of homestead entries to the local Land Agents, who would make the actual cancellation. He was also empowered to receive applications for re-entry, to issue receipts if homestead fees were paid and to administer the naturalization oath.

5. These paragraphs seem to contain a printing error. In the original, the text of the second paragraph repeats the previous paragraph, whereas the content implies that those who do not accept British citizenship would not be given the same treatment. It is also likely that the original announcement was supposed to indicate that those individuals who did swear the oath of allegiance and also wanted to cultivate land individually in homesteads were entitled to get 160 acres. For a more complete picture of the Canadian government's reversal regarding land ownership and the Hamlet Clause, see: http://www.larrysdesk.com/sklandseizure.html.

CHAPTER 36

A Move to British Columbia. An Explanation to the Government

Doukhobor village near Grand Forks, British Columbia

The cancellation of land entries by the government for the refusal to accept citizenship showed how unjust the government was. It did not keep its promise given at our arrival that this country had freedom of religion. In this way it lost all confidence among the Doukhobors. They understood that the governments were the same, both in Russia and here, and that the entire government structure was sustained by the immoral law that went contrary to the teachings of Christ. Then it was decided to leave Saskatchewan and to move somewhere else to a more suitable place. The designated individuals were appointed by the community and they set off on a journey. The designated people were Pëtr Vasil'evich, Nikolaĭ Zibarov and Semën Rybin, the latter was our interpreter from English. They went on one trip and looked around. Then they went the second time, and on the third time, they bought some land in Columbia[1] and the move began.

Thus the Doukhobors moved to Columbia for two reasons. The first and the main reason was the unjust cancellation of the land entries by the government. And the second was that as vegetarians, we wanted a warmer climate so that we could grow various vegetables and fruits for our sustenance. This untimely move caused us a lot of effort, losses and worries. As mentioned earlier, we had invested a tremendous amount of labour into buildings and cultivating the land. The land there [in Saskatchewan] was deserted and barren by nature. Until our arrival, it had not been walked upon by people, and there had only been wild goats, deer, moose and other animals. Therefore every furrow demanded tremendous labour, and as soon as we completed this labour, we had to move again. We petitioned to the Minister of the Interior to consider our situation and to pay us at least something for our labour of cultivating the land, as in Saskatchewan, cultivated land cost up to 30 dollars per acre. Even if the treasury paid us five of six dollars per acre, it would enable us to settle down in the new places where we had to buy the land for 50 to 500 dollars per acre. But whether the government pays attention to our legitimate request, or not, is yet to be seen.[2]

In Columbia, the terrain has mountains and forests, so the Doukhobors have to work even harder here than in Saskatchewan. However, it is much warmer here, various fruit trees grow very well, such as apples, pears, plums, prunes, sweet and sour cherries, and all the vegetables, including watermelons and tomatoes, ripen nicely. A lot that was bought by our designated individuals was located between the towns of Nelson and Trail. There is a railway passing along the ravine, and the big Columbia river flows through. Its tributary is the river Kootenay that flows from Nelson. The lot was on the other side of the river and the railway, and as it was all covered by a huge forest, the move started with the workers [who could do the heavy work of clearing].

In May of 1908, the first group went there which consisted of two men from each village. All the women and children stayed at home. These workers had to clear as much land as they could and build houses for living, and then the families would join them in the fall. This is how the move continued: each year, in early spring, workers from each village moved over, prepared the land and the houses, and then in the fall, their families would move over as well. They also maintained their households in Saskatchewan.

The Doukhobors believed that after their move to Columbia, the government would stop bothering them with their organizational orders since the Doukhobors did not accept the citizenship in Saskatchewan, and they were punished for this already. Here in Columbia, however, we bought the land with our available capital that we saved through hard physical labour. With every year of the move, the land area increased, as we kept buying more lots. The government did not pay attention to this and minded its own business.

Here we live on two lots separated from each other by 70 miles. The first lot is called Uteshenie[3] and Brilliant.[4] The second lot is called Fruktovaia,[5] which was so called because the land there was mostly bought with orchards, and the fruit from them was supplied to Uteshenie.

Here in Columbia we are forced to attend governmental schools and to register births, marriages and deaths. School education works for the benefit of the government, and the registries—of the clergy, and these two sides are closely connected. And as we understood it and are further learning, these two [schools and registries] strongly contradict the teachings of Jesus Christ, and consequently, our understanding of the religious beliefs as well. In Uteshenie, following our request, the government school was closed and replaced with our school, and the children are taught in both English and Russian languages.

In January this year, the blank forms for the registry of births, marriages and deaths were delivered from the government. We did not accept these forms and wrote the following explanation.

Brilliant, January 25, 1912

To Stephen Haskin, The manager of government affairs in Nelson

On January 21, through Shcherbinin, we received the blank forms that you forwarded to us in order to register births, marriages and deaths. We do not reject the registry and the rules established by your law, but they should apply exclusively to individuals who voluntarily accepted citizenship and who are willing to participate in this registry. As is known to you, we have not accepted citizenship, which should take precedence over the rejection of registry [of births, deaths and marriages]. Therefore, we are requesting you not to force us into this. We do not think that this would bring you either any benefit or honour if you persecute us for this, because we are doing this not because of a whim of some kind but due to the religious considerations of the law of God. Because of these considerations, we disagreed with the Russian government, left our motherland Russia and moved here, as we thought it was the land of freedom.

The people of the town of Grand Forks did not treat their [Doukhobor] neighbours in good faith and fairness only because the power is not on our side. And this is what happens, "The powerful always faults the powerless."[6] This is how it is done in Russia, but this is the reason why Russia is considered a backward country. The English are considered advanced people as compared to other nations, and this country is called "Freedom." Is this the way to execute this freedom? In the neighbourhood, a man died who had only one son. As everyone knows, death brings grief and sadness to the relatives. But the people on the outside did not sympathize with them, they even started causing them more grief and suffering, they took the son of the deceased as a miscreant and threw him into jail, because he had not called a doctor to examine the dead body. Is this reasonable? And how will God look upon this?

With respect,
The Christian Community of Universal Brotherhood, residing in Brilliant.

There was no response to this explanation. In the Fruktovaia area, the children are forced to attend a government school, and the Doukhobors are also investigated when one of them dies. In the first two investigations, one person in each case was put into jail for one month. In the second two investigations, two individuals per case were incarcerated for three months' terms. The wives and children of the arrested individuals wrote an explanation and submitted it to the judge who issued the arrests. This was the content of the explanation:

Explanation to the Judge

The unfair and cruel judge, following your order that reflects the rule of arbitrary violence, the police took away our husbands and fathers from us and put them into jail for three months for the following reasons. The first [of the arrested], Nikolaĭ Zybin and son, did not invite a doctor to examine the dead body of his brother. The second ones, Ivan and Vasiliĭ Dymovskiĭ, did not invite a doctor to examine the dead body of their mother. Because of this all four were forcibly arrested and put into jail. We are now left to the power of providence, and in order to protect our lives, we relate to you our sincere feelings. You are following the laws established in the ancient days, and these laws perhaps were necessary in those days when they were established. In our time, perhaps not all the people, but at least the people who have accepted the teaching of Christ, based on love, mercy and compassion to all living on earth, can do without these laws. Now you took away from us our bread winners and providers by force. Please tell us what we [women and children], powerless and weak in all respects should do now?

Perhaps you may tell us that we live in the commune and that the commune should take care of us, but the commune comprises private individuals who sustain their lives through the arduous, hard and honest labour of farming, and if you keep taking our work force away for no reason and throw them into jail, we repeat, what should the weak ones do? Isn't this unjust and cruel of you? Isn't this an embarrassment not only to you but to your whole country that has gained fame around the whole world as a country of freedom? We list below the losses incurred by you that you should seriously take into account. Nikolaĭ Zybin is not only the head of his household, he is also the senior gardener responsible for all the vegetables of the commune. His responsibilities and labour are remunerated with 10 dollars per every 10 hours of work. The other three are ordinary strong workers who sustain their families: wives and children, the total number of 12 individuals. To count the incurred expenses even by the lowest estimates, they are paid 5 dollars a day each for 10 hours of work. These are our legitimate requirements essential to our livelihoods that you should satisfy immediately. We turn to you, as you are the person directly responsible for our ruin, but if it does not depend on you, then you should promptly forward this to the person responsible.

This is because the life emanating from the Heavenly Father cannot be stopped, and it is given not for the suffering and torture but for joy. Yet we continue suffering because of your personal whims. Please seriously consider whether you can inflict sufferings onto people who are trying to absolutely follow the law of the Heavenly Father that was explained by Jesus Christ as the son of God.

We are expecting the results from you.

The wives and children of the husbands and fathers taken by you to prison from Grand Forks area.

Notes

1. The author often refers to British Columbia as Columbia.
2. No compensation for land losses in Saskatchewan has ever been provided to the Doukhobors.
3. Uteshenie (Ootishenia) is an area in present day Castlegar, BC, spelled as Ootischenia; the word means *consolation* in Russian.
4. Brilliant is an area in present day Castlegar; the word means *a diamond* in Russian.
5. Fruktovaia (Fruktova, Fruktovoe) is one of the former Doukhobor villages established in BC in Grand Forks area. The word means *fruit* or *fruit orchard* in Russian.
6. "The powerful always faults the powerless." The letter quotes the opening line of a fable (very famous in Russia but unknown in Canada) by Ivan Krylov called "The Wolf and the Lamb," which is based on Aesop's fable of the same name. The fable is also known via its rendition by Jean de La Fontaine. The initial line of the fable in La Fontaine's fable is somewhat different: "The reason of those best able to have their way is always the best" (translation by Eli Siegel http://www.aestheticrealism.net/poetry/Wolf-Lamb-LaFontaine.htm).

CHAPTER 37

Detailed Inquiry and Investigation by Royal Commissioner William Blakemore

The arrival of the Royal Commissioner William Blakemore in our midst was caused by a misunderstanding between the local government and the Doukhobors in regard to the acceptance of schools and registry books. There were also all sorts of misrepresentations from our former brethren who withdrew from the communal life. The reader of this book already knows that the major rule of communal life was established by the common voluntary wish of all the people. The one who would deviate from this common rule would no longer belong to the brotherhood. Those having forgotten the Lord's warning that one cannot serve two masters—God and Mammon,[1] first voluntarily joined the commune and then also voluntarily left it, in particular there were many individuals who left after the confiscation of the land registries [in Saskatchewan]. They left, first, because they were afraid of the government; that it could take away the rest of the land and inflict great misfortunes and sufferings.

Second, they were tempted by the land and those farms that had been developed together by the joint labour of the commune and taken away by the government. They hastened to accept these lands by swearing the oath to King Edward. And the third and the major reason was that they betrayed their convictions for which everyone suffered so much. Upon leaving the commune, they immediately started consuming meat, drinking vodka and smoking tobacco. This pertains to the Yorkton area, but of those who lived in Prince Albert area, many remained true to the same convictions: they did not eat meat, did not drink vodka and did not smoke tobacco.

In Yorkton, however, while leaving the commune, they took their share, and often took whatever they wanted irrespective of the share. The government respected them and helped them since they were now living under the government's rule. A testimony to this can be found in the report by Commissioner Bowes from Kamsack to the Minister of the Interior. Among other items he reported that individuals leaving the Commune should be provided with more support and assistance as they could vote during the elections.

In Columbia,[2] some people also started leaving [the commune] and reported misrepresentations and various untruths about Pëtr Vasil'evich as the official designate and the manager of all the communal affairs. All these facts together caused the appearance of the Royal Commissioner Blakemore.

On August 22, 1912, the Royal Commissioner called Pëtr Vasil'evich to Nelson and started a detailed inquiry. The inquiry was held in the public court. The general public was allowed to attend and listen, if they wished so. The inquiry was held by the Royal Commissioner in the presence of two legal representatives. The interpreter was Evalenko, a Russian who was not a Doukhobor. Ivan Shcherbinin also participated in interpreting. There were also two clerks present who took the written record of all the questions and the testimonies.

The inquiry started with Pëtr Vasil'evich's birth, childhood, upbringing and assuming the position of the leader of the Doukhobors. The interrogation lasted for two days. The Commissioner raised various serious matters, such as questions about how we believed in Christ and since when our religion existed. Pëtr Vasil'evich responded in the following words.

> I recognize Christ in the full sense as the Son of God, as Christ brought peace on earth and with His teaching, opened the way to the Heavenly Kingdom and united our souls with eternity and solemnly proclaimed that all the inhabitants of the earth are children of one God, the Father, and should live as brothers, and provided the law that enabled communion with eternity. The first commandment is: love God, your Lord, with all your heart, soul, and mind. The second commandment is similar to the first one: love thy neighbour as yourself. This is the entire Law and the Prophets.[3] With the second commandment he brings all the people together into one united brotherhood, through which the kingdom of God would come to being on earth.

The Commissioner addressed the question how Verigin and all the Doukhobors viewed the government. Pëtr Vasil'evich in his response denied all the governments of the earth, wherever they were, since every government only protected itself with the power of immoral law. By doing so every government prevented the advent of God's kingdom on earth that was called upon by Christ. Firmly following His teaching, all the governments should be abolished and merged into one God's kingdom, where peace, love, truth and equality of all people as God's children would abide instead of discord and terrible wars that made rivers of brothers' blood flow. The time for this was gone and people should abandon such lawlessness and enlighten their minds from the Holy Spirit above. This Spirit would lead all the people to the wisdom of God, and only then the people would understand their destiny in front of God and the great happiness of all the people on earth would follow.

The Commissioner was angry and agitated at first, as he was embarrassed in front of the public, as the court was packed full of people. But Pëtr Vasil'evich in his turn did not remain silent and proved their wrongdoing solidly and soundly. These were two forces: the power of this world and the spiritual power from above.

Thus the Commissioner understood that Pëtr Vasil'evich was a serious and earnest person in his spiritual understanding, who was not shy in front of anyone and not frightened by anything.

On September 5, this year, the Commissioner visited Uteshenie,[4] where he was greeted in the Prayer Home with bread and salt by the whole assembly of brothers and sisters. He was addressed with a speech on behalf of the whole community. This is the speech.

"We heard that you arrived in Columbia, and now we can see you in person. We are very grateful for your visit to us. In general, we consider people visiting other people a good deed, particularly when the visit can bring some benefits in deed, or at least in a simple verbal conversation." After these words, he thanked us and approached the table where bread, salt and water had been placed, and it was explained to him that in our assemblies we put these things because bread is the flesh of Christ, and the water is the source of His teaching in its spiritual meaning. He then asked to get a small slice of bread and took some water and said, "I am doing this because in my words, there will be only a good wish to you." We thanked him for this.

He started talking about Christ, "Christ is the only one on the whole earth that we have to honour and obey, as the Son of God. Now already all the states believe in Him. Sometimes if we, that is all the people, divert from His teaching, this is only a manifestation of our imperfection and weakness. You cannot say that you are perfect in everything either." After this he turned the talk to praising the local governors of this country, both past and present. He started praising them tremendously for their good laws that they came up with for the good of the people's lives, and differentiated this country from Russia: "In Russia, the government is rough and cruel, and to the best of my knowledge, you were persecuted and tormented a lot because of your practice of your faith. It does not happen here that anyone is persecuted based on their beliefs, this is the country of freedom in all aspects, this is the country of great education, and it is available to everyone." Then he turned to the children and asked them: "Are you going to school and learning to read and write?" The children responded, "No."—"Why not?"—"Because people educated in schools take our parents and brothers for no reason and put them in jail." The Commissioner said, "I will discuss this with your parents, as you are yet too young." Next, he immediately proceeded to explain the benefits of literacy. "After your children have been educated, that is they have gone to schools and become citizens of this country, this would be beneficial for them in all respects. They will have a vote in elections of new government, and they can even reach up to this level [be elected]. In general, literacy improves a person's life. You may have noticed that educated people work less physically and live the lives of plenty. The registries of births and marriages also serve to your benefit: couples that have a record in the registry books cannot split apart under any circumstances, this registry binds them and supports in this way the whole country. In case anything happens, such as the death of parents, the registered children will not be left destitute. The government will know about them through the registries and take care of them. The dead need to be registered to prevent murders, since people here live on their own, so this can cause murders and such other bad things. A doctor needs to examine the deceased: if he died on his own, this is fine, but if he is killed, the doctor needs to immediately report to the police, that have to take measures, find the culprit and punish him."

Following his every explanation, the Commissioner repeated that he was sure that based on Doukhobor lifestyle, nothing like a murder, a divorce of the newlyweds or children's sufferings could happen among them. However, he repeated that the law of this country demanded this, and all the people living here had to follow it fully. He spoke for about two hours and everybody listened to him attentively. We saw that the Commissioner was a clever, honest and truthful person. He was born in this country, he received a good education in terms of literacy. As a part of his education, he learned all the laws of this country, and he was so convinced by them that he did not notice any other laws in other countries and only noticed his own. He met us for the first time in his life, and without any treacherous thought or goal, in earnest, he started explaining these laws to us as if we were incapable of understanding them on our own. It was new to him that we refused to follow these highly praised laws as he probably had never met such people in his life, and to the best of his ability, he was trying to explain his laws to us.

After this we asked him whether we could provide some explanations on the matter. He said it was fine. We started explaining to him the law of God through which all the people on earth would be united in the teachings of Jesus Christ and would live as one great family of all humanity.

> God's law will be the same for all and all will follow it. Human laws, no matter how good and accepted they could be, contain many bad things, such as wars in which lots of brotherly blood is spilled, and all this happens in accordance with the laws that you approve. One person in the country signs an abominable declaration of war, which leads to a terrible material waste of the whole income that has been accumulated for hundreds of years through great labour. Millions of people's lives are prematurely terminated, and the relatives left behind suffer and grieve; elderly parents, wives and orphaned children are left without care to suffer for the rest of their lives. Nobody explains why and how it all happened and there is nobody responsible for this sacrifice of millions of people consumed by Baal.[5]
>
> If people start blaming the leader of this grief and misfortune who signed the insane declaration, the latter also relieves himself of responsibility and explains it in this way: "I signed it based on the laws of our ancestors who lived hundreds and thousands of years before us." Thus, you cannot find a single person responsible for this terrible deed. This is a great misfortune for all humanity. How does education relate to this, why does it not help to get away from this gloomy situation, which is like a shadow of death and darkness? This could still be comprehensible in the old times, when people whom we no longer remember now were not yet educated. This was still justifiable before the birth of Christ. However, after the birth of Christ, whose life and teaching ended with a terrible painful death on the cross to which he voluntarily sacrificed himself for the great cause of God entrusted with Him by the heavenly Father, war is no longer justifiable. The sacrifice of Christ should remain in the memory of the whole humanity as a lesson. It was the covenant established between God and people. Even after this great deed of Jesus Christ, the humanity still has not learned anything and keeps treading the path of Cain, at the same time pretending to believe in Christ. This is a terrible injustice. Isn't this the common faith of all the states, and have not they strongly deviated from the teaching of Christ? The teaching of Christ and human laws are as far from each other as the sky and the earth. What you are praising to us can hardly be called laws.

Then in a similar manner we explained our attitude to schools and public education, which involved military training. "We reject this education based on the legal basis of the teaching of Jesus Christ, the same relates to the registries that are not needed by people. Let this be left in God's hands, as it is by His will that people are born and die, and He surely knows about it all."

After this oral explanation, the Commissioner said, "I understood you well."

He was also handed an explanatory letter on behalf of the community. He accepted it and parted with us cordially. He thanked us for the reception and earnest conversation and left. He also visited Fruktovaia.[6] There, after a conversation, he was also handed an explanatory letter. He also visited Saskatchewan, Veregin Station, and audited the office for three days. Mikhail Vasil'evich Kazakov showed him all the records in good order, and the Commissioner said: "It is the first time that I find an office to be so clean." In conclusion of his detailed investigation, he wrote a report to the federal government.

Notes

1. Mammon in the Biblical tradition is considered a symbol or a deity of greed, material wealth and earthly possessions.
2. The author often refers to British Columbia as Columbia.
3. The Law and the Prophets are two parts of the Bible (the Torah that describes the laws of Moses and the Prophets that relates to the other books of the Bible).
4. Uteshenie (Ootishenia) is an area in present day Castlegar, BC, spelled locally as Ootischenia; the word means *consolation* in Russian.
5. Baal is an ancient god of storm and fertility worshipped by the Canaanites (Ancient Phoenicians). Baal is mentioned in the Bible; and in the Christian tradition, he became an allegory of a false God, a blood-thirsty demon and one of the Princes of Hell.
6. Fruktovaia (Fruktova, Fruktovoe) is one of the former Doukhobor villages established in BC in Grand Forks area. The word means *fruit* or *fruit orchard* in Russian.

CHAPTER 38

The Explanatory Letters of Doukhobors to Blakemore

I quote below the explanatory letter of the Doukhobors to the Royal Commissioner.

September 4, 1912. Brilliant,[1] BC. The valley of Uteshenie[2]

To the Royal Commissioner Blakemore

We have been known as Doukhoborsty for 300 years. Over this time in Russia, Russian clergy, priests and government officials have repeatedly raised questions about our Doukhobor beliefs, which our ancestors and ourselves have accepted from Jesus Christ. And we are trying to implement this teaching in life to the best of our abilities through our deeds.

Our ancestors have refused to recognize materialistic church services and worship of handmade objects. For this they were tortured and incarcerated in monastery jails, sent to hard labour; their children were taken away from them and brought up the way the clergy and the government wanted. However, none of this helped the Russian government and the clergy. God is mighty in His truth. Doukhobors in Russia were exempt from any church rites and they never signed up in any registry books. This matter of registry is closely connected with Doukhobor beliefs. Now as ever we wish to be citizens of the whole earth, and we wish our children to be free. Therefore we do not want to enter our children's names into the official government registry books, and we think that entering the names of the deceased is senseless. The essence of our religion is that we believe in the divine power of the eternal Spirit. Through the will of the eternal Divine Spirit, the whole universe is formed and maintained. Jesus Christ has brought the light of reason from the Father of the eternal Spirit from heaven to us, so that through the belief in the divine power, a person born on earth can transition into the everlasting Spirit after the physical death.

We are not against providing you with information about the growth or decline of our Doukhobor community, about the number of our people, once every five or ten years. However, we will not ever register in your books because we consider ourselves already registered by the Creator himself into the Book of Life which is called eternity. By the will of God, the creator of the entire universe, a human is born and lives in this world. It is also by the holy God's will that a person dies in flesh, but his soul returns to the Eternal Father in order to connect with its origin. Our God the Father is the power of the eternal Spirit, the power of love, the force of life that gave the origin to all that exists. And as Christ understood it, He revealed to us the Father of His eternal Spirit in this power. "Father and I are one," as Christ taught. School and literacy were not accepted by Doukhobors previously in Russia, and Doukhobors rarely taught children to read and write, and if they did occasionally teach them, they did this at home. We are raising children based on the oral tradition and instruction in order to avoid the expenses of paper and book printing. We reject school education for many reasons, but here are the main three.

The first reason: school education teaches and prepares children for military actions, where innocent blood of people is shed with no reason. The best educated people acknowledge this terrible sinful act of war as legal, whereas we consider it to be a great sin.

The second reason: education and literacy nowadays are only achieved as a source of easy profit, machinations, deceit and severe exploitation of the working class, of the people toiling the earth. We belong to the class of working people and are trying to earn our sustenance through honest labour. This is what we are teaching our children as well—to learn in the boundless school of eternal nature.

The third reason: the school and literacy separate people on earth. As soon as people get literate and educated, they very soon leave their parents and relatives and plunge irreversibly into various corrupt endeavours harmful to the soul and life. They no longer think about their duty of honouring their parents, and they themselves enslave people for their insatiable and corrupt gluttony. It is scary even to talk about school education, how insane people become in the higher university royal educational institutions, where thank God, common people are not admitted. But it grieves us immensely that the higher education and science consume all the people's labour and the capital produced by their work, and the people suffer without land and without a piece of daily bread.

This is why we clearly understand the teaching of Christ and we follow a communal lifestyle and consider all the people on earth our brethren and children of the same God the Father. We understand that all the people are equal in front of God and nobody can enslave a person. We strictly remember the teaching of Christ: if anyone wants to be the first, he must be a servant to all.[3]

Based on this, we avoid pronouncing any type of oaths, promises, swearing allegiance to submit to following the orders of people who are equal to us. We only submit to the law of God, about which Jesus said to His disciples: take the law of God into your mind and heart and preach it to the world. Therefore we, as followers of Christ and His teaching, are even against Russian literacy, whereas English literacy is entirely useless to us. We consider spiritual rebirth to be the necessity above all others for a person. We consider this essential as Christ was a simple man, without school or university education, but He was a spiritual person with a great worldview in His mind, who penetrated the depth of past and future centuries. The educated rulers of the world and the high priests in their bookish delusion and cruelty crucified the great king, reformer and divine genius, from whom all the tsars and kings, governors, judges and spiritual instructors, in fact everyone all the way down to a simple peasant, should have learned. If now the executives of government power want to be cruel to us yet again, this would only add to that old cruelty a perpetual shame of senseless ruining of peaceful dwellers whom Jesus calls towards universal equality and brotherhood of all the people on earth.

This is the essence of our belief and of the aspirations of our ancestors that ultimate peace will be established on earth and good will—amongst humans.

Based on past experiences we see that we cannot count on permanent residence here in British Columbia. This is not because of our personal whims or inability to select good land and so on, but because we are not understood by the surrounding people, who are pedantic in their laws, the laws that are based on material property and exclude any right for apostle prophecy about peaceful labour and equality of all people on earth. We are the descendants of the tribe of Israel, of the three youths, Ananiĭ, Azariĭ and Misail, whom the tsar Nebuchadnezzar threw into a blazing furnace.[4] We are the followers of Jesus Christ, the King of eternal glory and our Lord, the Saviour of the world.

An explanatory letter of the Doukhobors from the valley Fruktovaia.[5]

September 10, 1912. Grand Forks, BC.

Fruktovaia Valley.

To the Royal Commissioner Blakemore.

We come from Russian Transcaucasia and moved to Canada in 1899. The reason for our move from the beautiful Caucasus was the Russian government, which because of our refusal to be soldiers, relentlessly tortured us in jails. Some of those who were due for military duty were lashed with terrible force until they were half-dead, and after lengthy tortures and sufferings, up to 200 people—young men and 70-year-old elderly who were considered by the Russian government to be the leaders of the Doukhobor community—were exiled to the Iakutsk area. We should point out that everybody is a leader because Christ in His teaching clearly says, "All who do the will of my heavenly Father are my brothers and sisters,"[6] and therefore we are all for one and one for all.[7] It was not easy for us to undergo material ruin and suffer through the recent persecutions by the Russian government, but we deeply believe in the force of Divine providence that God sees all and will protect us with His own hand from the evil people.

In Russia, Leo N. Tolstoy, Dmitriĭ A. Khilkov, Vladimir G. Chertkov, P. I. Biriukov and other good people tried to help us via written petitions and personal requests to soften our punishment and alleviate the rough treatment of officials that we were subjected to for our faith accepted by us from Christ. And in the end, we were allowed to move to Canada. We were glad that we would get into the country of freedom, and we willingly left behind our wonderful fields, the abundant fruit orchards and temperate healthy climate, where we had good agricultural wealth.

In Canada, we received a warm welcome, and we thought that we would live here in peace protected by the freedom of religious practice of Christ's teachings and that we would no longer be tormented as in Russia. The Canadian government gave us plots of free land, over 2000 homesteads in the wild deserted prairies of Saskatchewan, that were covered by forest and shrubs, with large spaces of wet marsh and milliards of strong flies and mosquitoes that could not be tolerated either by people or by animals. However, we decided to stay there only because we were promised complete freedom of communal life, that we could settle in colonies and toil the land together in one lot, as it was suitable for the commune. Together we started clearing and cultivating the wet deserted prairies. Our women, in 10 or 12 pairs would pull the plough and furrow the land, and the men left to earn money. We paid 10 dollars per homestead, the total of 20,000 dollars, although that land did not suit our life's purpose, that is our vegetarian sustenance, as vegetables and fruit did not grow in the cold climate of Saskatchewan.

At the same time, the government of Canada sent us a few copies of a statute that made us exempt from military duty, and, in a separate document, we were allowed to settle in colonies and cultivate land together. As the result of this, we were beginning to believe in complete freedom. However, three years later, the government requested us to sign up for 160 acres of land individually in homesteads and accept citizenship. It became clear to us that we were deceived in a cunning way through the ministerial paperwork and all the oral promises of the Canadian government. This made us think hard and look for a way out of this voluntary confinement. There is a folk saying: "while escaping a bear, ran into wolves." We tried many times to explain our beliefs to the Canadian government, that we are the followers of Christ, and that neither our ancestors could, nor we can violate God's law for the sake of earthly benefits. Then we were directly told that our homesteads would be taken over by other people who would sign off the sworn allegiance to the English king and we would be driven out with a stick.

Doukhobors at meetings in all the colonies decided to let their cattle loose, and they all grouped together and went to prophesy the words of God and the teaching of Christ. The largest part of the Doukhobors stayed behind though as they were toiling the land and felt too sad to leave their labour behind. However, eventually they would have all been gone if the Canadian government did not forcibly terminate the march of the first group. The government applied force to return the Doukhobors to their villages and again started promising freedom of religion and life in the colonies and such other things.

At this time, Pëtr Vasil'evich Verigin arrived from Siberia where he had spent 16 years in exile for our Doukhobor cause. He started explaining to us that we have to live honestly and peacefully among any kind of people. Here there was a complete freedom of religion, and this should be enough for us for the time being. We, Doukhobors, decided once more to trust the promises of the government and we invested much effort into clearing up the fields, draining wetland and building good gravel roads. We bought good horses, bulls and cows and began sowing the fields together. We also bought a few steam-driven tractors and grain threshers. We also installed a few portable sawmills and built a lumber mill where grooved boards were dried and prepared with a steam-run equipment as building materials for house finishing. We constructed a big steam mill at Verigin station[8] that also functioned for rolling and sorting grain, which cost us up to 50,000 dollars. We built a few small mills in the villages. In winter, steam-driven machines were operating there, and in summer, we used them for cutting wood for construction. Close to Verigin station and in other areas, we bought over 70 homesteads of land, which cost about 150,000 dollars. We built two large double and three single elevators along the railway line, one at Verigin station and in other places, for selling our grain. We began selling about 1.5 million bushels of grain from our own harvested crops each year. We started demonstrating our agricultural well-being: we had a full set of agricultural tools; we had stables, barns, steam mills, brick plants, two to three common warehouses for the Doukhobor commune; and we manufactured goods and agricultural tools. We bought everything directly from the plants or from big warehouses at large discounts at very moderate prices.

The whistles of the steam-driven machines could be heard in the deserted prairies of Saskatchewan. Wherever possible, we ploughed all the land in the dry areas. Each steam tractor dragged eight or ten ploughs.

In sum, thanks to God's good will, everything had been arranged and taken care of very well. We acquired the best machines and steam tractors. We had over 1000 good horses, about 1500 good milk cows, about 2000 strong working oxen and about the same number of other domestic cattle, we also had over 3000 young sheep. We managed this entire household on our own. We had our own machinists and turners. We planned to bring the crop harvest up to two million bushels and sell the surplus. We were absolutely certain about this.

However, unexpectedly, in 1907, the government declared to us that all the Doukhobors should immediately accept British citizenship and follow all the laws, and if the citizenship were not accepted, the land would be taken away and given to others. We wrote to the ministry and sent deputies for personal explanations because we did not believe that such hypocrisy and cunning deceit could happen. This was the second godless deceit after which we had to decrease our household by more than half. We sold the sheep and the cattle very cheaply to whomsoever. Our homesteads that we cleared through hard toil were taken away and given to others. All our hard toil and the money paid for each homestead (10 dollars) was lost forever.

After this, the third deceit and plutocracy of Canadian officials followed. Through the agent John McDougall, we were informed as follows: if Doukhobors lived here on the purchased lands, the government would not pester them with its laws. The same person John McDougall provided 15 acres of land to each person for our temporary use for as long as the government pleased.

Trusting this, we immediately delegated three individuals: Nikolaĭ Zibarev, Pëtr Verigin and Semën Rybin (the latter was an interpreter from English) to buy land in British Columbia, where it was easier for us as vegetarians to procure vegetable nourishment, such as fruit and vegetables, and it was easier to follow a Christian peaceful lifestyle in our honest labour.

The first lot was bought at Brilliant and then at Grand Forks, BC. Until the present time, we have purchased 650,000 dollars worth of land. In the last five years, we have turned wild forests into a beautiful picture of flourishing gardens and orchards. We have planted over 70,000 good fruit trees: various apples, pears, plums, peaches, apricots, cherries, sour cherries, grapes as well as many types of berries such as raspberries, gooseberries, blackcurrants, strawberries and others. We have also built good houses for people with plumbing and good drinking water, as well as irrigation lines for watering gardens and orchards, along with large water reservoirs; the estimated costs of which are a few thousand dollars. We have also constructed lumber mills, where we manufacture construction materials for future communal buildings. In Brilliant, we have installed a big steam-driven water pump that pumps water from the Kootenay river over the whole Uteshenie valley. We are also installing electric power for lights over the whole colony and for using electricity for other work.

We are building a bridge over the Kootenay river, for which we have already purchased all the iron parts. While we do not yet have any surplus capital, we, thank God, have good health and physical power to work honestly, as humans should, and we hope that with God's will, we will overcome everything. Here we have good horses, cows from the best milk breeders and free-range horses from breeders.

All this property, earned in honest labour, we evaluate at 2–3 million dollars. In Saskatchewan, due to our refusal to accept citizenship, we sacrificed for the teaching of Christ about 7–8 million dollars' worth of land that the government was supposed to pass over into our property, there were over 2000 homesteads. We hope that in the near future, people will understand us, that we did this for the equality and brotherhood of all the people on earth. We will forever continue this apostolic mission of honest labour and peaceful life. Therefore, we turn to you with our sincere request. In the name of Jesus Christ, please give us an opportunity to live here as passers-by on earth. If you do not exclude the communal Doukhobors from signing in the registry books and do not liberate us from the English schools and literacy, with time, we will pack up and leave for another country, where we can be accepted as harmless people, and we would be practising in peace the holy teaching of Lord Jesus Christ, the Saviour of our whole world.

Glory be to our God.

The Doukhobor Commune of Universal Brotherhood, living around Grand Forks.

Notes

1. Brilliant is an area in present day Castlegar; the word means *a diamond* in Russian.
2. Uteshenie (Ootishenia) is an area in present day Castlegar, BC, spelled locally as Ootischenia; the word means *consolation* in Russian.
3. "If anyone wants to be the first, he must be a servant to all." The text is based on Matthew 20:26.
4. Ananiĭ, Azariĭ and Misail are legendary ancestors of the Doukhobors. The names are Russian versions of the names of the three Biblical youths, Hanania, Mishael and Azaria, also known under their Babylonian names of Shadrach, Meshach and Abednego. They were thrown into a blazing furnace for their refusal to worship the golden statue of king Nebuchadnezzar.

The youths came out of the furnace unharmed as they were protected by God. This narrative is based on Daniel 3:23.
5. Fruktovaia (Fruktova, Fruktovoe) is one of the former Doukhobor villages established in BC in Grand Forks area. The word means *fruit* or *fruit orchard* in Russian.
6. "All who do the will of my heavenly Father are my brothers and sisters." This text is based on Matthew 12:50 and Mark 3:31.
7. The expression "One for all and all for one" is found in many languages. It goes back to a Latin proverb "Unus pro omnibus, omnes pro uno."
8. Verigin (Veregin) is a village in south-eastern Saskatchewan founded by the Doukhobors in the early twentieth century and named in honour of Pëtr Verigin. At some point, the name of the village was incorrectly recorded by the railway officials as "Veregin" instead of "Verigin." Nowadays Veregin houses the National Doukhobor Heritage Village http://www.ndhv.ca/.

CHAPTER 39

The Inquiry Report and the Recommendation of the Royal Commissioner William Blakemore

Doukhobors are found to be "desirable settlers."
Recommendations towards more lenient measures.
Victoria, BC. 24 December 1912
The following general findings and recommendations were included in the report which was submitted to the honourable Lieutenant-Governor Council-Deputy Attorney-General in the city of Victoria by William Blakemore,[1] appointed as the Royal Commissioner for a public inquiry of the matter of the Doukhobor Sect in British Columbia.[2]

1. Doukhobors were found to be desirable settlers from the standpoint of their farming skill, piousness, devotion to agriculture, and general industry.
2. This investigation has failed to establish any valid objection to them, except their refusal to comply with the registration laws and the school.
3. Their customs and teachings have no evidence of bad inclinations that could be detrimental to the general well-being of the community.
4. Such minor objections as have been raised against them should not be taken into account in view of their many good features, typical of their lifestyle, and especially in consideration of their qualifications as agriculturists.
5. Their refusal to comply with the registration laws is their decision.
6. There is sufficient evidence to justify the conclusion that their views will be modified as soon as they become better acquainted with the true nature of our law.

7. The head of the Doukhobor Community, Pëtr Vasil'evich Verigin, has sufficient influence and authority to bring about full compliance with these laws—if not at once, at any rate within a reasonable time.
8. There is reason to believe that the Doukhobors have been kept in the dark as to their obligations under Canadian laws.
9. They are certain that as long as they do not become Canadian citizens, they would not be called upon to obey the existing law.
10. While moving to British Columbia and acquiring their land there by purchase with cash, they were certain that they would not be obliged to obey the laws, as it was in Saskatchewan, where they acquired their land from the Government.
11. Punishments, such as imprisonments, will fail to take effect, because they will regard it as persecution for their beliefs. The spirit of distrust towards the government has been developed in them since ancient times in consequence of the persecution to which they have been subjected for more than three hundred years.

Attached recommendations

(a) The membership of the Doukhobor Community is based on a firm religious foundation. Their opposition to accept the registration and the schools is also grounded in religious foundation. Therefore, no drastic steps should be taken to force their immediate compliance, but that should be left to Pëtr Verigin, their leader, who would convince them to comply with the government. Meanwhile, if it is found necessary to resort to punishment, it should take the form of fines rather than imprisonment, as the imposition of fines would be more effective, and would bring the matter home to the parties directly responsible—to their leaders.
(b) The Government system is advised to adopt a policy of patience with the people and putting pressure on their leaders.
(c) During the registration of births, deaths, and marriages, a responsible member of the Doukhobor Community should be appointed Sub-Registrar. This would facilitate and shorten registration.
(d) With respect to the schools, some leniency is required here, in order to give the Doukhobors confidence and secure their sympathy, some working arrangement might be made under which Russian teachers could be invited to schools; in conjunction with Canadian teachers, they could teach elementary literacy subjects.
(e) It would be good policy to appoint in each province a permanent Doukhobor Agent on somewhat similar lines to the Indian Agents.
(f) Doukhobors are exempt from military service in the interests of the country.

(g) Doukhobors should only be admitted to Canada if they have a clear understanding that no exemptions of any kind will be allowed in the matter of observance of laws.

The report of the Royal Commissioner Blakemore and all its 11 points are fully truthful; he understood our beliefs precisely and honestly expressed them in his report. There was nothing in this inquiry beyond sincerity and understanding. After his report was printed, some individuals could have dark thoughts about him as a traitor to his home country due to a monetary bribe. A blatant lie was told about this honest man. People have to understand that such things as belief in the power of God through the teaching of Jesus Christ cannot be acquired with money. One can see this from the past history of humankind: if the belief in the existence of eternity was to be proven, it was proven through mortal physical death. This can happen in our time as well. For his honesty and sincerity, William Blakemore deserves enormous gratitude from the entire community of Doukhobors. Let his good name be passed over to our descendants forever with a good memory.

And this is what the Doukhobors wrote to Blakemore.

Brilliant, BC, January 24, 1913
To the Royal Commissioner William Blakemore,
Victoria, BC

Dear friend, the first point of your report to your government dated December 24, 1912 mentions that Doukhobors are industrious and pious in character, but later you think and hope in vain that the views of the Doukhobors will be modified as soon as they become better acquainted with the true character of your law. In the course of your long inquiry, have you not yet become sufficiently acquainted with the Doukhobor religion to understand that Doukhobors are not as unenlightened as the government imagines them to be, and that they cannot by any means agree to accept and follow your human laws that act against the teaching of Christ? These laws allow wars, where thousands of people perish in the fields, where blood flows in torrents, and the soul is being torn apart by fear, and the heart throbs in fear and pain. The misery, cries and shrieks of mutilated people fill the air. Their fathers, wives and children are left hungry, without anyone looking after them, without anyone needing them. Besides human victims, another loss is milliards of capital that could have saved a whole country from hunger but which are instead spent on this terrible deed of war. You, educated and civilized people, should think about the fact that overseas

European wars have been long flooding the fields with blood. God's bounty grows on those fields that feeds people and cattle. And the earth no longer blesses these areas with its harvest, so millions of people die there from hunger, and along with them, their poor innocent children also die as martyrs.

In your rich palaces, with your luxurious food and clothing, you do not feel much of this. You, the English, only add fuel to the fire, as in your arsenals, you create weapons with the longest range among nations. You take pride in the fact that your deadly weapons are used somewhere very far away from you by other people to tear each other into pieces. Do you not think that you will pass over your bravery onto the sword that would be raised against you? Jesus said, "All who take the sword will perish by the sword.[3]" You do this yourselves and you invite us to accept such cruel laws splattered with human blood. Since the early days of their existence, Doukhobors have attempted to follow one law of Jesus Christ that forbids any murder and violence directed against people. For this divine law, Doukhobors have endured a lot of suffering and even death on earth. This is what Christ said, "All those who believe in me will be persecuted."[4]

You also want Doukhobors to become citizens of your country. But Doukhobors in their beliefs consider themselves to be the free citizens of the whole world and the brothers of all people living on earth, without the distinctions of any religions or nations, and the human laws have no purpose in the lives of the Doukhobors.

Your report also says that in the matter of schools, imprisonments should be substituted with monetary fines and Doukhobor leaders should pay these fines. Does the government really think that only the leaders and not all the Doukhobors are responsible for this issue which all the Doukhobors have been following since ancient times? Each Doukhobor is taught and brought up in Christ's faith since youth. Dear friend William, why did you not tell the government that on September 5, 1912, in Brilliant, 2000 men, women and children unanimously declared to you that we would not accept schools. Indeed, for us Doukhobors, school education is not required, as we are trying to teach our children honest labour in our fields and the divine religious understanding. Doukhobor teaching is based not on the books with dead letters but it is passed from one generation to another, from the father to the son, as the living word. Therefore, Doukhobors have no need for literacy. Doukhobors even reject the books of the Bible, which are considered in the world to be holy, and only accept in them the words which agree with the law of God. The Doukhobors cannot ever believe what the Bible allegedly says about military victories in the holy land being won by the will of Israeli leaders, prophets and God himself or that God the Lord could ever permit the killing of people. There are many other stories there that contradict the teaching of Christ. For centuries, people have wandered through the scriptures as though in the dark. While reading the Bible, some seek an easier way of entering the Kingdom of Heaven. Christ told a rich youth, "Give away your possessions to the poor and follow me."[5] And Jesus also told one of his disciples, "Put your sword back into its place; for all those who take up the sword, shall perish by the sword.[6]" Over 2000 years have passed, and His commandment is not yet taken to fulfillment by any of the literate and educated. There are some people who want to follow Christ's teaching, but these are illiterate and uneducated peasants, like the Doukhobors. In each country, the government prevents them from doing so. They are prevented by laws and parliaments to install the kingdom of God on earth, as it is in heaven. If the government imposes monetary fines for such an insignificant matter as schools, the government will inflict the second major wound to the Doukhobors. It seems that the Canadian government is pleased by the Doukhobors as good workers and agrarians. But why isn't the government happy that some people came to their country from far away as wanderers to have a peaceful life here, to have no weapons in their homes and to pursue perfection? On the contrary, you are going to punish the Doukhobors even more, and they have not inflicted any harm to your country. This would be terribly unfair.

A member of the Christian Community of Universal Brotherhood, Semën V. Vereshchagin.

Notes

1. William Blakemore was a Victoria journalist who was authorized to investigate the Doukhobors in 1912. The investigation was called "Royal Commission on Matters Relating to the Sect of Doukhobors in the Province of British Columbia (1912)."
2. It appears that the author G. Verigin attempted to translate the Blakemore report closely to the original. However, in some cases, there were some deviations from the original text based on the narrator's understanding of the text and the matter at hand. Therefore, the text was retranslated from Russian. The translator left as much of the original report as possible, while at the same time incorporating the modifications by the author G. Verigin. The original section of the Blakemore report can be found on https://open.library.ubc.ca/collections/bcsessional/items/1.0065738.
3. The text is based on Matthew 26:52.
4. The text is based on Timothy 3:2.
5. The text is based on Matthew 19:21.
6. The text is based on Matthew 26:52.

CHAPTER 40

A Conversation Between Military Minister Bowser and the Doukhobors About Registries and Schools

Fruktova (Fruktovaia) heritage site school in Grand Forks area, now a museum

The Doukhobor community was visited by Minister Bowser of the province of BC from Victoria.[1] The Lands minister Ross and some others were there as well. There was a total of six people visiting on December 17, 1914, in Brilliant.

When they arrived at the sobranie (Doukhobor Assembly), Pëtr Vasil'evich came out and explained, "I am a member and a representative of this community, Pëtr Verigin." Both ministers shook his hand and said, "Pleased to meet you and glad to make your acquaintance." Pëtr Vasil'evich told them with the reciprocal sense of politeness: "We welcome you."

After this, the meeting of the ministers with the Doukhobors began with greetings.

Minister: "I am very pleased that a few days ago I met the Doukhobors in Grand Forks. We had a very pleasant conversation about their life and settlement in British Columbia. I am accompanied by the Minister of Lands and we are both happy to have the pleasure of meeting you in such a large assembly, and this day is highly esteemed by us."

Doukhobors: "We are also very glad to see you and thank you for taking the trouble of coming here."

Minister: "This event will always remain a pleasant memory of our friendly meetings."

Doukhobors: "We are always ready and glad to see you in the future if you visit us."

Minister: "I have never met Doukhobors before, and I am very pleased to be here. Your community which now has a large number of men, women and children interests us a lot, we are also interested in your communal household. Within a short period of time, you have achieved tremendous progress, which can only be attained through joint forces, as your commune. Our government is now installing experimental exemplary farms in many places in order to improve the cultivation of land in the country and the growing of various fruits and vegetables. Our government invests lots of capital in this, but as compared to what your commune has achieved in the area of agriculture and gardening,

40 A CONVERSATION BETWEEN MILITARY MINISTER BOWSER... 247

	our enterprises seem small. We are very interested in your cultivation of land, planting of fruit gardens and growing of plants, installation of water irrigation pumps, building fruit canning and jam factories, flour mills, a lumber processing plant and your wonderful family houses. All these can also attract and interest the local population in the improvement of their farms, and serve as a positive learning example for them. This exemplary household and cultivation of land can provide our country with a good flourishing profit in the areas of cultivated gardening and agriculture. You deserve the complete and highest approval and appreciation of your hard labour. A considerable contribution to this, we believe, belongs to your communal representative Pëtr Vasil'evich Verigin."
Doukhobors:	"We are very grateful that you find our affairs and household in a good order, but we have always considered it essential to work and settle in, so that we could earn our nourishment from land with our own labour. It is a pity that you are visiting us in winter: the summer view of plants and gardens would be more beautiful."
Minister:	"Mr. Verigin wrote to me, and I am grateful for his invitation to come for a holiday last summer in order for me and the accompanying officials to enjoy eating your cherries. We had the intention with the Minister of Lands to visit you last July or August, but at that time, as you know, war was declared. Premier McBride was called to Ottawa, and I was too overwhelmed with other matters and could not visit you until now, when we could make this journey."
Doukhobor women:	"We will be very glad if you could visit us next summer when the fruits ripen, and we request you to also invite your wives and friends to try the cherries."
Minister:	"I am very grateful to you for your cordial invitation, and I must say that we are very interested in

	the fact that Doukhobor women take part as far as they can in the cultivation of land on equal terms with men."
Doukhobor women:	"We are very glad that you approve of our labour. We think that your wives should engage in agricultural labour as well, the way we do. We request you to pass over our opinion to all your women."
Minister:	"I will gladly pass over your opinion to our women, but unfortunately, I doubt that they would be capable of engaging in agricultural labour as you do, but in general, I consider our women to be great supporters for us, men, in life, wherever it is."
Doukhobor women:	"If they are not capable of engaging in agricultural labour the way we do, they can help you to cut down expenses on their outfits because their luxury strongly reflects on the workers of the poor class."
Minister:	"I promise to pass this over to our women, although I do not cherish much hope that it will take effect on them. In all this I see friendly relationship with you, and I hope that we will always remain in full trust of each other, so that there would be no misunderstandings arising between the Doukhobors and the government. The government is always ready to protect your interests against trespasses of whatever bad people, and you will be protected by law on par with all other people living in the country."
Doukhobors:	"We are very grateful to you for this."
Minister:	"Today at the Brilliant station, a few Doukhobors delegated by those who withdrew from your commune, requested me to charge you for their money that you owe them for their previous work together with you while they were still living in the commune. I explained to them that this is not a matter of authority either for me or the government."
Doukhobors:	"These individuals who withdrew from the commune, our brothers, are bothering you with their

	requests unfairly. In Saskatchewan, we still have communal property left from which all people leaving the commune receive their full share."
Minister:	"I will tell you once again that you have achieved very good results here in developing land, gardens and orchards. We are very interested how you, Doukhobors, have achieved such great progress without schools or science. I can tell you directly that in Grand Forks and here we saw your communal household, and we were very interested in it. But there is one small matter left that disturbs this pleasant side of your life: your disagreement with the laws of this country when it comes to the registry of the deceased, newly born and newlyweds. This legal system of the country equally protects all the people, whether citizens or non-citizens, no matter which religion or nation they belong to. Moreover, our government does not interfere in the matters of religion because we have complete freedom of belief in God here, as long as the laws of the country are not violated. The laws of this country give the complete freedom of religious practice to all. I hope you also agree with my arguments related to the freedom in our country."
Doukhobors:	"The reason we left Russia and came here to the country of freedom was to get rid of all the persecutions for the teaching of Jesus Christ, which our ancestors and we carried to freedom in this country through the hard journey of suffering inflicted by the Russian government and priests."
Minister:	"I can assure you once again that the law of the government of Canada does not touch upon the religions of all the people in Canada. However, for the purposes of governing the country, we have certain laws that are acknowledged by the citizens as being useful and indispensable. These laws have to be followed by all without any exceptions, so that children in case of parents' death, could receive inheritance. In addition, this gives us an

	opportunity to learn the increase or decrease of the population in the country."
Doukhobors:	"Such registry of increase and decrease of the Doukhobor community is done in our office in Brilliant, and the government is always welcome to learn the exact data. As far as inheritance is concerned, all our children are provided for since we do not have individual properties. The heirs of the deceased or live parents have the same legal brotherly right to the entire property."
Minister:	"Also, the registration of the deceased requires the presence of a doctor in order to get information about the danger of epidemic diseases and successfully prevent them in this way."
Doukhobors:	"Registry of the deceased is also done in the Doukhobor office in Brilliant, and as far as the epidemic diseases are concerned, we have no intention of concealing them."
Minister:	"Now we have one more question left about school education. As I know, two years ago, you built this nice big building for a school, and you taught children here for one year. Some positive reports of progress were received from the teacher. However, later, for some reasons, you closed the school. Now I suggest that you open the school again to continue the learning of literacy. The government considers this to be good and useful."
Doukhobors:	"We have already explained to you before that school education of children is very harmful because in public schools children are taught to kill in wars, they are given wooden rifles and taught military discipline."
Minister:	"I agree that children are given wooden guns in public schools, but this is only done to develop muscles in children."
Doukhobors:	"We believe that the best way to develop muscles in children would be to give them iron spades to soften the land for vegetable beds and around trees in orchards. We find this the most useful way

	of developing muscles among children. School education has a detrimental effect on the whole life of a person. You can see that all the literate people try to secure livelihoods by the easiest ways. After a short period of school education, our children started being disobedient to parents, avoiding agricultural labour and household duties at the most vulnerable age. This is why we unanimously declined the school and literacy."
Minister:	"I am perplexed: if you consider education so harmful to your children, why did you ask to open schools and built this house suitable for use as a school?"
Doukhobors:	"We built this house not for a school, but for prayer meetings. It cost us no more than 500 dollars."
P. V. Verigin:	"I would like to provide you with a short explanation about school. Doukhobors agreed to accept a school following my suggestion, as I thought that learning literacy would be very useful for Doukhobor children. But when the parents saw a big change in the personal character of their children, that the influence of the school brings forth a certain mood which goes contrary to ordinary Doukhobor life, Doukhobors closed the school."
Minister:	"I deeply regret that you refuse to accept the school and registry books in a peaceful way. Please understand that as a representative of the power and of the crown I am giving you a legal warning to accept the school and registry books."
Doukhobors:	"We are glad to hear that you represent the crown, but we request that you understand that the Doukhobor commune represents the teaching of Jesus Christ. We compare governmental law with a thick rope, which is woven from many parts. These parts have three major most dangerous components: registry books, school and swearing allegiance. This is why we will never agree to be woven into this thick rope. Our ancestors in

	Russia suffered brutally for this cause and here we are also ready to submit ourselves to suffering. It is 2000 years since people should have accepted the law of Jesus Christ and followed it, but unfortunately, in these 2000 years, people have issued many human laws, but the law of Jesus Christ remains without execution."
Minister:	"The teaching of Jesus Christ is not understood by everyone in exactly the same way. We also believe in Jesus Christ and live in agreement with His teaching. Our government will not put you into prisons and torment you as the Russian government did to you. But a special law was passed for you, you will be fined through a court system including the paying of the fines through the estimate and sale of your properties."
Doukhobors:	"You said yourself that you also believe in Jesus Christ and live following His teaching, and now you are threatening us with the fines and sales of our properties. We see clearly that the law of Christ and your faith are violated by your deeds because faith without deeds is dead. What will you evaluate, and what will you take away from us if all our possessions are mortgaged with a downpayment of 6000 dollars? We had to accumulate this debt because the Canadian government treated us unfairly. During our first settlement in Saskatchewan, the government gave us land, and after seven or eight years, the government took this land away. We invested our physical labour and material means into the clearing and development of this land, and then we were forced to move here to Columbia. You think that literacy and education are good things but we would like to explain to you again that your education brings nothing except a terrible bloody war. Education separates people into two halves. One half are social parasites who live off other people's labour and the second half are the eternal agricultural labourers,

	who often do not even have their daily bread, and you want to ruin us for this harmful education? Do you consider it a crime not to accept schools and registry?"
Minister:	"One cannot consider this directly a crime, but by violating a law, in a certain sense, you are committing a crime."
Doukhobors:	"Do you consider wars a crime?"
Minister:	"A war is a separate matter. It arises due to misunderstandings between states, which are always trying to resolve such misunderstandings by means of war. All the enlightened people understand that wars are wrong, and that it would be better to resolve these misunderstandings peacefully through arbitration."
Doukhobors:	"Whose fault is this?"
Minister:	"We think that this is the fault of the German emperor, and the Germans and their emperor probably think that this is the fault of England."
Doukhobors:	"And what is your personal opinion about this?"
Minister:	"I do not approve of any murder, but since I am a loyal citizen and subject of the King, if our advanced government in England considered it necessary to go to war and protect a country such as Belgium, then I would probably go willingly. But this would fully depend on my personal will. If I did not want to go to war, the government would have no right to force me into going to war."
Doukhobors:	"It would be very unfair to you, you would have to go to war, or else you would be violating your oath of allegiance. But who starts all these wars? Kings, emperors and educated people or the common working people? And can they be tried in court for this?"
Minister:	"Of course, they are started by people in power, but you are posing very deep questions. Wouldn't it be better for us to address the matters that brought me here. I think you realize the usefulness

	of literacy, as a literate person can always be a better agriculturist than an illiterate one."
Doukhbors:	"We consider all schools and universities to be harmful science. Because of them civilized people have come to many inventions and for their own ruin prepared long range weapons, airplanes, fast trains and armoured cars. Because of these inventions, millions of people die in the battlefields, as locusts. And all the educated people who hold administrative positions, including you, Bowser, are eating bread produced by other people's labour."
Minister:	"It is true that many harmful inventions came from educated people, but we should not forget all the things useful to people that were discovered by science. It is true that I eat the bread created by the hands of the farmers, but in my turn, I work for the benefit of these farmers. I think we should turn to the resolution of these two issues: the schools and the registries, that I hope you would agree to accept, otherwise you would subject yourselves to unpleasant consequences."
Doukhobors:	"Please also take into consideration that these two issues: schools and registries are closely connected to our religious beliefs and we will stand by our beliefs in the name of Jesus Christ. We request you on behalf of the whole assembly to take back your words that you will be ruining us through property evaluations and fines. As a people's governor, elected by the people to sort out various unfair matters happening in their lives, you should not treat us as Pilate treated Christ. Following the demands of the people, Pilate delivered Christ to mortal execution. Even if the people demanded our punishment, as a people's ruler, in the name of justice you should be protecting us, in particular, when you have personally seen our good household and you are well aware of our peaceful life. In 15 years, not a single crime has been committed.

	You can ask that police official who is required to know about his region, whether a single crime has been committed during our time in Columbia." The policeman Black answered, "There has not been a single crime."
Minister:	"It is unnecessary to ask the policeman. We are well aware of the peaceful life of Doukhobors and that they are obedient. But the issue is that the law about registries and schools that I informed you about cannot make exceptions, neither for your commune, nor for the Methodist church, nor for Masons, nor for any other communities."
Doukhobors:	"Our Doukhobor Commune includes between 7000 and 8000 people, and we all live following the law of God. There are no policemen or judges in our community. We know well that you have the power of your laws to ruin and torture us as much as you want. But we are all ready to submit ourselves to no matter what kind of sufferings and tortures, in order to save our faith in Jesus Christ."
Pëtr V. Verigin:	"I want to tell you my opinion about Doukhobors. The best for you would be to leave them alone. Doukhobors do not wish for your name to go into the Doukhobor history and into archives as the name of a cruel tyrant. What good would it do the government to ruin 6000–7000 thousand Doukhobors and let them wander as paupers around Canada? There are too many poor people without them. As far as I know, when Doukhobors are persecuted, they stick even harder to the communal life, but when they are left alone, they leave the Commune on their own and gladly accept all your laws. For example, in Russia, they were strictly adhering to the communal lifestyle, but here in Canada, out of six or seven thousand, over a thousand have left for individual farms and accepted citizenship. In regard to the school issue, I honestly confess to you that it was my fault. I often wondered why my parents did not place me in school

where I could get a good education in literacy. When I came from Siberia to Canada, I was fully convinced that school education was necessary for Doukhobors. In response to my suggestion, many Doukhobors agreed to educate their children in English schools. However, when the parents saw that the children were showing signs of disobedience already at this age, they consulted about saving their children from school education, teaching the children themselves as far as possible, and decided to immediately close the school. I now remain very grateful to my parents that they did not educate me. Please consider the fact that Doukhobors in Russia did not agree to accept school education and this resulted in a split. Doukhobors who belonged to the commune did not accept schools and left for Canada, and those who accepted schools and education stayed in their previous places of residence, but in our time, they all went to war. And our commune, thank God, lives happily. Please consider what difference was created nowadays between literate and illiterate Doukhobors.

Our view on emperors and kings agrees with the allegory by Lev Nokolaevich Tolstoy. He writes, 'When a colony of bees settles down around the queen, then in order to free the queen, the bees on the periphery start flying away, and this flying away of the peripheral bees liberates the centre of gravity and the queen becomes free'. This is what all people should do to liberate emperors and kings from the pressure on them, otherwise emperors and kings could be suppressed and strangled. In this case, Doukhobors flew away as peripheral bees and liberated the emperor Nikolaĭ Romanov in Russia."

Doukhobor women: "As mothers of our children, we sincerely declare to you that we will never let our children be educated by other people. We consider it our responsibility and highest duty to teach our children and bring them up in the law of God, so that along with us, our children can provide for themselves and obtain their sustenance from land through their own labour. We have to share with you our understanding that nature is the best school in the broad meaning of this word, all our well-being and higher education in life depends on it. Therefore we request to be left alone."

Minister: "I will let you consider this seriously, and in three–four months you can write to me your final decision."

Doukhobor children sang "Lord's Day" very harmoniously.

> The Lord's Day is coming, you can already see the light from afar,
> And all the ones who are asleep are woken by the joyous dawn of the morning.
> Chorus:
> We can hear the call, everyone brace up, hold the spiritual blade,
> Fight for the truth, protected with the helmet of salvation.
>
> Our leader is true in battles, let us be brave at heart,
> The legion of the chosen ones is led by Christ himself, we will win!
> Chorus
>
> All ahead, do not get sad, do not be afraid of the treachery of the enemies,
> As we are looking at the Saviour, our victory is precious.
> Chorus
>
> All banners unfolded, passing through all the places,
> Sing as loud as organs, that the kingdom of Christ is near.
> Chorus
>
> Glory be to our God.

The sobranie (assembly) was attended by over 2000 men, women and children.

They sang the following hymn loud and melodiously:

> The good shepherd is looking for a poor sheep, it will perish without him, and he feels sorry for it.
> Chorus:
> He looks for it, he looks for it, and the Lord wishes to save it.

A precious coin is acquired again, it was raised from the earth and darkness.
Chorus.

The Doukhobor women offered the ministers and the accompanying officials to partake bread and salt. The ministers gladly agreed and they were invited by Pëtr Vasil'evich to his quarters to have dinner.

The sobranie assembly was then declared closed and everybody parted very cordially.

Glory be to our God.

Note

1. William John Bowser was not a "Military" minister, there was no "Military" or "Militia and Defence" ministry in BC. In 1914, Bowser was serving as an "Attorney-General" in the cabinet of Premier Richard McBride. The position of the Attorney-General was more like a minister of justice.

CHAPTER 41

The Resolution by Soldiers Who Returned from the War Reached at a Big Meeting in Nelson on February 13, 1919

At this meeting, by a majority vote, the soldiers passed a resolution: "to request the government to deport the Doukhobors back into the country they came from, because the Doukhobors do not follow Canadian laws, do not enter the records of their newlyweds, newborn and the deceased in the registry books, and because they did not participate in the war."

The Doukhobors were accepted in Canada on a special condition, so that they would engage only in agriculture. The government then made a promise not to take soldiers from among Doukhobors. Now Doukhobors have started a lumbering business, they are building lumberyards and selling lumber. They also set up other kinds of factories with commercial purposes. Therefore, at the soldiers' meeting, it was decided that Doukhobors should return to Russia, particularly as the government that had been oppressing Doukhobors there had been removed. All the lands occupied by the Doukhobors should be taken away and given for settlement to soldiers who returned from the war.

The Doukhobors' Response to the Soldiers Who Returned from the War in Regard to Their Resolution of February 13, 1919

Toil and Peaceful Life

The elected representatives of the Christian Community of Universal Brotherhood were sad to see in the Nelson newspaper that the soldiers who returned from war had passed a resolution to take away the land from the Doukhobors in the Nelson district as well as elsewhere in Canada and give it over to the soldiers.

The Christian Community Committee decided that it was necessary to have an emergency meeting in Brilliant. The February 13th resolution by the soldiers who recently returned from the war was read and listened to attentively by the whole assembly. The entire assembly attended by over 2000 people, mostly women, passed a resolution: "To inform the public via the respectable newspaper 'Nelson Daily News' that the Doukhobors have solemnly decided to offer all the land that Doukhobors occupy in Canada to the soldiers who had suffered so much from the past four-year war." In particular, all the women unanimously expressed their wish to give this land to the soldiers. The women and children can procure nourishment in Canada without the land properties. Since all of the Doukhobor women, starting with 12-year-old girls, can fully support themselves through their own labour, it does not matter whether they would procure their nourishment from the land or through other occupations. On their home distaffs, all the Doukhobor women can spin yarn of various quality from wool, flax, cotton and other plant fibres. From this yarn, on home looms, they also weave good cloth and materials for their own use.

For the better convenience of engaging in various kinds of work, such as mentioned above, and to cultivate the land in Columbia, to clear the land of heavy stumps and stones, as well as for raising and nurturing children, already a long time ago, Doukhobor women cut their hair short, so that they would not spend time on hair styling. Doukhobor women, however, are taking good care of themselves otherwise: they often take baths in the steam bathhouses and use plenty of soap. There is also another reason for the women to cut their hair: so that there would be less hair falling off a woman's head when she is preparing home food or kneading bread dough because hair can fall off if it is not cut short frequently. In order not to have any extra expenses in their family lives, Doukhobor women have not been wearing any jewellery such as metal objects, like bracelets, rings, etc., for a long time.

Many men at the meeting asked the women with surprise why they demanded that the land should be given over to the soldiers. The women loudly voiced their unanimous opinion that the soldiers who returned from the war deserve this.

In general, the women said, the soldiers who returned from the war have to be satisfied and immediately taken care of in all respects. Although, seriously speaking, the soldiers should understand that they were fighting for the king and the British Empire and not for the Doukhobors.

Since the Doukhobor commune has no special valuable assets, the women are demanding to give the land to the soldiers who returned from the war. It is necessary however to notify the Canadian public and the soldiers that the Doukhobor lands in Canada are subject to significant mortgage payments of about a million dollars. There are report sheets to show this.

The commune does not own a single acre of the governmental land. All the Doukhobor land has been purchased, and therefore there is still debt against it.

Many have left the Christian Community of Universal Brotherhood and have taken over the homesteads of government lands. The communal Doukhobors who have no government land are sincerely requesting the public not to confuse them with those Doukhobors who accepted the allegiance to the royal government but did not go to war to protect the British state.

According to the principles of the Christian Community of Universal Brotherhood, it is not allowed to kill people under any circumstances because those who follow the principles of Doukhobor religion have no enemies on earth. The words "to consider Doukhobors hostile to the British nation" used in the February 13 resolution are totally erroneous, and the members of the Christian Community of Universal Brotherhood strongly protest this expression because the Doukhobors are sincerely grateful to the English nation and the government for providing them with a happy living in Canada for 20 years. While in these 20 years Doukhobors have not accumulated too much for their livelihoods, they have always managed to procure nourishment for themselves. Of course, Doukhobor diet is very limited. After moving from Russia, Doukhobors were placed in Saskatchewan, and they were given 3000 homesteads and 480,000 acres of land. Then, after the Doukhobors due to their religious beliefs did not swear the oath of allegiance required for this land, the government took away all the land, all the 3000 homesteads. This happened in 1907.

A lot of land was cultivated, many bushes cleared, marshes were drained and roads were laid through. Doukhobor women and children injured their hands a lot when they cleared the land from the roots, since in the first years, men mostly had to go for outside work in order to build houses and maintain households. This cultivated land was taken away from the Doukhobors. Forty villages that they built with costs estimated around one million dollars were left behind without any compensation. The veterans who returned from the war should know this by all means if they are talking about Doukhobors at their meetings.

The reason Doukhobors did not go to war is because they have the fundamental major principle: toil and peaceful life.

Doukhobors consider war to be a relic left from the barbarian knights of the past, as evidenced by the old story of Tamerlane, Goliath, and others, and of David who, according to the Bible, massacred thousands of people. In the modern times there are also famous military leaders: the French Napoleon, and the last Barbarian knight, the German Kaiser.

Doukhobors shudder while talking about such despotic animals, as Doukhobors consider that no murder of any human being can be allowed under any pretext. This is the principle of their deep faith.

Before moving to Canada, Doukhobors sent in deputy representatives who clearly explained to the Canadian government that Doukhobors had been persecuted in Russia for their refusal to become soldiers, and it had been over 300 years that they had been subjected to sufferings and oppression in Russia for their anti-militarism.

The Canadian government accepted the Doukhobors and gave them an honest promise never to take Doukhobors for soldiers. Therefore all the Doukhobors: the elderly, men, women and children are feeling deep gratitude to the English nation and the government for taking the Doukhobors into their country and thus protecting them from the oppression and the despotism of the Russian government.

In 20 years, the Doukhobors have not accumulated exorbitant assets and their nutrition is limited and poor, because when their land in Saskatchewan was taken away, community Doukhobors had to buy land in Columbia that was covered with stones and forest. Here again, Doukhobor women and children bruised their hands on roots and stones in order to clear the land from the stones that are in such abundance in Columbia. In the first years here, men cut heavy lumber, cleared the land from stumps and built houses. Women have always been given an easier workload in the commune.

We can seriously recommend that the leaders of soldiers' associations visit all the lands in Columbia where they will see piles of stones gathered from the land, so that we could plant potatoes and other vital vegetables. Doukhobors are vegetarians and never eat meat and fish.

Doukhobor lots are all equipped with machines that are very important for agriculture. For example, a river pump was built on the bank of the Kootenay river for irrigation in Brilliant. Within five or six hours, it can pump up to 10 million gallons of water into a water reservoir. The water reservoir was built three miles away from the river on elevated ground. Thanks to this pump, 2000 acres of land will be irrigated.

A wooden pipe factory is ready, but in order to meet the irrigation plans, we need to invest at least 100,000 dollars. When men asked where the soldiers can get such a considerable amount of money to finish the irrigation system plan, the women responded that the government would probably provide it. The government would then have to lend this money at low interest rates, so that the land would bear good harvest in the future since everybody knows that the land in Columbia is not worth anything without irrigation.

In Nelson and Grand Forks districts, the Doukhobor commune already has over 4000 acres of recently planted fruit gardens, and over half of it already bears fruit. The fruits are apples, plums, sweet cherries, pears, peaches and apricots, as well as some berry bushes, such as gooseberry, different kinds of currants and lots of strawberry patches. There is a well-equipped jam factory in Brilliant for processing berries, and it produces up to 50 railway car loads full of good jam.

During the four years of the war, a few railway cars of jam from this factory were given for free to the soldiers who fought in the war. Doukhobors also donated a few thousand dollars in cash to the Red Cross and to the Patriotic Fund. In short, Doukhobors donated as much as they could because they did not have large assets.

As far as the February 13 resolution point that Doukhobors should return to their previous country, Doukhobors have nothing against it, particularly since the despotic government in Russia has been eliminated. However, this question deserves a separate consideration and the attention of the British nation and the government.

Doukhobor women strongly request the exclusion of the words "to consider Doukhobors hostile to the English nation" from the February 13 resolution. This expression is completely unfair, as was already mentioned above. All of the Doukhobors, particularly women, are very grateful to the English nation and government for the peaceful life of Doukhobors in Canada and have no hostile feelings to the English people. If possible, Doukhobor women pass over their sincere gratitude to the English King and his family for their lives in Canada.

The major principle of the Doukhobors is "Toil and Peaceful Life."

Glory be to our God.

This resolution was passed at the meeting in Brilliant on February 17, 1919 and was edited by Semën Rybin, a member of the Christian Community of Universal Brotherhood.

CHAPTER 42

Canada and Doukhobors

Professor Mavor,[1] the head of political studies at the University of Toronto addressed the following open letter to Sir Thomas White, Prime Minister of Canada. He also offered it for publication to the newspaper "Citizen."

Open letter to Sir Thomas White, the Prime Minister of Canada,

Sir:

I desire to appeal to the high-minded public of Canada to prevent, as they can, if they will, the perpetration of what appears to me to be a monstrous national crime. It is known that between 7000 and 8000 Doukhobors emigrated from Russia in 1899. The oppression they endured from the government there was well known and they applied to be allowed to come to this country. They raised two conditions, both of which were accepted by the Minister of the Interior of the time. The first of these conditions—exemption from military service—was embodied in an Order-in-Council. The second condition—freedom to settle in villages—was also fully accepted, although it was not embodied in a formal document. When they came here, the people of Canada received them with open arms. This was the largest mass immigration to Canada. The fame of Canada as the refuge for the unfortunate was spread and even trumpeted throughout the world. The Doukhobor immigration represented the beginning of a great movement from Europe which was looked upon at the time as of the utmost importance in building up this country.

The European immigrants built the railways in the North-west and contributed enormously to the increase of production. Had this immigration not taken place it is doubtful if the North-west would now be in its present economical position.

Perhaps due to the severe persecutions by the Russian Government that must have affected their minds, in the last few years, the Doukhobors were subject to outbreaks of religious fanaticism. These outbreaks did not, however, affect more than one-fifth to one-quarter of the Doukhobor people and did not last long. There have been no such outbreaks for several years.

When the arrangements were being made about their settlement, I was invited by the Department of the Interior to make some suggestions; and I suggested that the land allotted to the Doukhobors by the Government surveyors should not be in one area and that it should be suitable for practical settlement. In this way, the land left between the Doukhobor settlements would soon be filled up. My suggestion was adopted, and the anticipation proved to be correct. The intervening areas did fill up very rapidly and the lands quickly rose in value. What I did not anticipate was that the Government would break faith and trust with the people so soon and become subject to pressure by land speculators, who sought to deprive the Doukhobors of the lands which had been explicitly reserved for them and given to them.

Had I known about this, nothing would have induced me to encourage any immigrants to come to this country. The process of attacks upon the Doukhobor lands began in 1906. It is necessary to explain certain peculiarities of these people that made them vulnerable and defenceless against such attacks. About three-fourths of them practised rigid co-operation. They bought collectively and they sold collectively. The local merchants disliked the Doukhobors because the merchants did not profit from them on account of the purchases of Doukhobors being made principally in Toronto and Vancouver, where, soon after their settlement, they began to buy on a large scale. The local farmers professed to believe that the sale of Doukhobor produce by them caused reduced prices.

The Doukhobors had no votes because they did not accept citizenship conceiving that citizenship would give the Government a power over them, which they could not understand. For this reason, their case was handled so shamelessly. In 1907, the government simply cancelled the Doukhobor land registries and took away nearly 400,000 acres of land from these people. Large areas of that land had been brought into cultivation by these people.

Technically the Government may have acted within their powers. However, morally, their action was unfair. One of the peculiarities of the Doukhobors is their adherence to the teaching of Tolstoy and to his maxim "Resist not evil" that strongly influenced them in recent years. They also believed that like the Government of Russia—the Canadian Government was simply an instrument of oppression. They decided that even the small portion of land left to them was held as a very insecure tenure, and that instead of relying on government land, they should buy land privately. They bought large plots of land in British Columbia with the knowledge of the government of that province. This action was suggested by their previous experience, for in 1912, further encroachment upon their Saskatchewan lands was made.

Some thousands of Doukhobors were transferred to the British Columbia lands. There they arduously engaged in the agriculture to which they had been accustomed in Russia. They established large fruit orchards, built a jam factory and produced various vegetables on a large scale. During the war, they presented the government with large quantities of jam for the soldiers.

Now comes the crime—these peaceable if obstinate and peculiar people are being forced out of their purchased lands as they were forced out of their homesteads by the same conspiracy of local tradesmen, local farmers, local politicians and speculators. These local people decided to exploit the soldiers who returned from the war in order to deprive the Doukhobors of their cultivated lands. The intention of the scheme is obvious as it is discreditable. Based on the plea that the returned soldiers must have land, they have induced the government to buy out the Doukhobor lands at forced sale, and then give it to the returned soldiers.

There is plenty of land in British Columbia and in the northwest for all the returned soldiers who desire to settle down to an agricultural life. Of course, they should be generously provided with land. However, there can be no sound policy in turning out established settlers who have achieved a significant success in land cultivation and who have bought their land believing in the good faith and honour of the people of Canada.

The soldiers can also expect that the lands granted to them may be similarly expropriated under some pretext. Canada needs immigrants to occupy its wide spaces; but how can they be expected to come, if following some excuse they can be deprived of their homesteads or even of the lands they have paid for, as is about to happen now?

And what are the dispossessed Doukhobors to do? They cannot go back to Russia, the conditions for them would not be any better there than they are here. It is useless for them to think of buying land in this country because some excuse might be found at any time to deprive them of this land in the same way as is being done now.

The Doukhobors must inevitably be turned into vagrants—unable to obtain land in a country where there are millions of acres waiting for the plough. The life of these unfortunate people has been torn up by the roots again and again by the governments, not only in Russia, but in this country as well. It is little wonder that they distrust the good intentions of the state organization. Their factual experience has convinced them that the government is merely an instrument of oppression. The short-sighted policy of the government with regard to the Doukhobors during the past thirteen years has borne its fruit: their view of the state has been strongly confirmed in their minds.

The distrust inspired in their minds by the actions of the government has a great deal to do with their objections to the education of their children, as well as with their isolation from their neighbours. They feel, and have reason to feel, that they have been treated without regard to justice by their neighbours, and by the government. These proceedings have nothing in common with a policy of "reconstruction," on the contrary they amount to deliberate destruction. If the Government expropriated the fruit farms in the Niagara District, turned the farmers adrift and bestowed the land to returned soldiers with the liberty to sell to speculators, the case would be precisely the same. Care for our returned soldiers is a national duty; it cannot with justice be made a special burden upon a few. When a government breaks the fundamental laws of its own country and of society, it is little wonder that law in general should be held in light esteem.

If Canada is ever to be emancipated from slavery to the petty politicians, this can only be done only by a clear expression of public opinion. If there is anything to be done, there is no time to be lost. Appraisers sent by the Federal Government are already on the spot estimating the value of the land which is intended to be confiscated. The whole matter has been rushed with extreme haste.

I would suggest that the Federal government immediately launch a serious inquiry conducted by competent persons into the entire circumstances of the case. Canada cannot afford to have it compromised by such an unjust transaction that goes contrary to everything the country stands for. It should also be taken into account that the Doukhobor people, who have been and are being again plundered, are innocent and inoffensive people unacquainted with political guile. Every high-minded citizen of this country ought to insist upon justice being done for them and upon their right in the enjoyment of their peaceful and productive life.

Yours Truly,

James Mavor,
Toronto,
May 1, 1919.

николай

1. There are some minor deviations from the original text of Mavor's letter. We therefore provide the translation of the Author's rendition of this letter and the exact text of the letter in Appendix 2. James Mavor was born in Britain. He moved to Canada to became a professor of Political Economy in the University of Toronto. He assisted in the early negotiations of the Doukhobor migration.

CHAPTER 43

Death and Funeral of Pëtr the Lordly

Pëtr Verigin's funeral. Mourners gathered at the burial site.

On October 26, 1924, at 10 pm Pëtr Vasil'evich left Brilliant[1] for Fruktovaia,[2] Grand Forks, on a passenger train of the CPR railway line. After the train left the Farron station, and within one mile from it, it exploded. It was the carriage in which Pëtr Vasil'evich was sitting that exploded. It happened at 1 am. An evil person placed a machine from hell under Verigin's seat, a bomb which blew up the whole carriage. At that moment, he was asleep as a quiet angel, leaning on the arms rest without suspecting anything. His body was thrown about ten feet away from the carriage onto the railway embankment, where a tiny brook was flowing. Pëtr Vasil'evich lay with his face down on the left side of his face. The train still kept moving and the carriage was all on fire. After about 100 more feet the train stopped. In this way, Verigin's body was spared from fire. There were two corpses of a woman and a girl of about 18 years old that completely burned in the carriage.

Before leaving Brilliant, Pëtr Vasil'evich notified Fruktovaia by telephone that he was going there and that they should meet him at the station. When the train came, they learned that Verigin died on the way, 30 miles before Fruktovaia. In the morning, they notified everyone about his death over the phone. The unexpected news struck everyone from children to the elders as lightening. There were no more passenger trains on that day, and we had to take a special courier train from Nelson. In an hour, it arrived at Brilliant, and about 15 of us including Anastasia,[3] left for the accident site.

When we got there, the body of Pëtr Vasil'evich was already placed in the carriage. Two brothers, Semën Makhortov and Pëtr Kuchin, made their way from Grand Forks with some other people and they placed the body into a carriage. An investigation was already conducted there. Two chief doctors and a few other representatives of Grand Forks arrived.

The investigation commission did not allow us to take the body back to Brilliant immediately, and according to their law, it had to be taken first to Grand Forks to be examined by higher officials. We arrived in Grand Forks at 6 pm. All the Doukhobors from Fruktovaia village, from the elders to children, were at the railway station, and the whole town was disturbed by his death.

Grand Forks municipal authorities suggested that the body of Verigin should be taken to the police station for an examination, but we all asked for this to be done in the carriage, and our request was respected. The officials conducted the examination in the carriage. There were 12 of them. The face was not covered, and they took turns making sure it was him, and this was the end of the investigation.

Then all the brothers and sisters who wanted to say their good-byes to their great beloved leader took turns passing through the carriage and everyone got on their knees. This farewell took about three hours, and when it was finished, the train gave a whistle and it hurried to Brilliant.

The whole square in Brilliant was already filled with people. About a mile before Brilliant, the machinist gave three train whistle signals as a sign of a misfortune. At that time, it seemed that not only the earth but also the heavens trembled, all the people were terribly frightened and did not know what to do.

When the body was taken out of the carriage and brought to the house, all the people cried bitterly and could not believe their own eyes. The body was brought directly to the bath house that had been already specially prepared for it. Four men were designated to wash the body, and I was one of them. As we were undoing the buttons and taking off the clothes, we saw that half of the upper shirt was torn apart, and so evenly as one cannot even cut with scissors. Such an incredible force of hell struck our irreplaceable leader. Anastasiia participated in dressing the body and was shedding tears of grief over his body.

The site of his body reminded us of the body of Jesus Christ who was crucified on Golgotha, as we see it depicted. His left hand was placed behind the back of his head, as he put it in his sleep in the seat. His right hand was placed on his chest. There were no major wounds on his body, except for the left leg that was completely smashed together with the bone, but was still there, although his left shoe was not found. His right leg was all intact, except above the knee where it was pierced with a piece of metal about a foot long, four inches wide and one inch thick. This was iron from the seat.

When his body was dressed, it was taken to his bedroom and placed on his bed. The bed was moved into the middle of the room, so that it would be easier for people to take their last look at him. When all this was arranged, Anastasiia and all the relatives who gathered there got on their knees, everyone recited the psalm for the eternal peace and then they recited Christ's prayer "Our Father who art in Heaven."

Then all the other people did the same. There were no distinctions as to foreign, or Jewish, all were the children of one God the Father, and everyone had the same access. There were not only the communal Doukhobors from all the districts and from Saskatchewan, but all those who left the commune also came. There were many people from Prince Albert. All gathered at his body. There were many Englishmen and people of other nations, there were also many blacks and people with Indian origins. Men and women entered his bedroom, knelt and remained on their knees for a very long time saying their spiritual prayers and crying in grief.

His wake continued in this way for five days until his body was buried. People did not want to leave, only when their bodies weakened, they would leave for a while. The sad singing, crying and tears did not stop for a minute. Even nature looked saddened, it was very quiet, and once in a while, it would drizzle, like a mother lamenting its child. In all the five days, there was no night, and the day was day, and the night served as day, as there was an incessant flow of people to say their prayers in the service of God.

On the last day, it was Sunday, the day of the resurrection of Christ,[4] it was announced in newspapers that the body would be buried after lunch at 2 pm. By this time, a special courier train arrived from Nelson that carried over 500 of the English. There were noble and rich among them, there were also a lot of common people. Besides the train from Nelson and Trail, the towns closest to Brilliant, there were at least 100 cars. These people were honoured by a special arrangement: at that time the coffin was moved from the bedroom to the dining room, where there was free passage for people, they could enter through one door and leave through the other, and so everyone could see Verigin's face. Many friends bowed on their knees and lamented his unexpected death.

At 1.20 pm, his coffin was taken out into the yard, where people could say their last good-byes to his body. Everyone knew that his foot would no longer step on the neighbourhood walk, his hand would never open doors to his room and his warm greetings to his people would never come again from his mouth. In flesh, he was departing from his people forever. It was as if the great mystery beyond any words was suddenly revealed at that moment. All the people became silent for a moment in awe and grief. The moment went by, and the people broke again into crying and lamentations. Larion, Verigin's nephew, delivered an obituary speech in English. Except for the choir, all the people from all the districts were placed on both sides of the road half an hour before the coffin was to be carried along the way. This procession took about a mile and a half.

At last, at 2 pm exactly the coffin was raised and carried forth. In front of it, they carried a banner that said in large letters "The Emblem of Peace. Toil and Peaceful Life. Pëtr the Lordly." Children and young lads and maids between 17 and 18 years of age walked on both sides of his coffin carrying in their hands bunches of flowers and branches of evergreen pine trees. The choirs followed the coffin. The first behind the coffin were choirs from Uteshenie and Brilliant, followed by Fruktovaia, Plodorodnoe, Lugovskoe and Krestova. The Krestova choirs were followed by Blagodatnoe, and finally, by the farmers who had left the commune and the Svobodniki (Freedomites). Each district choir sang its distinctive psalm.

When the coffin was carried, nature took an entirely different appearance: all the rain clouds dissipated in an instant as if they had never appeared before. The huge orb of the sun shone in all the corners of the globe as if the sun itself participated in the burial of this great and mighty son of the Earth. All of nature helped. During the entire procession of carrying the coffin right up to the grave the coffin was open and the sun poured the last rays on his pure and radiant face.

About 100 feet before the grave, there was an elevated spot from which one could see all of Uteshenie and all of Brilliant, his house, the office, warehouse, factory, the workers' canteen and the high elevator. All this was constructed by the Doukhobors themselves following his advice. The inscriptions on these buildings bear witness to this: "Christian Community of Universal Brotherhood." There, the coffin was placed down on a stone so that Verigin could say good-bye to his entire earthly life, with its incessant labours, and all his efforts to create God's kingdom on earth. He worked so sincerely at it, in his labour, he often did not eat enough, did not sleep long enough, and now he could rest from all the earthly labours. The heavenly Father released him from all of this. His body was going back to earth. His deeds remain here among people. His soul goes back to the beginning from which it came originally to the eternal dwelling, to the realms of infinity. While living on earth, he believed in this sincerely and unequivocally. Here, over the coffin, they sang his favourite verse:

>   *Nearer my God to Thee, nearer to Thee.*
>   Even though it be a cross that raiseth me,
>   I only need to get nearer to Thee, my Lord. Nearer to Thee.
>   I am a wanderer in a desert, and the night is dark.
>   There is only a stone for me to rest my head on.
>   Yet in my dreams my heart gets nearer to Thee, nearer to Thee.
>   Wake up from the sleep, sing a hymn.
>   Glory to You, Christ, glory from the Father.
>   I find joy in grief.
>   Nearer my God to Thee, nearer to Thee.
>   When I finish my life on earth,
>   You will then lead me to glory.
>   Eternal joy to me, nearer my God to Thee, nearer to Thee.
>   Glory be to our God.

Then they resumed carrying the coffin to the grave. When it was brought to the grave, following the Doukhobor custom, all the close relatives recited one psalm each. After this, E. Konkin delivered a eulogy. There was also an obituary delivered in English. Then the coffin was lowered into the grave. It did not go without more tears and laments. They sang the psalm "I call upon the Lord, I pray upon the Lord, I will pour my prayer in front of Him, I will announce my grief in front of Him." With these words, the people addressed their grief to God, both with the text and the sad melody. The choir was very strong, but they could not maintain singing perfectly, as they were all crying their hearts out. It was as if the souls of all the people who were present faced God himself and pleaded to Him to comfort them in their grief. Then they sang one more hymn.

> ***Suffering from unbearable imprisonment***[5]
> He died an honorable death.
> While fighting for people's and God's cause
> He lay down his head honestly.
> You have served long and faithfully
> For the benefits of your native land,
> And we, your brothers in the cause
> Have taken you to the graveyard.
> Grief pressed on our souls,
> And the tears shone in our eyes
> As we lowered you in the grave
> And threw earth on your ashes.
> Our enemy did not defile you,
> There were only your loved ones around,
> We closed your beloved eyes ourselves, our dear.
> We have the same path with you,
> As you we will walk into prisons,
> As you, we will give our lives for God's cause.
>
> Glory be to our God.

These were his personal wishes. When he was still alive, he said, "When I die, I want this hymn sung over my grave." The singing continued for a very long time, all the people did not want to leave his grave. The sun set behind the mountains and the shadows descended on earth. The dusk was approaching. All the people knelt once again and went back along the same road that they followed to carry his coffin.

All the people from different backgrounds who participated in the funeral conducted themselves politely and honestly, and they only wished one thing—to put to rest the body of this great man in peace. We reached the house where Verigin lived, sang one more psalm and bowed to the ground one more time.

Everybody thanked Anastasiia for maintaining everything in good order. Anastasiia also thanked all for their participation in the funerals. Wishes of good will for the future were exchanged, and people parted to make way to their own homes.

This was how the funeral of Pëtr the Lordly ended. Living in our time, he was the great and mighty spiritual leader of the Doukhobors. Let him enter the Kingdom of Heaven, let eternal peace be with him.

A monument that cost 5000 dollars was placed on his grave. He had nothing to do with this. It was not his personal wish, but the wish of the people. When he was alive, and it came up in a conversation, he would always say, "The life of each individual person should be his memory. And there is no need for anything else." Glory be to our God.

I attach here two hymns. The first of them "This happened in the Caucasus" was dedicated by Doukhobor youth to Pëtr Verigin, the Lordly.[6] The second—"Sleep on, Brave Eagles"[7]—to all the brothers and sisters who died in Russia beginning with their move to Transcaucasia and finishing with exile in the Iakutsk area.

> *This happened in the Caucasus.*
> This happened in the Caucasus. It was a glorious deed, friends.
> Our fathers burned weapons under Peter's banner.
> Our great leader, let him be remembered forever.
> He sacrificed himself, and was the first to put himself on the line.
> In the struggle with the enemy, he achieved victory.
> Go ahead, brothers, go ahead, brothers! We will reach our goal.
> The youth should strongly hold on to one principle:
> The banner of toil and peaceful life and forgiveness of all trespasses.
> In order to overcome the untruth we will live with this forever.
> And in our homeland, our Savior will reward us.
>
> *Sleep on, brave eagles.*
> Sleep on, brave eagles, sleep with your souls at peace,
> Our dear, you have earned eternal memory and rest.
> It is now easy for all of us to tread the path you have prepared for us.
> But you have acquired it for us with a precious price.
> You have suffered terribly for your homeland for a long time.

You have lived for a long time in the tundra of cold Siberia.
Today we will remember the past, your sufferings and effort,
We will get together as one, we will tighten our ranks.
Sleep on, brave eagles, sleep with your souls at peace.
Our dear, we will overcome everything, and we will walk the path of Christ.

Notes

1. Brilliant is an area in present day Castlegar; the word means *a diamond* in Russian.
2. Fruktovaia (Fruktova, Fruktovoe) is one of the former Doukhobor villages established in BC in Grand Forks area. The word means *fruit* or *fruit orchard* in Russian.
3. Anastasiia—Anastasiia (Nastas'ia) Golubova, in the English transliteration known as Anastasia F. Holoboff) was P. Verigin's partner, who after his death expected to be recognized as his successor. When the majority of the community disagreed, and P.V. Verigin's son (P.P. Verigin "Chistiakov") was proclaimed the Doukhobor leader, she broke off from the "Orthodox" Doukhobors and, with a group of followers, founded a village commune in Alberta.
4. In Russian, the name for "Sunday" is "voskresenje," which means resurrection (of Christ).
5. The lyrics of this song "Zamuchen tiazhëloĭ nevoleĭ" were composed by Grigoriĭ Machtet, a Russian nineteenth-century writer and a revolutionary, a member of the Narodnaya Volya radical revolutionary group. The song was very popular among Russian revolutionaries and political prisoners. The author omits two last stanzas of the song about the rise of a new avenger that were probably discarded by the Doukhobors as incompatible with their peaceful non-resistance concept. The Doukhobor version of the song also substitutes "people's cause" with "God's cause" in the lyrics.
6. The author provided the following note in this place of the text:

    "The word 'Lordly' means that he lived the most part of his life in the name of the Lord." The translator and editor would also like to point out that the nickname "Lordly" was bestowed upon him by Luker'ia Kalmakova while he was still a child.

7. The hymn "Sleep on, brave eagles" (Spite, orly boevye) was originally composed by I. Kornilov, a Russian composer. The lyrics were written by K. Olenin. The song created in 1906 commemorated the victims of the Russo-Japanese war of 1904–1905 and also possibly the first Russian revolution of 1905 (http://a-pesni.org/starrev/spiteorly.php). Doukhobors adopted the first stanza of the lyrics and modified the rest to reflect Doukhobor history. The melody became modified in the Doukhobor version, but is still recognizable.

Addendum 1: A Visit of Molokan Brothers and Sisters by Pëtr Vasil'evich

At one time, Pëtr Vasil'evich personally visited all the Molokan[1] brothers and sisters who lived in Los Angeles and also around Oregon. Pavel Planidin and Mikhail Kazakov accompanied him. Brothers and sisters in Los Angeles knew the day of his arrival, and respectable old men, the so called elders, met him at the railway station. From the station they went to their settlements on automobiles, where many brothers and sisters greeted him with lots of respect. Pëtr Vasil'evich was thanked for his bravery of having endured 16 years of suffering in the most remote parts of northern Siberia with its terrible frost and living conditions unsuitable for a human being. They praised the Lord for his liberation and arrival in Canada among the Doukhobors and also thanked Pëtr Vasil'evich for coming to visit them in person. There was no end to the spiritual joy experienced by all brothers and sisters as well as by Pëtr Vasil'evich and his companions. This joy was expressed in the singing of spiritual psalms and hymns, as well as in words.

Brothers and sisters organized meetings attended by thousands and invited Pëtr Vasil'evich to give talks about the matters of spiritual, moral as well as material life. He talked a lot about the past and present and about the situation of all the people. He said about the past that

> We, Doukhobors and Molokans, were one family and one people. Our ancestor and precursor in the understanding of God and of the true path is Jesus Christ, but with the flow of time, one family divided into two. You

believe in Christ the same as Doukhobors do, but there are some differences in concepts. Doukhoborism is based mostly in the oral tradition, and many words were borrowed from the Gospel, such as the Sermon on the Mount, and others. These psalms were passed orally to the young generation. Molokans, on the other hand, based their teaching on the scriptures: on the Bible—the Old Testament and the Gospel—the New Testament. Thus, this family became completely separated with time.

Spiritual and moral life was supported by both sides, but there has also been some leeway. I will point out some leeway among Doukhobors, particularly in my own lifetime. Doukhobors started drinking and smoking tobacco; some of them were getting richer and some poorer. The rich started treating the poor not in a brotherly way and hired them as "hands." Even the word itself "a hired hand" contradicts Doukhoborism. Our ancestors did not have any of these. I was born and raised in a Doukhobor family, and I know the village and their whole life. When after the death of Luker'ia Vasil'evna Kalmakova I took the position of Doukhobor leader, I advised everyone to leave all this behind and live as our ancestors did. You also are aware of this, and I advised so following the ancestors. And it appears that the new thing that I introduced on my own is not consuming animal meat. It became revealed to me in my own mind that this is not a natural food for people, people should take nourishment from the land. I was in exile for two years and tried eating food that was not killed. Of course, it was a little disagreeable to the tongue and the stomach, but my spiritual considerations compelled me to follow this new rule, and after this I also offered it to Doukhobors. And not all of them, but the majority followed my advice.

You, the Molokans, have been maintaining spiritual and moral lives better. You saved yourselves from drinking, smoking and many other bad habits. And now I offer to you, if you wish so, it is time for us to get reunited into one family. However, you should give up eating meat. Of course, this would require understanding and effort, but it is only through effort that the Kingdom of God can be achieved. Look, you only need to make an effort not to eat meat, and Doukhobors had to make efforts also against drinking and smoking. You know that these harmful habits were so deeply rooted among Doukhobors that some old men would only wake up with the purpose of smoking. Then I also advised them to leave the cities and settle on the land. Cities are dens of vice, particularly for the young generation, and besides the old commandment also says: "In the sweat of your face you will earn your bread from the earth."[2]

Brothers and sisters listened to this, did not raise significant objections, but could not secure general acceptance either. Pëtr Vasil'evich himself only brought this up as a simple suggestion that would take lots of time for a complete acceptance. Mikhail Petrovich Pivovarov, now deceased, liked this suggestion by Pëtr Vasil'evich very much, and he started working very hard on this, and after some time he became a vegetarian. He expressed his understanding in a poem that I attach here.

Grigoriĭ Verigin

> The King, the ruler of the Universe, please forgive
> The sin that I committed against you.
> All living things, please also forgive me
> For your blood that I shed.
> Cattle, fish, feathered birds,
> I will not kill you,
> And I will not raise my hand to take away your lives.
> I promised in front of God
> Not to kill you anymore,
> And I will not enter the ranks of those madmen
> Who spill their brothers' blood.
> The psalm singer loudly praises
> That a man is created for glory.
> For the sake of my weaker brother
> I will never eat meat.
> I will no longer be a grave
> For burying the corpses of animals,
> I will also not be tempted
> To ever drink wine.
> Apostle Paul proclaimed:
> Blessed is the one who is merciful to his domestic animals,
> And lets them free
> And does not spill their blood.
> All the creatures are waiting for mercy
> From God's sons,
> And they appeal loudly to God,
> And they will soon be sent assistance.
> The people will change their thoughts,
> They will not raise a sword,
> The meek Lamb will be set free
> And the animals will be given freedom.
> Do not be afraid of me, living things,
> I will not be your enemy.

> All the creations should glorify God
> Glory be to God forever. Amen.
> Glory be to our God.
> *Mikhail Pivovarov*

When Pëtr Vasil'evich died, the Molokans were notified with a telegram. They responded to it with the following letter.

> To our dear brothers and sisters,
> We received from you the unexpected sad notification about the death of Pëtr Vasil'evich Verigin and we were very saddened by it. We would have liked to come to bury the body of Pëtr Vasil'evich and share with you this great grief, but as there was very little time, we realized that we would not make it on time for his funeral. Therefore, we gave up the trip and remembered him in our prayers. However, there is no peace in our hearts and we are rebuked by our conscience. We request the deceased friend Pëtr Vasil'evich as well as your whole assembly to forgive us this fault in our attitude to you. You are right, and we are wrong, we put ourselves on trial for not being able to lay to rest such a great man.
> One of our ancestors, a famous man with his small regiment armed with the power of God, stepped out into the battlefield against the world Beast. He raised the life of God with the hand of his people and pierced the world's power with God's arrow, he dispelled all the tricks of Devil and liberated his people from slavery and death, and united all the like-thinkers into one brotherly family. No words are worthy of your holy heroic deed. Your memory will remain steadfast through centuries, you are the weapon of God and the hand of his governance. Amen.
> We wish eternal peace to Pëtr Vasil'evich in joyful heaven with our Lord Jesus Christ and all His holy martyrs. Let his name never be erased from the book of life, let his lamp shine forever, and those of you who are left to live, may God bless you to live in peace and love with one another. With a simple soul engage in your ancestral labour, do not forget the trail of your ancestors and their holy covenant, be in peace, love and union with one another. Do not do to others what you do not wish upon yourselves, and treat others as you wish to be treated. This is the Law of God and the Prophets, and the love of our Lord Jesus Christ, crucified on Golgotha. Glory and Honor to our Lord God and the Holy Spirit, and all our beloved ancestors, who set our feet on the path of true faith. Let their names be glorified in our kin for ever and ever. Amen.

Our dear brothers and sisters in Christ, we also request you to accept our sincere greetings and good wishes as well as condolences of your grief, and we hope to see you in the near future.

Your loving younger brother
Mikhail Petrovich Pivovarov.

PS: Please respond, we wish to come to visit you, but we are not sure when God allows us to.

Addendum 2: The Last Poem by Pëtr Verigin, "Oh, Lord, you are the light of my life"

On November 20, 1924, Pëtr Vasil'evich gave his last poem to Konkin so that a melody could be found to go with it. He died on November 29, 1924.[3]

> Oh Lord, you are the light of my life, I want to praise you forever.
> You created me from earth, and you gave me a comprehending soul.
> The order of the world above evokes in me divine joy.
> You created me from earth, and you gave me a comprehending soul.
> The whole nature in an ecstasy of powers praises you, the Lord.
> You created me from earth, and gave me a comprehending soul.
> The stars are shining in the skies as if they want to tell us about the brotherhood of the world.
> You created me from earth, and you gave me a comprehending soul.
> *Pëtr Verigin*

Appendix 1: The Author's Appendix Information

The author placed in appendix an article by Lev Nikolaevich Tolstoy entitled "Two wars." Tolstoy is held in high regard by Doukhobors.

The translation of the text can be found on the Internet at http://www.nonresistance.org/docs_pdf/Tolstoy/Two_Wars.pdf

Appendix 2: Oath of Allegiance (the Early Twentieth Century)

Downloaded from http://www.larrysdesk.com/oath%2D%2Dbc-move-verigins-watch-gmo-speech-tolstoy-quote.html

I, A.B., formerly of (former place of residence to be started here), in (country of origin to be stated here), and known there by the name of (name and surname of alien in his country of origin to be stated here), and now residing at (place of residence in Canada and occupation to be stated here), do sincerely promise and swear (or, being a person allowed by law to affirm in judicial cases, do affirm) that I will be faithful and bear true allegiance to His Majesty King Edward VII (or reigning sovereign for the time being) as lawful Sovereign of the United Kingdom of Great Britain and Ireland, and of the Dominion of Canada, dependent on and belonging to said Kingdom, and that I will defend Him to the utmost of my power against all traitorous conspiracies or attempts whatsoever which shall be made against His Person, Crown and Dignity; and that I will do my utmost endeavor to disclose and make known to His Majesty, His heirs or successors, all treasons or traitorous conspiracies and attempts which I shall know to be against Him or any of them; and all this I do swear (or affirm) without any equivocation, mental evasion or secret reservation. So help me God.

Sworn before me at.... this ... day of ....
A.B.

Appendix 3: The English Original of a Letter by James Mavor

OPEN LETTER TO SIR THOMAS WHITE
Acting Prime Minister of Canada,
8 University Crescent, Toronto
May 1st, 1919.

Downloaded from
http://www.larrysdesk.com/queen-victoriafrank-oliverjames-mavor-move-to-bc.html

Sir:

I desire to appeal to the high-minded public of Canada to prevent, as they can, if they will, the perpetration of what appears to me to be a monstrous national crime. It is known that between 7000 and 8000 Doukhobors emigrated from Russia in 1899. The oppression they endured from the government there was well known and they applied to be allotted to come to this country. They made two conditions, both of which were accepted by the Minister of the Interior of the time. The first of these conditions—exemption from military service—was embodied in an Order-in-Council. The second condition—freedom to settle in villages—was as fully accepted, although it was not embodied in so formal a document. When they came, the people were received with open arms. The immigration was the largest which had ever come to Canada in one mass. The fame of Canada as the refuge of the unfortunate was spread and even trumpeted throughout the world. Other circumstances, no doubt conspired, but the Doukhobor immigration represented the beginning of a great movement, from Europe which was looked upon at the time as of the utmost importance in building up this country.

The European immigrants built the railways in the North-west and contributed enormously to the increase of production. Had this immigration not taken place it is doubtful if the North-west would now have been in the economical position in which it finds itself.

Whether the disturbance to their village and family life due to the frequent harassing conduct of the Russian Government affected their minds or not, it is the fact that for some years before and for some years after their arrival in Canada, the Doukhobors were subject to outbreaks of religious fanaticism. These outbreaks did not, however, affect more than one-fifth to one-quarter of the people and in no case were the outbreaks of long duration. There have been no outbreaks for several years.

When the arrangements were being made about their settlement, I was invited by the Department of the Interior to make some suggestions; and I suggested that the land allotted to the Doukhobors should be on the outer limit of what was considered by the Government surveyors, at that time, as suitable for practical settlement. I pointed out that the fact of their being a "hard knot" in a country otherwise occupied by farmers cultivating individually, would not be so inconvenient as it might be if the settlement were in the heart of the country, and that the area intervening between the existing settlements and the Doukhobor lands would be filled up all the more readily, if they were beyond that area. This suggestion was adopted, and the anticipation proved to be correct. The intervening area did fill up very rapidly and the lands quickly rose in value. What I did not anticipate was that the Government would break faith with the people so soon and becoming subject to pressure by land speculators, seek to deprive the Doukhobors of the lands which had been given to them, or explicitly reserved for them.

Had I done so, nothing would have induced me to encourage any immigrants to come to this country.

The process of attacks upon the Doukhobor lands began in 1906. It is necessary to explain certain peculiarities before it. About three-fourths of them practiced rigid co-operation. They bought collectively and they sold collectively. The local merchants disliked them because they did not profit by their proximity on account of the purchases of Doukhobors being made principally in Toronto and Vancouver, where, soon after their settlement, they began to buy on a large scale. The local farmers professed to believe that the sale by Doukhobors produced reduced prices.

Together with the land speculators—many farmers being among these—and aided by the local politicians, the groups mentioned organized a raid upon Sir Wilfred Laurier and Mr. Frank Oliver. Neither of these had ever been in the Doukhobor Settlement, nor did they know anything about the people or their character. The Doukhobors had no votes because they objected to the oath of allegiance—conceiving that to swear it, gave the Government a power over them which they could not understand. For this reason their case was regarded with cynical indifference. Instead of dealing with the question in a diplomatic manner, the Government in 1907, simply cancelled the Doukhobor grants and took away from the people nearly 400,000 acres of land. Large areas of that land had been brought into cultivation by the people. Technically the Government may have acted within their powers—morally, their action was without justification. One of the peculiarities of the Doukhobors is adherence to the maxim of Tolstoy, by whom in recent years they have been much influenced—that maxim is "Resist not evil." They accepted the situation and of course believed that like the Government of Russia—the Canadian Government was simply an instrument of oppression. They decided that even the small portion of land left to them was held a very insecure tenure and therefore they should buy land in British Columbia from and with the knowledge of the Government of that province. They were well advised, at all events for the time, for in 1912 further encroachment upon their Saskatchewan lands was made, at the instance of Conservative Politicians and others.

Some thousands of Doukhobors were transferred to the British Columbia lands. There they engaged in the intensive agriculture to which they had been accustomed in Russia, this form of agriculture not being possible in northern Saskatchewan. They established large fruit farms, built a jam factory and produced on a large scale. During the war they presented the Government with great quantities of jam as their contribution to the war fund.

Now comes the crime—these peaceable if obstinate and peculiar people are being forced out of their purchased lands as they were forced out of their homesteads by the same conspiracy of local tradesmen, local farmers, local Politicians and local speculators.

These people have entertained the idea of exploiting the returned soldier in order to deprive the Doukhobors of their cultivated lands.

The intention of the scheme is obvious as it is discreditable. On the plea that the returned soldier must have land, they have induced the

Government to buy out the Doukhobors at forced sale, and then give the returned soldiers grants of their land. The experience of such military grants in this country and elsewhere, is that the soldier quickly realizes upon his grant and then the opportunity of the speculator comes. He buys the grants thus suddenly thrown upon the market, at a low price, and holds the land for a profit, meanwhile allowing it to fall out of cultivation.

There is plenty of land in British Columbia and in the northwest for all the returned soldiers who genuinely desire to settle down to an agricultural life. They should be generously treated in the distribution of land but there can be no sound policy in turning out established settlers who are making a success of intensive cultivation and who have bought and paid for their land believing in the good faith of the people of Canada and in their respect for civil rights. The soldier, unless he is also a politician, may find his grant similarly expropriated and the plea that he has not fulfilled precisely all the conditions. This country needs immigrants to occupy its wide spaces; how can they be expected to come, if the prospect lies before them of being deprived on one excuse or another of their homesteads or even of the lands they have paid for?

What are dispossessed Doukhobors to do? They cannot go back to Russia, the conditions there would be for them not any better than they are here. It is useless for them to think of buying land in this country, because some plausible excuse might at any time be invited to deprive them of it in the same way as is being done now.

They must inevitably be turned into vagrants—unable to obtain land in a country where there are millions of acres waiting for the plough.

The life of these unfortunate people has been again and again torn up by the roots, not only in Russia, but in this country, by the action of the respective Governments. It is little wonder that they distrust the organization of the State. Their experience of it has been that when for some reason its attention is spasmodically drawn to them, it is an occasion merely an instrument of oppression and disturbance.

The short-sighted policy of the Government with regard to the Doukhobors during the past thirteen years has borne the fruit, that this adverse or even perverse view of the state has been strongly confirmed in the minds of the Doukhobors, and if the policy is further persisted it must affect in a similar way others who are not so simple-minded as they are.

The distrust inspired in their minds by the past actions of the Government has a great deal to do with their objections to the education of their children, as well as with their isolation from their neighbours.

They may be self-righteous and afflicted with spiritual pride; but they feel, and have reason to feel, that they have been, and are now being, treated without regard to justice by their neighbours, and through their influence, by the Government.

These proceedings have nothing in common with a policy of "reconstruction," on the contrary they amount to deliberate destruction. If the Government expropriated the fruit farms in the Niagara District, turned the farmers adrift, and bestowed the land in grants to returned soldiers with the liberty to sell to speculators, the case would be precisely similar. Care for our returned men is a national duty; it cannot with justice be made a special burden upon a few. Disregard of civil rights is an infectious disease. When a Government breaks the fundamental laws of a country and of society, it is little wonder that law in general should be held in light esteem.

If Canada is ever to be emancipated from slavery to the petty politician whose eye is bent exclusively on the main chance, this can only be done by a wider and less self-interested public opinion making its influence felt upon the Government. This seems to be an occasion when such influence ought somehow to be made manifest.

If there is anything to be done, there is no time to be lost. Appraisers sent by the Dominion Government are already on the spot estimating the value of the land which is intended to be confiscated. The whole matter has been rushed with indecent haste.

I would suggest that the Dominion Government institute without delay a serious inquiry conducted by competent persons into the whole circumstances of the case. Canada cannot afford to have its public character compromised by a transaction which will not bear the light of day. The fact that the people who have been and are being again plundered, are innocent, inoffensive, industrious people unacquainted with political guile, ought to make every high-minded citizen of this country insist upon justice being done for them and upon their right in the enjoyment of their peaceful and productive life.

Yours Truly,
JAMES MAVOR,
Professor of Political Economy
University of Toronto.

NOTES

1. Molokans are a sectarian religious group that split off the Russian Orthodox Church. At present, Doukhobors of Canada and Molokans of the United States retain amicable relationships and send representatives to each other's major events.
2. "In the *sweat* of thy face shalt thou eat *bread,* till thou return unto the *ground*" Genesis 3:19. *The wording quoted by the author is closer to the Russian Orthodox version of the Bible.*
3. This is likely a typo or printing error, as according to Chap. 43, and to other sources, P. Verigin died on October 29, and not in November.

Name Index[1]

A

Agafonov, Vasiliĭ, 20
Aniutushkin, Ivan A., 79, 100, 205
Arekhov, Vasiliĭ Ivanovich, 80
Arekhov (Verigin), Arefiĭ Ivanovich, 80
Argatov, Ignatiĭ, 25
Arishchenkov, Mikhaĭlo, 116
Aslamov, Aleksandr Il'ich, 147
Astafurov, Dmitriĭ, 106, 107, 116
Astafurov, Grigoriĭ, 100, 106–107
Avsinskiĭ, Evgeniĭ, 43

B

Barabanov, Danila, 99
Baturin, Ivan Vasil'evich, 16
Baulin, Alistrat, 116
Biriukov, Pavel Ivanovich, ix, xvi, xviin1, xviiin13, 63, 171, 176, 234
Blakemore, William, 225–230, 239–243, 243n1
Bol'shov, Nikolaĭ N., 140

C

Chernenkov, Semën, 78
Chernov, Nikolaĭ Timofeevich, 80, 121
Chertkov, Vladimir Grigor'evich, 71, 148, 165, 167, 171, 188, 234
Chertkova, Anna Konstantinovna, 167, 168
Chivil'deev, Kirila Nikolaevich, 116, 143
Chutskov, Ivan, 107, 108, 116, 117

D

Dadiani, Georgiĭ Alksandrovich, 72, 95
Darofeev, Vasiliĭ Ivanovich, 99
Dergousov, Ivan, 80
Dergousov, Nikolaĭ, 80
Dmitriev, Emel'ian Dmitrievich, 24
Domashchenko, Semën Ivanovich, 146, 147
Dorofeev, Grigoriĭ A., 99
Dymovskiĭ, Ivan, 223

[1] Note: Page numbers followed by 'n' refer to notes.

© The Author(s) 2019
G. V. Verigin, *The Chronicles of Spirit Wrestlers' Immigration to Canada*, https://doi.org/10.1007/978-3-030-18525-1

Dymovskiĭ, Pëtr Fëdorovich, 80, 133
Dymovskiĭ, Vasiliĭ, 223

E
Eletskiĭ, Vasiliĭ, 102

F
Filipov, Pëtr Dmitrievich, 140, 141
Filipova, Mar'ia Iakovlevna, 140
Fofanov, Nikolaĭ, 117

G
Golubev, Fëdor Ivanovich, 102
Golubov, Fëdor, 79
Golubov, Vasiliĭ, 80
Golubova, Nastas'ia, 205, 278n3
Goncharov, Nikolaĭ, 144
Gratchin, Aleksandr, 116
Grigoriĭ, Astafurov, 100
Gritchin, Aleksandr, 117
Gromova, Anna Ivanovna, 136, 143, 144
Gubanov, Ignat, 16
Gubanov, Mikhail, 15
Gubanova, Praskov'ia, 15
Gubanova, Tatiana, 15

I
Ivin, Ivan, 177

K
Kalmykov, Ivan, 102
Kalmykova (Gubanova), Luker'ia Vasil'evna, xiv, xviin8, xx, xxiiin6, 2, 9–16, 17n11, 19
Kazakov, Mikhail Vasil'evich, 230, 279

Khaminov, Fëdor Akimovich, 116, 117
Khilkov, Dmitriĭ Aleksandrovich, 72, 179n8, 234
Khudiakov, Nikolaĭ, 89, 91
Kiniakin, Pëtr Stepanovich, 116
Konkin, Evseĭ, 20, 276
Konkin, Fëdor Vasil'ievich, 12, 25, 27
Konkin, Ivan Evseevich, xiv, 7, 130, 155
Konkin, Ivan Vasil'ievich, 43–49, 52–53, 100
Konkin, Vasiliĭ Mikhajlovich, 80, 131
Konkina, Varvara Vasil'evna, 25
Kotel'nikov, Gregoriĭ, 11, 20, 78, 79
Kotel'nikova, Avdotia Grigor'evna, 8
Kuchin, Pëtr, 272
Kuftinov, Ivan, 116, 117
Kuftinov, Nikolaĭ, 117

L
Lebedev, Matveĭ (Timofeĭ) Vasil'evich, 69, 116
Lezhebokov, Dmitriĭ Vasil'evich, 28, 35, 37, 44, 65
Lezhebokova, Arina Vasil'evna, 35

M
MacDougall, John, 212, 214, 216n4
Makhortov, 28, 36, 44, 65
Makhortov, Alekseĭ, 116
Makhortov, Ivan Fadeevich, 19, 25
Makhortov, Pëtr, 177
Makhortov, Semën, 272
Malakhov, Ivan Vasil'evich, 105, 112
Malov, Fëdor Nikolaevich, 116, 117
Malov, Nikolai, 144
Malov, Nikolaĭ Potap'evich, 80
Markin, Fëdor, 211
Markov, Andreĭ, 20

Maude, Aylmer, 166, 167, 169n2, 169n3
Mavor, James, 265, 291–295
Morozov, Pëtr M., 100
Morozov, Vasiliĭ Vasil'evich, 91

N
Nakashidze, 20, 21, 81
Nanasov, Efrem, 20
Negreev, Semën, 204
Novokshonov, Luk'ian Fëdorovich, 116, 117
Novokshonov, Osip Fëdorovich, 80

O
Ob'edkov, Vasiliĭ, 49, 52, 62–64

P
Pivovarov, Mikhail Petrovich, 281–283
Planidin, Larion L., 131
Planidin, Pavel Vasil'evich, 95, 97, 159, 160, 188, 189, 199, 204, 279
Plotnikov, Fëdor Ivanovich, 116
Podavinnikov, Ivan Vasil'evich, 96, 100–102
Polovnikov, Mikhail Iakovlevich, 102
Popov, Evgeniĭ Ivanovich, xv, 63, 65n6
Popov, Filipp, 117
Popov, Mikhail, 144
Popov, Mikhaĭlo Petrovich, 80
Popov, Vladimir F., 154
Pugachëv, Kuz'ma Nikolaevich, 116

R
Repin, Andreĭ Alekseevich, 102
Romanov, Aleksandr Nikolaevich, 13, 17n8

Romanov, Mikhail Nikolaevich, 13, 17n8
Rybalkin, Stepan, 116
Rybin, Fëdor, 25, 28, 36, 44, 65, 189
Rybin, Semën, 211, 220, 236, 263
Ryl'kov, Fëdor A., 89, 107–109, 111, 112, 133
Ryl'kov, Nikolai Ivanovich, 116
Ryl'kov, Nikolaĭ Vasil'evich, 111–113, 116

S
Safonov, Pëtr, 116
Sakhvonov, Nikifor Nikolaevich, 116
Salykin, Fëdor, 80
Salykin, Pëtr Fedorovich, 116
Samorodin, Fëdor Pavlovich, 116, 117
Semënov, Vasiliĭ Fëdorovich, 80
Shcherbakov, Nikolaĭ Vasil'evich, 117
Shcherbakov, Vasiliĭ Nikiforovich, 80
Shcherbinin, Ivan, 226
Shcherbinin, Mikhaĭlo, 117, 221
Shchukin, Larion Ivanovich, 116
Sherstobitov, Vasiliĭ, 107, 108, 116, 117
Shishkin, Mikhail Alekseevich, 80
Sokol'nikov, Prokofiĭ N., 143
Streliaev, Vasiliĭ, 20
Sukhachëv, Fëdor, 204
Sukhachëv, Nikolaĭ, 116
Sukharev, Grigoriĭ Ivanovich, 116

T
Terekhov, Larion Fëdorovich, 80
Tikhomirov, Ivan Semënovich, 37
Tolstoy, Lev Nikolaevich, xv, xvi, 143, 171, 176, 211, 234, 256, 287
Tregubov, Ivan Mikhaĭlovich, xvi, 71, 172
Tsybul'kin, Nikolaĭ, 25, 28, 36, 44, 65, 117

U

Usachëv, Ivan Ivanovich, 71, 76, 144
Usachov, Semën Semënovich, 117

V

Vanin, Grigoriĭ, 116
Vereshchagin, Vasiliĭ Gavrilovich, xiv, 55–60, 129–136
Verigin (Arekhov), Anton Fëdorovich, 102
Verigin, Fëdor Fëdorovich, 102
Verigin, Fëdor Vasil'evich, 79
Verigin, Grigoriĭ Vasil'evich, viii, ix, xi, xv, xx
Verigin, Ivan Stepanovich, 24
Verigin, Ivan Vasil'evich, 25
Verigin, Lukeian Vasil'evich, 7
Verigin, Lukian Prokof'evich, 6
Verigin, Pëtr Vasil'evich, xiv, xx, xxiiin6, 3, 5–8, 20, 33, 171–173, 235, 240, 247, 282
Verigin, Vasiliĭ Lukianovich, 20
Verigin, Vasiliĭ Vasil'evich, xiv, xv, 67, 69

Verigina (Kapustina), Anastasiia Vasil'evna, 6, 181–182
Verigina, Anna Vasil'evna, 6
Verigina, Avdot'ia Luk'ianovna, 205
Verigina, Fedos'ia Luk'ianovna, 205
Verigina (Konkina), Varvara Vasil'evna, 25
Verigin-Orekhov, Grigoriĭ Nikolaevich, 116
Vertsynskiĭ, Aleksandr, 28
Vorob'ev, Alekseĭ, 68, 83, 84, 86
Voronin, Nikolaĭ Ivanovich, 25, 36, 37
Voronina, Katerina Vasil'evna, 36

W

White, Thomas, 265, 291–295

Z

Zibarov, Grigoriĭ Savel'evich, 116
Zibarov, Nikolaĭ, 199
Zubkov, Alekseĭ, 16, 25
Zybin, Nikolaĭ, 222, 223
Zybin, Vasiliĭ Nikolaevich, 80
Zymovskiĭ, Danilo, 116

Subject Index[1]

A

Agriculture/agriculturalist, 178, 200, 204, 213, 234, 235, 239, 246–248, 251, 252, 254, 259, 262, 267, 293, 294

Alcohol, ix, 46, 146, 150

Anarchism/anarchist, 182

Animal(s), ix, xx, 40, 47, 57, 79, 149, 150, 172, 178, 184, 194, 220, 234, 261, 280

B

Blagodatnoe, 275

Bogdanovka, 65, 83

The Book of Life, 232

Brilliant, xvii, xxii, 221, 222, 231, 236, 237, 241, 242, 246, 250, 260, 262, 263, 272–275

British Columbia, vii, 219–223, 233, 236, 239, 240, 246, 267, 293, 294

Brotherhood, ix, xvi, 72, 225, 226, 233, 237

Burning of the weapons, xiv, xv, 68, 77, 78, 80, 83, 86

C

Canada, vii, viii, xiv, xv, xvii, 147, 155, 159, 160, 165, 166, 171, 175–177, 181–183, 188–190, 205, 208, 211–216, 233, 234, 241, 249, 255, 256, 259–263, 265–268

Christian Community of Universal Brotherhood (CCUB), 212–216, 222, 259, 261, 263, 275

Citizen, 208, 209, 228, 231, 240, 242, 249, 253, 265, 268, 295

free citizen(s) of the world, 242

Citizenship, 208, 209, 214, 217n5, 219, 221, 222, 234, 236, 237, 255, 266

---

[1] Note: Page numbers followed by 'n' refer to notes.

302 SUBJECT INDEX

Commune
  communal household, 204–206, 246, 249
  communal life, 35–41, 199, 205, 225, 234, 255
Conscription card, 76–80
Cossacks, 78, 81–83, 85, 100

D
Disciplinary battalion(s), xii, 70, 105–117, 122, 130, 135, 173
Doukhoborets/Doukhobors, vii–ix, xii–xv, xx–xxii, 2, 6, 7, 9, 19, 49, 70, 78, 95, 100, 119, 153, 160, 167, 172, 177, 185, 188, 189, 195n3, 199, 200, 201n1, 203, 209, 222, 226, 228, 231, 232, 234, 235, 239–242, 246–248, 250, 251, 255–263, 265–268, 276, 277, 280, 292, 293
  Doukhobortsy, vii, 172

E
Education, xvii, 221, 228–230, 232, 233, 242, 250–253, 256, 257, 268, 294
Exile, viii, xiv–xvi, 19–21, 23–25, 27–29, 31, 36, 37, 39, 43, 44, 48, 52–53, 55–60, 64, 78, 83, 85, 86, 95, 96, 100, 115, 119–125, 130, 131, 133, 145, 148, 160, 168, 172, 173, 176, 181, 182, 190, 193, 234, 235, 277, 280

F
Farmstead, 208, 209
Freedom, vii, xxi, 15, 69, 88, 90, 92, 98, 116, 135, 176, 177, 184, 193, 209, 214, 219, 222, 223, 228, 234, 235, 249, 265, 291
Fruktovaia, 221, 222, 230, 233–237, 272, 275

G
Gendarmes, 23, 24, 27, 38, 56, 70, 78, 79, 97, 119
Goreloe, xx, 2, 10, 12, 14, 20, 80–82, 86, 200
Government of Canada, Canadian government, viii, 189, 208, 212, 214, 215, 234, 235, 243, 249, 252, 262, 266, 293
Government of Russia, Russian government, 166, 171, 188–190, 192, 193, 215, 222, 231, 233, 234, 249, 252, 262, 266, 292, 293
Grand Forks, 222, 233, 236, 246, 249, 262, 272
Gun(s), 90, 105, 131, 153, 172, 250

H
Homestead(s), 209, 212, 234–237, 261, 267, 293, 294

K
Kholodnoe, 24, 86
Krestova, 275

L
Labour, xvi, 6, 12, 13, 40, 45, 87, 94, 96, 97, 99, 194, 199, 220, 221, 223, 225, 229, 231–233, 235–237, 242, 247, 248, 251, 252, 254, 257, 260
Land entries, 208–209, 211–216, 219, 220

cancellation of, 208–209, 211–216, 219, 220
Literacy, viii, ix, 105, 228, 232, 233, 237, 240, 242, 250–252, 254, 256
Lugovskoe, 275

M
Military
  service, xiv, xvi, 3, 57–59, 67–69, 78, 80, 91, 92, 99, 102, 105, 106, 108, 109, 111, 131, 153, 181, 240, 265, 291; refusal of, 67–72, 86, 112
Molenie, moleniia, molen'e, molen'ia, 8n4, 73n1, 80n3, 190n1

N
Novospasskoe, 80

O
Oath
  of allegiance, 57, 65, 184, 214, 253, 293
  swearing an, 57, 65, 225
Orphan's Home, 2, 15, 16, 19–21, 31–33, 81, 83
Otradnoe, 190, 204–206

P
Permanent residence, 233
Peter and Paul's day, 76
Plodorodnoe, xxii, 275
Pokrovka, 200
Prison, 76, 78, 89, 90, 92, 100
Prisoner transport, 57, 61–65, 119–125, 129–136, 154
Property, xii, 13, 16, 20, 24, 28, 31, 33, 45, 63, 96, 171, 177, 184, 198, 208, 216, 233, 237, 249, 250, 252, 254, 260
Psalm, 82

R
Registry/registry books, 184, 209, 221, 222, 225, 228, 230, 231, 237, 245–247, 259, 266
Russia, vii, viii, 121, 145, 153–156, 166, 171, 176, 177, 184, 189, 211, 215, 220, 222, 228, 231, 232, 234, 249, 252, 255, 256, 259, 261–263, 265, 267, 277, 291, 293, 294

S
Saskatchewan, vii, ix, 220, 221, 230, 234, 236, 237, 240, 249, 252, 261, 262, 267, 273, 293
School, 7, 10, 198, 221, 222, 225, 228, 230, 232, 233, 237, 239, 240, 242, 243, 245–247
School education, 221, 232, 250
Science, 232, 249, 254
Slavianka, 2, 5, 7, 11, 12, 20, 21, 49, 52, 67, 78–80, 96, 130, 131
Sobranie, sobraniia, sonran'e, sobran'ia, 7, 8n4, 20, 67, 73n1, 77, 80n3, 82, 91, 129, 188, 190, 190n1, 246, 257, 258
Spasskoe, 80, 90
Surveillance, 20, 21, 24, 39, 149, 156, 205
Svobodnik/Svobodniki, 194, 199, 275

T
Terpenie, 68, 194
Tobacco, ix, xiv, 46, 53, 146, 150, 225

Toil and Peaceful Life, 259–263, 274, 277
Tolstoyan, 63, 72, 154, 167
Transcaucasia, xx, 64, 65, 96, 160, 233, 277
Tribunal, 71, 72, 112
  military, 71, 72
Troitskoe, 80, 145

U

University, 232, 233, 254, 265
University education, 233
Uteshenie (Ootischenia), xxii, 221, 227, 231, 237, 275

V

Vegetarian, 37, 39, 41, 43, 65n6, 236, 281

Vegetarianism, 40, 63, 172, 177
Village(s), ix, xiv, xx, 2, 5, 7, 11, 12, 14, 52, 61, 62, 65, 67, 68, 70, 76–78, 80–83, 85, 90, 91, 95, 96, 100, 102, 121–124, 131, 139, 145, 147, 154, 168, 177, 181, 184, 185, 188, 190, 192–195, 197–200, 204–206, 208, 209, 211, 212, 215, 221, 235, 261, 265, 272, 280, 291, 292

W

War, xvii, 7, 13, 92, 106, 109, 115, 229, 232, 241, 247, 252, 253, 256, 259–263, 267, 293
Weapon, 76, 77
  burning of weapons, 76, 78